Y0-BVN-127

Patern

in a Sout

Paternalism
in a Southern City

RACE, RELIGION, AND GENDER

IN AUGUSTA, GEORGIA

Edited by Edward J. Cashin
and Glenn T. Eskew

THE UNIVERSITY OF GEORGIA PRESS

ATHENS AND LONDON

HM
821
.P38
2001
West

© 2001 by the University of Georgia Press
Athens, Georgia 30602
All rights reserved
Designed by Betty Palmer McDaniel
Set in eleven on thirteen Bulmer by Betty Palmer McDaniel
Printed and bound by McNaughton & Gunn
The paper in this book meets the guidelines for
permanence and durability of the Committee on
Production Guidelines for Book Longevity of the
Council on Library Resources.

Printed in the United States of America
05 04 03 02 01 C 5 4 3 2 1

Library of Congress Cataloging-in-Publication Data

Paternalism in a southern city : race, religion, and gender in
Augusta, Georgia / edited by Edward J. Cashin and Glenn T. Eskew.
p. cm.
Papers of a symposium held at Augusta State University in June 1996.
Includes bibliographical references and index.
ISBN 0-8203-2257-1 (alk. paper)
1. Equality—Georgia—Augusta—Congresses. 2. Paternalism—Georgia—
Augusta—Congresses. 3. Ideology—Georgia—Augusta—Congresses.
I. Cashin, Edward J., 1927– II. Eskew, Glenn T.
HM821 .P38 2001
305'.09758'61 dc21   00 019131

British Library Cataloging-in-Publication Data available

Contents

Foreword

THE AUGUSTA STATE UNIVERSITY CENTER for the Study of Georgia History is pleased to present this collection of essays, the result of a symposium held at Augusta State University in June 1996. The individual participants, independently of each other, had been conducting research on the city of Augusta and its people; the conference brought them together for the first time. As Georgia's second oldest city, Augusta presented an attractive field for research with valuable primary sources, including court records dating to the American Revolution and the files of the oldest continuously running newspaper in the South, dating from 1785 to the present. These scholars probed new areas of social history—especially those relating to race, class, and gender. Using previously neglected sources and asking new questions, each arrived at insights and fresh interpretations applicable to other southern cities. In essays of great originality, the authors explore the lives of artisans, millworkers, and African Americans. What becomes clear in a reading of their work is that the authors all, almost inadvertently, encountered a pervasive paternalism, manifested at times in unexpected places, underlying more obvious themes of protest, religion, family, and community. Edward J. Cashin, who has written extensively about Augusta's history, contributed a chapter tracing the development and erosion of paternalism. By exploring the dimensions of local history, this work expands the dimensions of history generally, demonstrating the enduring validity of Carl Becker's dictum that all history is local.

LEE ANN CALDWELL
Augusta State University

Introduction

AMONG MANY SCHOLARS OF SOUTHERN HISTORY, paternalism is a given, for the concept helps explain the complicated and messy nature of human relationships. Paternalism describes a personal association between individuals whereby an authority figure relates to someone under his influence as a parent treats a child: the person in power regulates the other's conduct and provides for the other's needs. In return, the other performs some service on the behalf of or remains committed to the person in power. It is a relationship based not on equality but on deference. Yet the dependence engendered by paternalism flows both ways, for it reflects the reciprocal duties and mutual obligations that can privilege or empower those involved. Scholars often use paternalism to address control from above, but it also can help explain reaction from below.

Paternalism is the key theme that runs through all the essays in this volume. Serendipity, rather than clever planning, accounts for this. The historians who participated in a symposium conducted by the Augusta State University Center for the Study of Georgia History were invited because, independently of one another, they had been working on various topics associated with Augusta history. Only during the symposium did it become obvious that all of the papers dealt with important but differing perspectives on paternalism and its significance for understanding southern history.

Illuminating paternalism as a framework for interpreting the South, the essays employ the analytical tools of race, class, and gender to address in a new way Augusta's history. In several instances this trinity is magnified through the lens of religion. The traditional paternalistic relations between masters and slaves, husbands and wives, parents and children, mill owners and workers, the elite and the masses, are expanded to explore the interconnections among race, class, and gender, which are maintained through social customs. In short, the essays demonstrate that paternalism profoundly shaped all aspects of nineteenth-century southern society.

This volume builds on the work of previous scholars who have recognized the value of paternalism as a useful concept for understanding southern history. The proslavery ideology of the planter class promoted paternalistic race relations between masters and slaves, as detailed in William Sumner Jenkins's study *Pro-Slavery Thought in the Old South* (1935). The ideology also found fruition through practice, as argued by U. B. Phillips in *American Negro Slavery* (1918) and other works. In *The World the Slaveholders Made* (1969), Eugene Genovese reinforced Phillips's findings regarding paternalism. Genovese advanced Antonio Gramsci's theoretical work on cultural hegemony and the class struggle, and applied this thinking to the Old South, arguing convincingly for paternalism. In his *Roll, Jordan, Roll: The World the Slaves Made* (1974), Genovese used the concept to illuminate the actions of slaves. Elizabeth Fox-Genovese, in *Within the Plantation Household: Black and White Women of the Old South* (1988), carried the argument into the domestic sphere by considering how paternalism maintained unequal relationships between mistresses and slave women.

Often seen as an anomaly in itself, the city in the Old South was not thought to harbor paternalistic relations. In the seminal *Slaves in the Cities: The South, 1820–1860* (1964), Richard C. Wade emphasized the distinctiveness of the urban South and reported no evidence of reciprocal duties between masters and slaves. Yet David Goldfield contends that the differences between the rural and urban South were less significant than the similarities. In a study of antebellum Virginia and a series of revisionist essays republished in *Region, Race, and Cities: Interpreting the Urban South* (1997), Goldfield used anecdotes replete with examples of paternalism to prove his point. As the essays in this volume suggest, Augusta bears witness to the prevalence of paternalism in the urban South.

Historians of the postbellum period have found paternalism helpful in describing the relations between owners and workers in mill villages. Broadus Mitchell made the connection in *The Rise of the Cotton Mills* (1921) by praising mill owners who acted as fathers when providing for their workers. In *The Mind of the South* (1941), W. J. Cash criticized the "paternalistic pattern" that welded white people together into a solid South and thus prevented reform. In *Paternalism and Protest: Southern Cotton Mill Workers and Organized Labor, 1875–1905* (1971), Melton McLauren discovered that millworkers protested childlike treatment they received and challenged the dominance of the mill owners. Although questioned by David Carlton, Douglas Flamming, and others who have found industrial paternalism to be nothing more than cynical welfare capitalism, the concept continues to shape the debate.

The essays here expand the discussion over paternalism by showing how millworkers, housewives, and African Americans used paternalism to demand reciprocity from people in authority. By considering agency, one can see how Augustans on the bottom took what is often seen as an ideology of control emanating from the top and turned it around to their own advantage.

In his introductory essay, Edward J. Cashin explains the dominance and decline of paternalism in Augusta. He traces the devolution of paternalism from its roots in medieval chivalry to the code of conduct of English country gentlemen, which influenced the aspirations and behavior of the rising gentry of Virginia and from thence spread across the South with the plantation system. Even though Augusta had been a commercial center from its origins in the Indian trade, when businessmen from Carolina arrived espousing a market ideology, the Virginia gentleman planter and his lady became the social models for the merchants and artisans who settled in the area.

Michele Gillespie writes of the subordinate status of women, even of elite white women. She assumes "a paternalistic ideology that legitimated white male dominance over the household, and by extension, over society." Slave women were not unaffected but challenged that system through their participation in informal economies and even through their dress. Free black women deliberately chose to work outside the white household. Inevitably, the pragmatic commercialism of the city compelled women to pursue the "unladylike" chores of helping artisan husbands and managing their own shops.

LeeAnn Whites expands Broadus Mitchell's portrayal of paternalistic mill owners who "behaved more like fathers than employers to 'their' mill people" by recovering the "maternalism" of the mill owners' wives and daughters, who devoted their attention to improving the condition of the workers. If mill owners took over the paternalistic legacy of slaveholders, she asks, "what or where did that leave the working man?" Her search for an answer to the intriguing query leads her to the rise of the Knights of Labor among white male mill employees. Workers as well as planters could try on the trappings of chivalry.

Glenn T. Eskew finds that the concept of paternalism helps explain the interracial cooperation that led to the founding of the Colored Methodist Episcopal Church as a denomination and the establishment of Augusta's historic Trinity CME Church. Moreover, paternalistic interracial cooperation contributed to the creation of important African American institutions in Augusta, such as Paine College. The willingness of some black and white Augustans to work together helped compensate for the brutality of the white-supremacist system under which they lived.

Kent Anderson Leslie investigates African American responses to the construction of the color line in Augusta. She observes that "the elite black community of Augusta based status on more than money—either earned or inherited—for community position depended on a constellation of attributes, including color, status before the Civil War, education, manners, family connections, and wealth." Using Amanda America Dickson to make her point, Leslie shows how the aristocracy of color—many of whom, like Amanda, were of mixed-race ancestry—behaved much like the white aristocracy. Despite the reality of a truly distinguished black society in Augusta at the turn of the century, segregation imposed a code of behavior that ignored class differences among African Americans. Leslie cites the frustration of Bishop Lucius Henry Holsey and members of the Harper and Ladeveze families with the new racial order. Yet some African Americans, such as Lucy Craft Laney, saw in segregation a way to improve conditions in the black community.

Though not a speaker at the original symposium, Bobby J. Donaldson attended the conference and was invited to compose for this volume an essay on William Jefferson White, a giant among Augusta's leaders, black and white. Donaldson finds that "as minister and newspaper editor, [White] dedicated himself to the uplift of African Americans in Augusta and throughout Georgia." White's contributions, including the founding of Morehouse College, earned him the title "Father of Negro Education." Yet by the end of the century White joined other African American leaders in expressing a profound sense of anguish at the cruelty and unfairness of segregation.

Julia Walsh addresses the religion of millworkers as it relates to paternalism. She is reluctant to label the action of paternalistic whites as "purely social control," as some historians have suggested, but instead she finds genuine religious motivation at work among white benefactors. She notes that the turn of the century "saw an increasing interest by the churches in the social welfare of the city's millworkers." The Reverend John Chipman, pastor of the church "rolled down the Hill" in Walsh's title, campaigned for safe working conditions and fair wages. J. S. Meynardie, a Baptist minister, went so far as to organize a local chapter of the Knights of Labor.

By exploring neglected sources and asking different questions, the writers have expanded the dimensions of local history. If the researcher is wise, clever and patient enough to plumb its secrets, history can reveal the inner workings of human nature. The contributors to this volume display originality and even brilliance in the questions they ask and the answers they find. The authors reinforce Genovese's warning issued a generation ago: "The South, white and black, has given America some of its finest traditions and sensibilities and certainly its best manners. These were once firmly rooted in the plantation way of life and especially in the master-slave relationship. Their preservation does not require the preservation of the injustice and brutality with which they were originally and inseparably linked, but it does require a full understanding and appreciation of those origins." The essays in this volume address the paternalism that underlay the system in an effort to heighten an understanding of the human relations that existed in the nineteenth-century South.

The Center for the Study of Georgia History at Augusta State University was established in 1996 to promote Georgia history in a variety of ways. The editors are pleased to present this collection of essays as the first publication under the aegis of the center. We appreciate the patience and good humor of the contributors during the lengthy process of publication. The Department of History at Georgia State University provided graduate assistants who drafted the bibliography, and a word-processing specialist, Elizabeth Adams, who standardized pagination. A subvention from Augusta State University Center for the Study of Georgia History covered the cost of illustrations, copyediting, maps, and indexing.

EDWARD J. CASHIN *and*
GLENN T. ESKEW

Paternalism
in a Southern City

Paternalism in Augusta:
The Impact of the Plantation Ethic
upon an Urban Society

EDWARD J. CASHIN

G EORGIA WAS CONCEIVED in paternalism. James Edward Oglethorpe and his friends thought, at first, that they would rescue debtors and give them a second chance in a far-off utopian colony. When their colleagues in Parliament failed to show enthusiasm for helping criminals of any stripe, Oglethorpe accommodated by focusing attention on the deserving poor, who could be put to work producing desirable products such as silk and wine, while protecting the valuable rice province of South Carolina. That idea touched the humanitarian heart of Parliament, especially since there were profits to be made in the process of doing good.[1]

Unfortunately, the early Georgia colonists became, in Daniel Boorstin's phrase, "victims of philanthropy." A case could be made that the Trustee period of Georgia history witnessed the first crisis in paternalism. The settlers, dubbed "malcontents" by the Trustees, objected to being ruled from afar by British gentlemen, however well-meaning and benevolent. Women started it by protesting the entailment of land in males only. Men followed with a chorus of complaints regarding restrictions on landholdings and the prohibition of slavery. The Trustees surrendered their ungrateful charges to royal rule in 1752. Then the first of Georgia's formative forces began to operate: Georgians started to comport themselves after the manner of the people in Carolina. That is, they celebrated their liberation from a paternalistic system by adopting a different kind of paternalism. Most of them, at least most males, aspired to become planters, owners of other people. Many of them succeeded, and what some have called a "plantation elite" rose in frontier Georgia.[2]

Gentlemen, Preachers, and Crackers

Under the inept administration of their first governor, John Reynolds, the brilliant but abbreviated government of Henry Ellis, and the lengthy tenure of the capable James Wright, Georgia society took shape. Because so many Carolinians crossed over the Savannah River after 1752, the Carolina standards of success became those of Georgia. Georgians adopted the South Carolina slave code and sought the same prerogatives the Carolina legislators enjoyed. Governor Henry Ellis, tutoring Georgians in the new business of self-government, disliked the way his charges harked across the river for role models. "It would be happy for us," he wrote his patron Lord Halifax, "if South Carolina was at a greater distance as our people are incessantly urging and aiming at all the privileges enjoyed there." Ellis had in mind the political privileges, but there were other features of Carolina life envied by Georgians. Charlestown, a transplant from Barbados, exemplified the good life, at least for white people. An enterprising man could purchase land and slaves on the installment plan. Thanks to a friendly climate, rice and indigo grew prodigiously. Proceeds from scattered plantations provided the means to live a comfortable life in a large house in town. Charlestown became noted for its fine houses and Charleston still is so known. The absentee planters exemplified the Charlestown characteristics. They were sociable and pragmatic. They did not burn with religious enthusiasm or intellectual curiosity. Savannah and its sister city Augusta took on Charlestown attitudes. The first inhabitants of Augusta were mostly Carolina merchants and Indian traders who moved across the Savannah River when Oglethorpe diverted the Indian trade to Georgia.[3]

The second formative influence, that of frontier religion, followed the peace settlement of 1763. In that year the Indian congress at Augusta opened a strip of land between the Savannah and the Ogeechee for settlement. The royal proclamation of the same year channeled restless pioneers down the mountain valleys and into the Georgia backcountry. The new gentlemen of Savannah and Augusta called these newcomers "banditti," "vagabonds," and other invidious names, before settling on "crackers." Lacking most of the refinements of civilization, these pioneers provided the raw material for the evolving Georgia social structure.

The frontier itself acted as a formative influence. The struggle for survival bred traits of self-reliance, adaptability, and ingenuity, along with less admirable characteristics such as waste, violence, and a culture of ignorance. Georgia had a long frontier history, and in certain back pockets of the state, some people still live like the first crackers. Georgia writers from Augustus Baldwin Longstreet to Erskine Caldwell have been intrigued by them.

More important than the environment was the religious climate. The uplifting leaven at work among the rough pioneers was the Great Awakening. Daniel Marshall and Shubal Stearns caught the seraphic fire from Jonathan Edwards and brought the torch to Georgia, establishing Kiokee Baptist Church in 1772. Even earlier, itinerant preachers roamed the backcountry, bringing their exciting message that salvation was possible for repenting sinners. One of these preachers, Wait Palmer of Connecticut, found eager listeners among the slaves of George Galphin's plantation at Silver Bluff, twelve miles below Augusta on the South Carolina side. Jesse Peters, one of the original congregants, moved with his followers to Augusta after the American Revolution to perpetuate the first independent African American church in the country.[4]

The evangelical denominations—Baptists, Methodists, and New Light Presbyterians—emphasized the central importance of the personal experience of salvation. Earlier Puritans thought in terms of individual experiences that followed upon careful preparation marked by Scripture study, prayer, and attention to learned sermons. Jonathan Edwards discovered that whole congregations could be moved by an intense sermon, and he equated the group experience with the traditional personal one. The experience meant that God saved the person from hell and destined the soul for heaven, changed the will to love the good and shun the evil, and assured blessings in this life as a prelude to happiness in the hereafter. No wonder that the experience became the pivotal point of existence.

An essential part of the neo-Puritan message, that which stressed paternalism, stemmed more from philosophers such as Peter Ramus than from theologians such as John Calvin.[5] God's order in nature carried over into societal relationships. The husband headed the family; the wife accepted her subservient role. Anne Hutchinson's fate was caused by her acting like a husband instead of a wife. The necessity of a God-ordained social order found acceptance in the Georgia backcountry and has survived through the years as one of the most recognizable aspects of evangelical religion. This statement might have been uttered by John Cotton: "The Holy Ghost forbids a woman to teach or to usurp authority over men, and commands her to be silent." In fact, the line is from a recent letter to the editor of the *Augusta Chronicle*. This is another: "When the wife wants to go her own way, to discover 'her place' in life, she not only does all in her power to destroy her home, but the home of her children." Preachers, uniformly male, had no doubt that God wrote paternalism into natural law and they frequently reminded their congregations of the fact.

When the emotionally charged Great Awakening came in contact with the cold pragmatism of the town, it lost much of its energy. Mrs. Gabriel Manigault listened to George Whitefield one night and attended the theater the next. She considered both events entertainment. Throughout the colonial period and well into the national, the Awakening remained a rural phenomenon. Preachers warned their listeners that the devil lurked in the theaters, gaming rooms, racetracks, and taverns in Charlestown, Savannah, and Augusta. When depressed economic conditions later forced farm families to move into cities, they constituted a self-conscious enclave, alienated from sophisticated urbanites. Erskine Caldwell's Jeeter Lester refused to go into Augusta and get a job in a factory. God didn't want him in no factory, Jeeter would say. God wanted him to stay on the farm and plant cotton.[6]

The paternalism of the new rural religion, seemingly rooted in the Bible, had a more profound impact on the southern psyche than the kind of paternalism practiced in towns. British law and tradition supported paternalism, but the demands of urban life modified gender differences somewhat. Cities generated wealth, and when women inherited wealth, their social standing appreciated. Charlestown's priority on entertainment, imitated in Savannah and Augusta, also enhanced the woman's role. The party planner became the social arbiter. Andrew Jackson might fume at John C. Calhoun, but it was Floride Calhoun who blackballed Peggy O'Neale Eaton at White House social functions. Cynthia Kierner has made the point that "the rise of genteel culture resulted in improvements in the status of elite white women decades before the Revolution unleashed its potentially liberating ideology."[7] Gentility required participation in fine dining, complicated dancing and polite (as opposed to vulgar) conversation. It is not enough to say that women were requisite to these social arts, women invented them, and used them to civilize men.

The French adventurer Louis Milfort related an incident in his tour of the Georgia backcountry that illustrates one way in which women began to civilize their men. Apparently the woman who dominated the household where Milfort lodged had not learned about the social order taught by the evangelical religions. She acted as the authority figure in her family. In honor of Milfort she decided to serve tea for the first time. She gave her husband money and sent him to Augusta to buy tea. In due time he returned with a thick wad of tea. She pretended to know what to do with it. After boiling the tea, she poured out the liquid and served the tea leaves on a platter. As the bemused Milfort looked on, she sampled a bite of the leaves, then cursed and threw the rest of the tea at her husband. She accused him of squandering her money on liquor and buying the worst tea she ever tasted.[8]

Mrs. Robert Mackay represented a different level of the same civilizing influence when she instructed her husband to purchase fine chinaware in Savannah for their Augusta home. Mrs. Mackay also required the use of a horse-drawn chaise. Her husband brought a new coach from Savannah. LeRoy Hammond ordered a Windsor chaise for his wife. "Mrs. Hammond is confined to Snow Hill until we can get another vehicle of some kind or other," he confided to a friend.[9] Only a few miles separated Mistresses Mackay and Hammond from the tea-throwing termagant, and only a few degrees of gentility.

Georgians may prefer to cite the example of Nancy Hart as the pregenteel independent pioneer woman. Her cabin on the Broad River was called "Nancy Hart's" because, according to George Gilmer, who chronicled the accounts of the first settlers, "her husband was nobody when she was by." Gilmer described Nancy as "a tall, muscular, red-headed, cross-eyed woman."[10] During the war she captured three Tories and delivered them at musket point over to Elijah Clarke's tender mercies. The prisoners could not tell which one of them she was looking at and correctly assumed that she would just as soon shoot them. The state of Georgia, as intimidated by Nancy as the Tories must have been, named a county after her.

Nancy served as an example of the mellowing influence of religion. Early in life, she brawled and cursed in the customary frontier fashion. Later in life, as she settled down on a farm in Edgefield County, South Carolina, she found herself in the midst of fervent Methodists. Deciding to attend their meeting, she found the church door fastened to keep out intruders. She took out her knife, cut the binding and stalked defiantly into the meeting. According to Gilmer, "She heard how the wicked might work out their salvation, became a shouting Christian, fought the Devil as manfully as she had fought the Tories, and died in good fellowship with the saints on earth, with the bright hope of being admitted into communion with those in heaven."[11]

With Charlestown and the Great Awakening the two major formative influences on the emerging Georgia society, a third infused and even more powerfully shaped social attitudes. The Virginians brought an agrarian paternalism to Georgia. Whereas Charlestown exemplified a pragmatic, urban, profit-minded commercialism, Virginians prided themselves on their disdain for those Charlestown characteristics. They convinced themselves that they presided over their plantations because nature endowed them with superior talents. It was their duty to care for the less well endowed. Virginians looked down on tradesmen; Charlestonians were tradesmen par excellence.

As Daniel Boorstin and others have noted, the Virginians of the seventeenth century modeled their lifestyle on that of English country gentlemen. It was only natural that these tobacco farmers, delighted and perhaps surprised by the profits they reaped, imitated the successful persons back home. And, of course, it followed that they accepted the feudal philosophy that nature divided people according to their talents. Those Virginians who did well assigned themselves to the category of natural aristocrats. Virginia society sorted out into classes. Douglas Southall Freeman counted eight strata of society in the Virginia of George Washington's birth.[12]

As in Carolina, wives played an essential role in the sophistication of the Virginia gentry. If the men thought of themselves as American lords of the manor, their womenfolk encouraged them to behave accordingly. The role of plantation wife required disparate skills. Women had to be efficient managers of a household staff and also charming ornaments for the guests. They had to engage in demanding physical activity while encased in whalebone stays, which made, in Edmund Morgan's phrase, the simple task of walking a problem in navigation. Morgan tells a priceless story about Mrs. Robert Carter of Nomini Hall. A long-term visitor, impressed by Mrs. Carter's supervision of the kitchen and her elegance of dress, expressed astonishment one day when she appeared without her figure-molding stays.[13] The poor woman must have suffered spasms of discomfort going about in the Virginia climate so tightly bound. The source of wonder is not so much that the women of eighteenth-century Virginia adopted such painful fashions but that southern women of succeeding generations followed the example.

Catherine Clinton paints a dismal portrait of the plantation mistress who "found herself trapped within a system over which she had no control, one from which she had no means of escape." Her only hope lay in God's mercy and an early death. Meanwhile, she endured, the "slave of slaves," "isolated unto herself," denied even the sense of community her servants enjoyed. Clinton saves her most trenchant barbs for the masters of the household. She has no use for Bertram Wyatt-Brown's term "Christian slaveholders"; she would rather call them "self-serving, profit-mongering, sin-ridden monsters." She proposes that "Southern honor" be dethroned and that "antebellum Southern dishonor take its rightful place at center stage."[14]

Clinton's strong views have rankled some women historians. Elizabeth Fox-Genovese states flatly that "slaves of slaves they were not." They knew that they led privileged lives and intended to keep it that way. In her opinion, "they emerge from their diaries and letters as remarkably attractive people who loved their children, their husbands, their families, and their friends, and who tried to do their best by their slaves, but who accepted and supported the social system that endowed them with power and privilege over black women." Shirley Abbott, in *Womenfolks: Growing Up Down South,* takes issue with feminist historians who blame "the patriarchy" for an assortment of evils, with the implication that the world would be a better place if women ran it. She warns, "Women are superb collaborators, none more so than the good old-fashioned Southern lady."[15]

Catherine Clinton's depiction of the plantation mistress, isolated and bereft of community, could not apply to slaveholding women in cities, whose social demands occupied much of their time and attention. Her suggestion that the notion of southern honor be dethroned is either facetious or a misunderstanding of the code. Honor represented an ideal to be striven for. (Perhaps historians of gender will some day undertake a study of men who were victims of the impossibly high demands of the ideals of chivalry. Jack Greene showed how Landon Carter suffered nervous depressions because he realized his own shortcomings.[16]) Though the notion of honor had some unfortunate consequences—it encouraged a proclivity to violence and an oversensitivity to slights, and it furnished a pretext for the mistreatment of women and servants—most of those failings occurred when men fell short of the ideal. Those who approached the ideal were accorded recognition as "true southern gentlemen." The reason that the memory of Robert E. Lee has such a hold upon the hearts of so many southerners is that he came closer than most to the ideal.

The Pragmatic Revolution

Because relatively few Virginians settled in Georgia before the American Revolution, the two earlier influences had more effect on people's conduct, for the Revolution reflected frontier characteristics marked by primitive behavior. The level of savagery astonished more conservative observers. They remarked that a "Georgia parole" meant death to the defeated. Georgians engaged in frontier-style fighting, with Creeks and Cherokees joining in on both sides. Elijah Clarke, after his 1780 raid on British-held Augusta, complained that Tories and Indians fell upon his retreating sick and wounded, scalping and torturing women and children: "Women and children strip'd, scalped and suffered to welter in their gore. Lads obliged to dance naked between two large fires until they were scorched to death." The patriots retaliated in kind. A Cherokee chief described patriot brutality: "They dyed their hands in the Blood of our Women and children, burnt 17 towns, destroyed all our provisions."[17] To observe a decline in civility during the Revolution is to understate the obvious.

What influence did the Great Awakening religions have upon the Revolution? Baptist preachers such as Abraham Marshall, Loveless Savage, Sanders Walker, and Silas Mercer (father of the more famous Jesse Mercer) exhorted their listeners to do God's work as they fought against British tyranny and the established church. Ministers of the Church of England, such as the Reverend James Seymour of Saint Paul's Church in Augusta, who had denounced dissenting ministers, fled to Florida in exile. As the result of the Revolution, religious enthusiasm penetrated the towns, hitherto the bastions of moderation.[18]

The evangelical religions had as much impact on the future of Georgia's black folk as on that of white people. David George, a slave on George Galphin's Silver Bluff plantation, began preaching to the other slaves at the outset of the Revolution. When the British army under Lieutenant Colonel Archibald Campbell marched from Savannah to Augusta in January 1779, David George and ninety of the Silver Bluff slaves sought protection in Savannah. Galphin was a good master, as George acknowledged, but George preferred the uncertainties of freedom to the security of paternalism. George Liele joined David George in Savannah later in the year. Like his master, Henry Sharpe, George Liele belonged to Buckhead Baptist Church, the second Baptist church in Georgia. Before hostilities Liele went about preaching to slaves on neighboring plantations, including Silver Bluff, where he met David George and Jesse Peters. During the war Liele rode with Henry Sharpe in the royalist militia and attended Sharpe when he suffered a fatal wound in March 1779. In Savannah, Liele and the Silver Bluff people organized a church and worshiped freely. When the British evacuated Savannah in 1782, Liele led a contingent of Baptists to Jamaica, where they were welcomed by the same Archibald Campbell, who had invaded Georgia in 1779 and in 1782 was governor of the island. David George led others to the less hospitable climate of Nova Scotia, where at Shelburne they established the first African American church in Canada. Later he moved again with his people, this time to found the first Baptist church in Sierra Leone. Meanwhile, Jesse Peters, his colleague and cofounder of the Silver Bluff church, had returned to Silver Bluff and submitted to the lenient supervision of Thomas Galphin, George's son. After the war Peters preached in Augusta as well as Silver Bluff; then he located his church permanently in Augusta as Springfield Baptist. The distinguished black historians Walter Brooks and Carter Woodson called Springfield the oldest African American church in the United States.[19]

The largest significance of Springfield and the two Savannah churches that trace their origins to Andrew Bryan is that the religions of the Great Awakening appealed to African Americans in a way the older religions had not. They found the enthusiasm and excitement of the preaching and prayer meetings much more congenial than the comparatively colder ritual of the traditional churches. In that sense the Great Awakening provided a threshold through which African people might become Americans. The thesis that black churches provided an entrée into American culture has stirred some controversy. The sociologist E. Franklin Frazier and the historian John Blasingame emphasize the dominance of American over African traditions; Sterling Stucky argues that blacks maintained African customs under cover of Christianity. Charles Joyner wisely concluded that a merger occurred between African and American traditions. The epochal fact is that so many black people found meaning and values in the evangelical religions. After two centuries Springfield Church stands in Augusta to witness and celebrate that reality.[20]

The case can be made that the Revolution represented the aggressive pragmatism of Charlestown. Backcountry Georgians recognized an opportunity to wrest land away from the Creeks and Cherokees. They considered those who did business with Indians as opposed to their interests. A British government that blocked expansion beyond the Ogeechee River did not represent them. The rumor that did most to inflame revolutionary passions in 1775 was that the British ministry intended to unleash an Indian war upon the backcountry. Though the rumor was false, the loyal Georgians thought it a good idea and eventually convinced the British high command to try the plan.

The British decision to bring Indians into the war proved fatal to their cause. The people of the backcountry would never ally themselves with the Indians whose land they coveted. It might be unfair to Charlestown to attribute greed and unbridled ambition to that elegant colonial town, but listen to William Henry Drayton, the hotspur of the Revolution in Carolina, as he urged war against the Cherokees: "It is expected that you make smooth work as you go—that is you put up every Indian cornfield and burn every Indian town and every Indian taken shall be the slave and property of the taker and that the nation be exterpated and the lands become the property of the public."[21] Whereas the frontiersmen might want to extirpate the Indians for the savage joy of it, the more sophisticated Drayton stressed the practical value of getting the Indians' land.

That the Georgians learned their Carolina lessons well is evidenced by a remarkable petition addressed to General Charles Lee, commander in the southern department, by the inhabitants of the backcountry parishes of Saint George and Saint Paul. The letter carried their complaint against the Indian traders who brought "those savages down into the settlements" and endangered the lives of the settlers. It went on to denounce Governor Wright for failing to extract the Ogeechee–Oconee strip land, "by nature formed for the benefit and advantage of the inhabitants, in giving them an opportunity of sending and exporting their produce to market." The petitioners concluded with the suggestion that General Lee consider "how far prudent it might be to make an attempt to exterminate and rout those savages out of their nation." In that event, "your petitioners will be ready, at the hazard of their lives and fortunes to unite together for so desirable a purpose."[22]

When actually called upon to cooperate with Carolina in a campaign against the Cherokees, the Georgia petitioners had second thoughts on the prudence of the matter. George Galphin, the Silver Bluff planter and longtime Indian trader, accepted the appointment as Indian commissioner from the Continental Congress, but he thought better of the Indians than he did of the backcountry braggarts. When he used the term "damned villains," he meant the Georgians who wanted to bring on an Indian war.[23]

Many undoubtedly were villains, but there was a rationale for their strategy. They saw land as the necessary foundation in their quest for economic betterment and increased political clout. The Treaty of Paris in 1783 fulfilled the brightest dreams of Georgia expansionists. The western border of the state lay on the remote Mississippi. A Georgian confided to the exiled Thomas Brown, "We are determined to possess ourselves of the territory and privilege of navigation agreeable to the treaty of peace—and 'tis an object richly worth contending for."[24] The war opened to Georgians the possibility of success enjoyed by the Charlestown gentry, a combination of planting and commerce, the object the accumulation of sufficient funds necessary to enjoy the good life in town.

The irony of the story of the struggle of Georgians for land is that they won the war but could not get at the prize of war, the land beyond the Ogeechee. The postrevolutionary state government carved the land into counties and issued paper money backed by the value of the land, but the land itself remained beyond their reach. The Charlestown-educated Alexander

McGillivray, son of the Scottish trader Lachlan McGillivray and Sehoy, a Creek woman of the powerful Wind Clan, would not let Georgia cross the Ogeechee. McGillivray, a deputy of John Stuart and later Thomas Brown, the British Indian superintendents, gained the respect of the Creek Nation and became its spokesman. Largely because of the state's inability to deal with McGillivray, Georgia delegates voted for a strong federal government at the Philadelphia convention, and the state quickly ratified the new constitution. George Washington invited McGillivray to New York to settle the land question. McGillivray witnessed the strange sight of the New York Sons of Saint Tammany dressed in Indian garb, presumably to make the Creeks feel welcome. By the terms of the Treaty of New York, Georgians gained the Oconee but were vastly disappointed at not getting a great deal more. At least one reason for George Washington's southern tour in 1791 was to quiet the grumbling Georgians.[25]

The conduct of the victors after the war confirmed the reason for waging war in the first place. Georgians wanted to be like Carolinians, especially Charlestown Carolinians. They turned away from Savannah and its historic links with Europe and turned toward the rich promise of the frontier. They moved the capital to Augusta while building a new capital at Louisville. Augusta imitated Charlestown with its racetrack, resident theater, dancing schools, social clubs, and a thriving commerce. Five tobacco warehouses lined the Savannah River. Tobacco roads led to Augusta; the one to John Twiggs's warehouse at New Savannah Bluff still bears the name. During the decade of the 1790s, cotton gin inventors—Eli Whitney, Joseph Eve, and William Longstreet—competed for business.

The great object of every would-be entrepreneur who flocked to Augusta was wealth, of course, and more specifically land as a means to the attainment of wealth. Inferior-court judges grew rich selling plots of land that did not exist. The files of the surveyor general's office in Atlanta contain hundreds of fictitious plots. Between 1789 and 1796 more than three times as much land was granted as existed in the area available for sale.[26]

The most blatant expression of the pragmatic opportunism that can be attributed to the Charlestown influence was the great Yazoo land fraud of 1795. After the Pinckney Treaty of that year confirmed Georgia's title to the western lands above the thirty-first parallel, the Georgia legislators decided to sell roughly fifty million acres, the future states of Alabama and Mississippi, to land speculators. Members of the Georgia legislature held stock in the companies which purchased the land for about five hundred thousand dollars. As this business of the legislators' transferring public land to themselves became known, it aroused a storm of indignation. James Jackson came home from the Senate to lead a reform party in the repeal of the Yazoo Act. The reformers moved out of Augusta, "the sink of iniquity," as Jackson called it, and took up residence in the new capital, Louisville. The original stockholders shrewdly sold out to unsuspecting Yankees and foreigners, so they were not bothered much by the repeal. The innocent victims fought back in court. After a long legal battle, they won. In the case of *Fletcher v. Peck*, Chief Justice John Marshall argued that the United States Constitution did not permit Georgia to cancel the Yazoo sale. Fraudulent or not, it was a valid contract.[27]

The important point about the Yazoo affair and the reform movement as far as this essay is concerned is that it represented both the supreme expression of the Charlestown influence and the first important example of the Virginia influence. With the end of the Revolution, a steady stream of people from Virginia moved to the Georgia backcountry to satisfy their ambition to acquire land and establish a Virginia-type plantation. They brought with them a well-defined code of paternalism. The Yazoo Act discredited the selfish profiteering of the Charlestonian gentlemen who fought and won the war, and installed the mores of Virginia as the social and political standard. One of the first Virginians, George Gilmer, expressed the opinion that Georgians "had but slight comprehension of government, and but little use for that which they had but as the instrument for satisfying their desire for land."[28]

When the Virginians came to frontier Georgia, the vision of a classical plantation house gave way to the reality of a log cabin the first year, an adjoining one connected by a breezeway the next year, and finally front and back doors, dormer windows, and corner rooms added as the family grew. Many Virginians brought at least a few slaves with them, and migration proved even more disruptive to the slave families, but the newcomers soon replicated their society in the Georgia backcountry. A modern student of history is caught in amazement at the inexorable pervasiveness of the Virginia influence in Georgia. The evangelical tradition ran as deeply as before, but now with an overlayer of Virginia behavior. The first Baptists and Methodists opposed slavery; but with the social acceptance of the plantation system, the ownership of slaves became fashionable, and justification for slavery was found in the Bible. The urban commercial class adopted the language and deportment of agrarian planters, though they had difficulty living up to the code.

In a major effort to enforce civilized behavior, the Georgia legislature outlawed the practice of biting various parts of the opponent's anatomy and gouging out of eyes. There followed an outbreak of dueling, much of it ridiculous posturing. It seemed that those who aspired to be gentlemen were especially sensitive to points of honor. Governor James Jackson, leader of the reform party, set the example by exchanging shots with Robert Watkins, whose fault lay merely in including the Yazoo Act in a compilation of laws. George Lamplugh tells how James Gunn, one of the new arrivals from Virginia, challenged General Nathanael Greene because of an imagined slight years before. Greene declined the challenge, perhaps because he did not have to prove that he was a gentleman.[29]

The Virginia Influence and Gender

The fact that artisan households as well as those of the merchant-planter class felt the effects of paternalism illustrates the growing influence of Virginia attitudes. The comparatively rapid progress in civility can be traced in comments by visitors to Augusta. All agree that the town bustled with commerce; several paid compliments to the good people of the place. In 1809 the Scot John Melish noticed the signs of the "very extensive and profitable trade" which Augusta enjoyed. He noted that the "inhabitants are in general well informed and have a considerable taste for literature. They are affable in their deportment and polite and hospitable to strangers." C. D. Arfwedson stopped in Augusta during his 1830 tour and wrote, "Of all the towns in the Southern States, none, with the exception of New Orleans, had a more agreeable exterior and inspires the stranger at first with a stronger idea of comfort and wealth than Augusta." He thought that the immense cotton warehouses, some holding nine thousand bales, ought to be tourist attractions. The Irish actor Tyrone Power in 1834 called Augusta "the most enterprising and most thriving community in Georgia." The travel writer James Silk Buckingham said that the residents of Augusta seemed to vie with one another about who could show the greatest kindness and attention. Further, the residents he met proved to be intelligent, hospitable, and agreeable.[30]

Land and slaves measured success, and by those measures several Augusta families attained success by 1818. Christopher Fitzsimmons owned 153 slaves; his brother-in-law Oswell Eve, 116; John Milledge, who corresponded with President Jefferson from his Overton plantation, 115; John Course, a merchant-planter, 100. Others who claimed at least 50 slaves included Valentine Walker, Nicholas Delaigle, Richard Tubman, and Ferdinand Phinizy. When Thomas Cumming bought his first 10 acres on "the Hill" overlooking Augusta in 1800, he signed himself "merchant." When he bought an additional 261 acres in 1818, he had become "Thomas Cumming, Gentleman." Thomas's son Henry H. Cumming was pointed out to a newcomer as one of the town's "ancien noblesse." The comment is a remarkable commentary on the era. A person in Augusta could become a gentleman or gentlewoman in one generation. By the twentieth century a family had to have invested several generations before it "belonged." Caroline Matheny Dillman, in *Southern Women*, made the cut-off point the Civil War. If a woman's ancestors lived in the South then, she was entitled to be called a southern woman, otherwise she was a woman in the South.[31]

How did members of the rising gentry comport themselves? In her diary Emmaline Eve gives us a glimpse of her father, Oswell. He operated a sawmill and a brewery, and he invented a "teamboat" (one propelled by horses on a circular treadmill) and put his money into plantations scattered about the countryside. He wore knee pants, silk stockings, and gold knee and shoe buckles; he curled and powdered his hair. He employed a tutor, a governess, and a dancing master for his children. Emmaline remembered that her doting father bought her a rocking bed that simulated the motion of the sea. When she went to the races, she wore a purple skirt, a scarlet velvet jacket, scarlet slippers, and a scarlet turban with white ostrich feathers. Sartorially, the Eves had come a long way from the frontier.[32]

Though the city differed essentially from the plantation, the plantation dictated behavior. While over a hundred stores lined Broad Street and hundreds of women worked in these stores, schools actually prepared women for the plantation. The female department at Richmond Academy taught languages and needlework. Although women had to do figures in their business, they were not taught mathematics for fear that it would addle their brains. Thomas Sandwich's Mount Salubrity school for girls on the Hill offered a typical curriculum: "Filigree, Tambour and Artificial Flower making" as well as "the useful and fashionable needleworks" and "polite literature."[33]

Husbands who were not and never would be planters objected to their wives' working outside the home. Susan Nye, a schoolteacher from Dutchess County, New York, married Adam Hutchinson, an Augusta cotton broker who had aspirations to the rank of gentleman. When the cotton market fell off and his income declined, Susan suggested that she could open a school. She confided to her diary that Mr. Hutchinson became so angry at the notion that he refused to talk to her or her child for two days. One can only imagine how it must have galled Hutchinson when his fortunes continued to decline and he had to ask his wife to start her school.[34]

Some would-be gentlemen cast their wives out for one reason or another, and then ran notices in the newspaper that they would not be responsible for their wives' future expenses. One Susanna Carson refused to act the part of the submissive wife when her husband published such an announcement. She sent in a rejoinder:

> To all good people who want him descripted
> To running away her has long been addicted.
> He deserted his country, being scared at a musket ball,
> And ran home the greatest hero of all.
> For such services as this he obtained a pension,
> How well he deserved it, I will not mention.
> But one thing for all I needs must acknowledge
> He's the worst husband God ever made to my knowledge.[35]

Clearly, Susanna's husband failed to live up to the code of a gentleman, but Susanna, in spite of her literary achievement, also failed to play the part of the long-suffering wife. She had too much steel and not enough magnolia.

Augustus Baldwin Longstreet grew up in Augusta during what he might have called "gentrification." His *Georgia Scenes* are a mild satire on a society emerging from the frontier. He admitted that he regretted the passing of the old "foot-stomping" dances and the introduction of the minuet, cotillions, and waltzes, all meant, as he said, "to teach us the graces."[36] In a chapter entitled "The Charming Creature as a Wife," he lampooned the shallow, superficial southern belle. In the story George Baldwin asks his bride, Evelina, what she wanted him to be.

> "I would have you think more of me than all the world beside," replied Evelina. "I would have you overcome your dislike of such innocent amusements as tea-parties and balls, and I would have you take me to the Springs or to New York, or Philadelphia every summer. Now, what would you have me do?"
>
> "I would have you rise when I do, regulate your servants with system, see that they perform their duties in the proper way and proper time. Let all provisions go through your hands and devote your spare time to reading valuable works, painting, music or any other improving employment, or innocent recreation."
>
> "Lord," rejoined Evelina, "if I do all these things you mention, I shall have no time for reading, music or painting."[37]

Evelina possessed the first essential of a southern lady: she had charm enough.

But she lacked the necessary counterpart, the ability to manage. Therefore she drove poor George to drink and to ruin. A study has not yet been made of the men whose lives were wrecked by such charming creatures.

Eleanor Boatwright wrote about the difficulty of balancing the duties of a good wife. An Augusta native and a teacher at a school named in honor of Emily Tubman, Boatwright grew up with the myths of southern history. At Duke University she learned the history as historians see it. Her 1939 master's thesis, entitled "Women in Georgia, 1783–1860," was so far ahead of the time that it went unread. Anne Firor Scott rescued it from the archives of Duke's library and published it in 1994. Boatwright wrote with wit and humor and a forthrightness she had learned from Tubman's Julia Flisch, an able historian who wrote novels about strong pioneer women and weak husbands. Boatwright described the problems of the southern lady: "In blindness and with unstudied cruelty, a southern gentleman expected a frivolous girl, kept ignorant in the name of innocence, trained under the theory of inferiority and selected as a bride for the very qualifications that she must renounce, to become on her wedding day a Roman matriarch with the wisdom of Solomon." Then she added the Boatwright touch: "And the astonishing thing is that many women accomplished it."[38]

Two noted Augusta women who negotiated the rites of passage from belle to matron were Octavia LeVert and Emily Tubman. Octavia Walton was born in Augusta's Hill section in 1810, the daughter of George Walton Jr. and Sarah Walker. Her prospects for achieving the status of lady benefited from the social position of her family: her grandfather George Walton signed the Declaration of Independence, and her uncle Freeman Walker became a United States senator. Her personal qualities also helped equip her for the role of belle. In Florida, where her father served as territorial governor, she mastered several languages, including French, Spanish, and Italian. The clever girl translated official documents for her father. When her mother took her to Mobile to meet the great Lafayette, the sixteen-year-old Octavia delighted the visitor by welcoming him in French. She moved to Mobile with her family, and her father became mayor of that city. Octavia married a wealthy physician, Henry LeVert, and excelled as wife, mother, hostess, and manager of the household. A consummate charmer, she collected a galaxy of famous admirers, including the writers Washington Irving, Edgar Allan Poe, and Henry Wadsworth Longfellow; the actors Joseph Jefferson and Edwin Booth; Senators Henry Clay, Daniel Webster, and John C. Calhoun; and Presidents Millard Fillmore and James Buchanan. She was Buchanan's special guest at a ball for the prince

Emily Tubman (1794–1885) combined social
graces with business acumen. (Courtesy
Reese Library, Augusta State University)

of Wales. Having conquered the great men of America, Octavia set her cap for Europe and wrote a two-volume work about her travels. She met Queen Victoria, Prince Napoleon, and Pope Pius IX, among others. The only flaw in an otherwise perfect portrait of a southern lady was a certain coolness regarding secession. That and the war interfered with her acting the part of sophisticated hostess and woman of the world, and she returned to her natal home on the Hill in Augusta, where she died in 1877.[39]

Emily Tubman is an even better candidate for perfect-lady status. She added shrewd business sense to charm and vivacity. She grew up in Kentucky, with Henry Clay her financial guardian after her father's death. She visited Augusta to attend the wedding of a friend in 1818, met the wealthy merchant Richard Tubman, and promptly married him. She was twenty-four; he, fifty-two. That Emily possessed the variety of talents required for ladyship is evidenced by her being chosen to manage the social event of the decade, the ball for the hero Lafayette on the occasion of his visit to Augusta in 1825. She led the distinguished visitor to the floor and opened the ball by dancing the minuet. The Lafayette ball marked an upward stride in Augusta's progress toward sophistication. When Richard Tubman died in 1836, Emily invested her money in Augusta's banks, railroads, and factories and built a fortune. She paid the way to Liberia for forty-two of her freed slaves. She donated churches, school buildings, and homes for the poor. She presided graciously over Augusta's society in the postwar years.[40] Somewhat after the manner of Lee, she demonstrated that real people could match the myth.

Turner Clanton, an Augusta merchant, strove to measure up to the Virginia ideal. He acquired several plantations and managed them from his mansion in Augusta. His adoring daughter Ella Gertrude regarded him as a model gentleman and tried her best to become an ideal lady. Her daily successes and failures, recorded faithfully in her journal, reveal how it was for a girl to grow up in antebellum Augusta. For years her journal fascinated scholars who perused it at Duke's Perkins Library. In 1990 Virginia Ingraham Burr presented an edited version of the journal under the title *The Secret Eye*. In it Gertrude is revealed as an intelligent, sensitive, warm person, and a woman of her time. When she was eighteen, she married Jefferson Thomas, one of a group of young men who had serenaded her under her window at half past eleven at night. She called her husband Mr. Thomas, even though he was only twenty-one. She thanked God for her husband: "Combining such moral qualities, such an affectionate heart, with just such a master will as suits my woman's nature, for true to my sex, I delight in looking up and love to feel my woman's weakness protected by man's superior strength." Unfortunately, Jefferson Thomas failed to measure up to Gertrude's expectations. The serenading ended with marriage. Gertrude recorded a poignant and painful moment. "With a heart filled with kind wishes and affectionate emotions filling my thoughts, I bent towards him and requested him to kiss me. He was reading and probably engaged, made rather an impatient gesture and did not appear inclined to respond with alacrity to my request. I drew back offended, I confess. I felt the blood rush to my face and tears of wounded pride filled my eyes." All her readers must cry out, "Shame on you, Jefferson Thomas." As for Gertrude, she knew what her role demanded of her: "The only remedy for faults discovered," she told herself, "must be to love them down."[41]

Joan Cashin concludes that many women shared Gertrude's attitude. She calls it a culture of resignation:

> They had to be chaste and pure, to live for the family before and after marriage. They should be devout, pray, attend church regularly, and read the Bible. They should defer to their fathers, husbands, brothers, cousins, and ministers, who would protect them from harm and advise them on any matter pertaining to the greater world beyond the household. In return women gave up their autonomy, but that was a small price to pay for acceptance, respectability, responsibility and security.[42]

Plantation models and mores became an obsession during the 1850s. The best defense of slavery consisted in the class-structured view of society. A refined upper class justified a menial lower class. Christopher C. G. Memminger, future Confederate secretary of the treasury, explained the system to the Augusta Young Men's Library Association, though his listeners probably needed no explanation. "The Slave Institution of the South increases the tendency to dignify the family. Each planter is in fact a Patriarch—his position compels him to be a ruler in his household. From early youth, his children and servants look up to him as the head, and obedience and subordination become important elements of education. . . . Domestic relations become those which are most prized." With leaders like Memminger expatiating on the patriarchy, no wonder that Jefferson Thomas comported himself as lord and master. Across the river, at Redcliffe, James Henry Hammond sincerely believed that he had done all he could "to make my sons well-educated and well-bred independent South Carolina Country Gentlemen, the nearest to noblemen of any possible in America."[43]

Many women like Gertrude Thomas muttered to their diaries about the posturing of the lords of creation and the unfairness of the system. In 1850 an anonymous woman who had reached the limits of her restraint wrote the editor of the *Augusta Chronicle*. The piece, published July 7 and entitled "Advice to Wives," noted that husbands rarely asked for advice, and on those rare occasions "they do not seek your opinion, but agreement." When your husband comes home and inquires how your day went, she continued, he does not want you to tell the truth—that things were difficult—so you ought to answer, "Quite well, as usual." Even though you know that his work is light and his office pleasant, and that he has an occasional julep with his friends, "he wishes you to think it as hard work for him to make money as the digger in the mines is up to his knees in mud."[44]

Such sober comments appeared rarely as the plantation ideal increased its hold upon nonplanting urban merchants and artisans. The irony is that while Virginia rhetoric filled the forums, Augusta took an antiagrarian, Yankee-like turn. Augusta built factories. This should not be surprising if one recalls that the old Charlestown commercial tradition ran deep under the veneer of Virginia manners.

The men who invested in steamships, banks, and railroads realized that Augusta, like other eastern cities, had to create jobs or its people would join the throngs moving west. Whether Henry Clay's visit to Augusta in 1844 suggested the idea or was coincidental, shortly afterward city leaders began talking about a bold scheme to dig a canal from the rapids seven miles above Augusta and run it into town to provide power for the factories. The leader of the enterprise, Henry H. Cumming, knew that he had to change public opinion: "To many the thought of competing with the North in industry was foolish; to others the very name manufacturer had become odious." Apologists for slavery denounced with increasing vehemence the cruel factory system of the North. Investment in land and cotton had become a test of Southern patriotism. Henry Cumming had to argue that industrial development would allow the South to be less dependent on the North. He could also couch his appeal in the language of paternalism. During the early 1840s the South experienced a depression. City leaders felt constrained to do something for the jobless. Under the leadership of Mayor Martin Dye and the presidency of a former mayor, Daniel Hook, a public subscription was held in 1841 for a "Home Industry Society." The society took as its purpose the employment of women who had to support themselves and their families. It collected money to buy raw materials and the women manufactured the finished product.[45] This kind of paternalism formed part of Henry H. Cumming's appeal. Augusta must provide for artisan families; they must have work, homes, and schools. The appeal was a bold one. Cumming and his partners said, in effect, "Forget your plantation South and save your city. You are not father figures on an American manor, but you can be father figures for the urban poor." Although Cumming might not have realized it, he and his friends acted from motives similar to Oglethorpe's and those of the Georgia Trustees. Humanitarianism motivated them; if profits might be made, so much the better.

The Augusta canal builders stole a march on William Gregg, whose essays on domestic manufacture appeared in the *Augusta Chronicle* beginning January 1845. Gregg warned that political leaders did a disservice by arguing against industry. The South had the resources, the capital, and the labor supply to do its own manufacturing. Gregg expressed particular concerns for poor white families. He counted twenty-nine thousand illiterates above the age of twelve in South Carolina alone who lived in conditions "but little elevated of the Indian of the forest." He wrote about the happy changes that would occur in their diet, health, and appearance if a factory employed and housed them. He painted an appealing picture of the mill village on the Sabbath, "when the females turn out in their gay colored gowns." Frustrated by the Augusta entrepreneurs in his bid to build his dream factory along the Augusta canal, Gregg developed his mill village at Graniteville, across the river from Augusta. Gregg's biographer, Broadus Mitchell, aptly observed that "Graniteville was like a feudal village, with the great stone factory substituted for the turreted castle and the wooden houses in place of thatched cottages; the Poor Whites came in for their protection of their overlord just as eagerly as did the peasants of centuries earlier. . . . Gregg was to be his retainer's landlord, employer, teacher, clergyman and judge."[46]

The Augusta Factory began operating in 1848, before Gregg's Graniteville Mill opened. The factory attracted so many visitors that tickets were required. A Lexington, Georgia, farmer wrote home to his wife, "I also went to the large factory in Augusta where there is 200 persons operating and was sorry when I got there I did not have you and Lou with me to see the greatest sight I ever saw."[47]

A grateful city honored the father of the canal, Henry Cumming, with a tribute and a seventeen-piece silver service. The canal produced two large flour mills, a sawmill, a grist mill, a machine shop, a railroad-car factory, and two cotton mills; it also brought twenty-five thousand bales of cotton yearly to the mills.[48]

Paternalism and Race

The growing obsession of city folk with plantation notions during the antebellum years manifested itself in race relations even more strikingly than in gender. The feudal system inherited from England required a menial class but not necessarily a black menial class. The belief that blacks must be servants evolved gradually in Virginia and in the West Indies. Jefferson warned about the way his contemporaries consigned the whole race to the lowest caste. Why not recognize that black persons exhibited the same range of talents as did people of other races? In his novel *Lancelot*, Walter Percy's hero recognized that the South took a wrong turn in this simplistic separation of the races: "We got stuck with the Negro thing and it was our fault."[49] The erroneous racial view ruined the potentially valuable Virginia system, where decency and manners were held in high regard.

Responding to the influence of the plantation, Augusta's city council enacted a bewildering array of ordinances calculated to keep blacks "in their place." Only aged blacks were allowed to sell beer, cakes, and trifles at public gatherings. Any person of color, slave or free, who used "saucy and insolent language" to a white person might get a switching. If they fought, danced, or drank in the streets, they could be punished by "a moderate whipping." No person of color could keep a light in his or her house after ten in the evening. The ordinance forbade the sale of liquor to slaves, and slaves were not to loiter in liquor stores. Persons of color were proscribed from attending military parades; they could not walk with a cane unless blind or infirm, nor smoke a pipe or cigar in a public place. They could not hold balls or other public gatherings without official permission. Prayer meetings had to be supervised by responsible whites. State law forbade traveling without a pass from the slaveowner, learning to read and write, owning property, and working in a printing shop.

These and other strictures, many of them petty, had the common purpose of enforcing childlike behavior among blacks. If on the plantation their assigned role was that of the contented children of the father figure, they should act like contented children in town also. Their place in society could not have been more minutely defined by legislation; the next nearest approach occurred in the massive segregation statutes of the first part of the twentieth century.

The problem with the black codes of the antebellum southern cities was that they were—in a word—silly. Cities were not plantations. It must have been obvious, even at the time, that cities existed for the buying and selling of things.

The codes assumed the inability of a person of color to acquire money. If such a person in fact had money, many of the codes no longer applied. A person with ready coin acquired sudden status in Augusta stores.

Slaveowners cooperated in the disregard of the codes by readily granting permission to travel and live apart, and to attend parades and circuses and the like. Some planters near Augusta confessed their inability to prevent their slaves from visiting Augusta. Malhurin Verdery appealed for the return of any of his people who could not show a pass.[50] Michael Fleck expressed his exasperation at the way his elderly slave kept running off to Augusta. He published this rhyme:

> This trip he has not gone alone
> He's carried off my horse.
> Likewise a borrowed saddle,
> Which is to me much worse.
> Pray, gentlemen, be friendly,
> If Shadrack you do see,
> Secure him well in limbo
> And straightway send for me.[51]

Augusta blacks ignored regulations when they could. They were not supposed to frequent taverns or liquor stores, but tavern owners and storekeepers willingly took their money. In 1805 a "publican" put a notice in the paper defending his practice of selling to slaves: "Slaves that go in boats or hire their own time get money by extra work." He argued that they should be allowed to spend it as they saw fit. By 1828 someone complained to the *Chronicle* that certain slaves had actually engaged in the retail liquor business in cooperation with white partners. The same critic noted that even though slaves were barred from owning property, everyone knew that an individual slave owned several shops. An 1834 grand jury complained that slaves crowded liquor stores "both day and night."[52]

The state code prohibited blacks from working in printing shops because they might learn to read. Nevertheless, blacks in Augusta worked in print shops, and the editor of the *Augusta Chronicle* defended the practice. The 1829 grand jury included such employment in its presentments, explaining that printing shops afforded "a source of information to that class of our population which sound policy forbids."[53]

Nothing illustrates the futility of white efforts to regulate black conduct more than the issue of unauthorized congregating. In 1823, 1826, and 1827 white persons wrote to the *Chronicle* complaining about blacks gathering in the streets on Sunday. The grand jury repeated the complaint in 1830 and again in 1846. In 1859 the grand jury protested "the nuisance of negroes congregating in the streets, particularly at night and on the Sabbath." Modern Augustans could readily understand why respectable people might object to persons dressing shabbily, but white antebellum Augustans seemed inordinately anxious about black Augustans dressing well. In 1829 the Richmond County Grand Jury objected to black persons driving carriages about the streets on Sundays. In 1859 the jury complained that too many blacks wore "showy and expensive dress." Such clothing "was not suited to their position" and constituted "a rapidly growing evil."[54]

Finally, in the list of ways in which reality confounded convention, black persons owned slaves. A city ordinance of September 9, 1806, attempted to stop the practice of hiring of slaves by free blacks, but the authorities never reached the next logical step demanded by the orthodoxy of the plantation, the banning of slave ownership by free persons of color. The Richmond County tax digest for 1818 showed that Caesar Kennedy owned eight slaves, as did Judy Kelly.[55] Twenty-three other free black persons owned slaves in that year. No matter what their motives, actual ownership should have demonstrated that black persons were not suitable subjects for Aristotle's category of natural slaves.

The editor of the *Journal of Negro History*, Carter Woodson, argued that black persons who owned slaves did so for humanitarian reasons, and others have echoed that idea. However, Michael P. Johnson and James R. Roark challenged that assumption in their perceptive article in Carol Bleser's *In Joy and Sorrow*. They calculate that only about 14 percent of the 3,600 free black slaveowners in 1830 owned family members. They assume that black people shared the same social attitudes as whites. Free blacks who wished to attain respectability went about it the same way whites did, by the acquisition of property, including slaves. They saw that the best way to "secure their own freedom and to separate themselves and their family members from slaves" was the ownership of slaves.[56]

In short, paternalism affected the behavior of black persons as well as white. If that idea is surprising, it is because one assumes that antebellum blacks, having suffered belittlement, injustice, and ignominy from white paternalism, must have become ardent egalitarians. In fact, as Johnson and Roark contend, free black women who married free black men "often encountered an exaggerated form of patriarchy." Strong fathers lessened the vulnerability of black families in a racist society. Consequently, the increasing influence of the plantation model upon white southerners also influenced black southerners. Johnson and Roark show that there was a dramatic increase—273 percent—in the number of black slaveowners between 1810 and 1830.[57]

George Lewis, a Scotch Presbyterian minister, visited Augusta in 1844 and commented on the way blacks imitated the manners and entertainment of the whites. "They have their formal parties, to which they invite each other a week or ten days before," he noted. Often the parties were held in a hotel or a public room hired for the purpose. When Henry Clay visited earlier in the same year, the authorities sent a coach to convey Clay to his reception. That same evening the free black community sent a coach to bring Clay's servant to a separate reception. George Lewis commented, "This high life below stairs indicates at least the comparative ease and freedom in which the coloured people live, and the more so that it occurs in a small city, where such things cannot be done in a corner."[58]

Springfield Church provides another example of how the black experience in Augusta contradicted the prevailing notions of class and caste. Jesse Peters, cofounder of the church, moved his congregation to Augusta from Silver Bluff after the Revolution. Springfield records indicate that within two years of the end of the war, the members met in the house owned by Dick Kelly. Perhaps Judy Kelly, who owned eight slaves and some real estate in 1818, was a member of Dick Kelly's family. White Augustans helped Peters secure the lot on which the church still stands two centuries later. The remarkable fact about Springfield is that by its independent existence it defied the prevailing belief that persons of color could not and should not manage for themselves. The church still has a letter written by its founder in 1798 in which he testified that he and his people worshiped without interference. In an era that forbade public gatherings of black people and required blacks to worship under the watchful eyes of whites, Springfield members gathered together without supervision. Not until 1836, when Nat Turner's insurrection raised white fears and some Augustans questioned Springfield's independence, was there a connection with a white congregation. Even then it was at Springfield's request that white First Baptist agreed to supervise.[59]

Despite all the evidence that the plantation ideal did not work well in cities, the plantation continued to dictate behavior and shape attitudes. The visitors who noticed Augusta's bustling commerce and enterprising black folk commented on the risk attending any criticism of slavery. James Silk Buckingham phrased it succinctly. In Augusta "slavery is a topic upon which no man, and

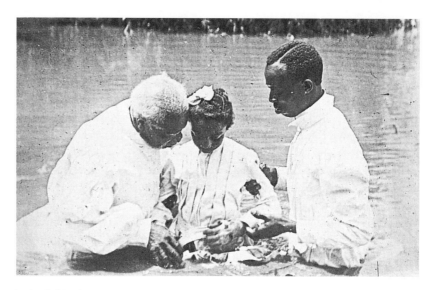

Springfield Church used the nearby Savannah River for baptisms. (Courtesy Reese Library, Augusta State University)

Springfield Church, originally founded at Silver Bluff in 1773, is the oldest African American congregation in the country. It has occupied the same site since shortly after the American Revolution. Shown is the Saint Johns Building (1800), now the church annex. (Courtesy Mark Albertin)

above all a foreigner, can open his lips without imminent personal danger unless it is to defend and uphold the system. . . . all public discussion of the question is as effectually suppressed, as if these were a censorship of the press, or a holy inquisition."[60]

The triumph of the Virginia philosophy over practical experience was almost complete in 1859, when the State of Georgia enacted legislation calculated to return troublesome free black persons to slavery, their proper place. Henry H. Cumming, "father of the canal," seemed able to preserve a rational attitude better than most others. He argued against the application of the legislation, which he termed arbitrary and unjust. Councilman William Gibson rebutted Cumming's argument. He favored selling all free black persons into slavery "as the most humane thing to do."[61]

The Decline of Paternalism

There is a great and continuing mystery about southerners' collective memory of the Civil War and Reconstruction. The recollection does not correspond with the reality in some essential aspects. The "Letters to the Editor" section on the editorial page of the *Augusta Chronicle* provides a key to public understanding. An occasional disparaging comment about the battle-flag emblem in the Georgia state flag brings a number of responses explaining that the war was about not slavery but other issues, such as industrialization versus agrarianism, unfair tariffs, and the meaning of the Constitution. Righteous indignation characterizes many of the letters, and the tone is of absolute certitude.[62]

A colleague commented that her entering college students were astonished when she told them that secession concerned the matter of slavery, a reaction this professor also has witnessed during his many years in the classroom. So what does history tell us? There can be no doubt that the question of slavery in the territories caused increasing controversy between slave and nonslave states, beginning with the Missouri Compromise in 1820 and escalating with the Compromise of 1850, the Kansas-Nebraska Act, the Dred Scott decision, and the Lincoln-Douglas Debates. In the critical election of 1860, the Lincoln Republicans opposed the extension of slavery, the Douglas Democrats favored a policy of letting the people of the territory decide, and the Breckinridge Democrats advocated a constitutional guarantee of slavery in the territories. Lincoln's election precipitated South Carolina's secession.

Undoubtedly, most men went off to war to defend home and family, not slavery. But they would not have denied that they fought for the southern way of life, and slavery had become an essential element in that way of life. Paternalism was another component of the ideal southern society, and it might correctly be said that the war was meant to preserve paternalism. Apologists for the southern way explained that if all people occupied the position for which nature fitted them and strove to fill that position as well as possible, then society would reach new heights of civilized achievement. Spokesmen talked about a civilization surpassing Greece and Rome, with scholars and statesmen doing great things. Confederate Vice-President Alexander Stephens said in a speech in Montgomery that the mission of the Confederacy was to "exhibit the highest type of civilization which is possible for human society to reach." Stephens assumed that slavery was an essential feature of the ideal society. "Our new government," he said in a speech in Savannah, "is founded upon, its cornerstone rests upon the great truth that the Negro is not equal to the white man, that slavery, subordination to the superior race is his natural and moral condition." He said that this great truth had been slow to evolve and that the Confederacy was "the first government ever instituted upon principles in strict conformity to nature and to the ordination of Providence." The Confederacy would be modeled on Aristotle's perfect society, a society of classes.[63]

The proclamations by Abraham Lincoln and Jefferson Davis reveal what might be called the official interpretations of the war's purpose. After waiting for the opportune moment, Lincoln declared that slaves in the Confederate States were to be free, depending upon the success of Union arms. At Gettysburg he framed the issue in classic language: the war was about equality, about a classless society. The response of Jefferson Davis to the Emancipation Proclamation is not part of our collective memory; it does not appear in school books; southern students do not memorize it for oratorical contests. His message rests in the obscurity of the Jefferson Davis Papers in the archives of Washington and Lee University. In a direct reply to Lincoln's Emancipation Proclamation, Davis addressed the people of the North and South: "All Negroes who shall be taken in any of the States in which slavery does not now exist, in the progress of our arms, shall be adjudged, immediately after such capture, to occupy the slave status, and in all states which shall be vanquished by our arms, all free Negroes shall, ipso facto, be reduced to the condition of helotism, so that the respective normal conditions of the white and black races may be ultimately placed on a permanent basis, so as to prevent the public peace from being thereafter endangered." Davis echoed Alexander

Stephens in reaffirming "slavery is the cornerstone of a Western Republic" and ended by voicing his belief that "the day is not distant when the old Union will be restored with slavery nationally declared to be the proper condition of all of African descent."[64]

How such a clear and emphatic statement by the chief officer of the Confederacy could be so completely forgotten by those who honor the Confederacy is a puzzle that invites investigation. A similar phenomenon happened in the case of Reconstruction, when the newly organized Republican Party fell into quarreling factions while Democrats waited to pick up the pieces of state government. The architects of the Republican Party, the so-called "Augusta Ring," included former Confederates. Foster Blodgett, chairman of the 1868 convention that drafted Georgia's Reconstruction constitution, was a native Augustan, a popular and successful prewar mayor, and a Confederate officer. His friend Rufus Bullock, the only Republican to be elected governor in Georgia, was also a Confederate officer. So was the lieutenant governor, Benjamin Conley, another former Augusta mayor. These men, along with the wartime governor, Joseph E. Brown, dominated the brief and ineffective Republican administration. None were carpetbaggers. Nor was there any black rule, not even any danger of Negro rule. Only twenty-three African Americans were elected to the Georgia house and three to the senate. As soon as the Union troops left, the black members were expelled. Bullock invited the troops back to prop up his fragile government for a year. The Democrats maintained their control of the legislature and in 1872 regained the governorship.[65]

That is not the image of the Reconstruction most white Georgians retain. When most think of Reconstruction, they picture a carpetbagger-black coalition creating unimaginable scandals and spending money lavishly. (Actually, the most important legislation to come out of the Bullock administration was a bill to establish public schools.) They further imagine rude black men insulting white women with the encouragement of boorish Union soldiers. There is no doubt that the Reconstruction era was traumatic for most white Georgians, but the shock was mainly psychological. Defeat meant the end of the goal of a class-oriented society and a victory for the notion of equality. When troops of the Thirty-third Colored Infantry marched boldly into Augusta, chanting their regimental song, it must have seemed to many onlookers that the world had turned upside down.[66] Those who had been consigned to a condition of helotism by Jefferson Davis were now in uniform and in charge! Even if they did nothing, the prospect of what they might do terrified white

Augustans. Gertrude Clanton Thomas confided to her diary that Lee's defeat made her doubt the Bible.[67]

Though it did not disprove the Bible, Lee's surrender signaled the end of the dominance of the Virginia plantation ideal as the official southern philosophy. Augustans had always been business-minded, and they made most of their opportunity. They built monuments to honor the dream of a higher civilization, now referred to as the "Lost Cause," and dedicated themselves to a new banner labeled "Progress." Colonel George W. Rains, who built and operated the Confederate Powderworks in Augusta, set the example. He suggested to the city council that the Powderworks chimney remain as a memorial to the Confederate dead, and that the canal be enlarged so that new factories might be built alongside. The city did both. The factories were constructed and Augusta called itself the "Lowell of the South."

The new element in the New South was not that businessmen sat in the seats of power—that had always been the case—but that business leaders no longer owned slaves. They no longer had to defend slavery as a necessary part of a classical civilization. New South standards did not emphasize paternalism. From the North came speakers bearing a new version of the old Puritan message that God blessed his elect in this life with material success. Henry Ward Beecher, speaking in Augusta in 1883, declared, "Show me a community that is rich and you will find it advanced in moral excellence." Russell Conwell, president of Temple University, toured the country telling young people to get rich. "God promises prosperity to the righteous man," he said. "You should be a righteous man. If you were, you would be rich."[68]

Defenders of the Old South traditions felt uncomfortable with this kind of talk. Money-getting and money-grubbing were frowned upon by the old code. Some Confederate veterans complained that there was too much talk of progress and too little about personal improvement. One of the most articulate critics of the new fashion was Augusta's Colonel Charles C. Jones Jr., whose family letters have been published under the title *Children of Pride*. In a speech on Confederate Memorial Day 1889, he contrasted the Old South and the New. He regretted the passing of "a civilization, patriarchal in its characteristics." Contrary to orators like Beecher, he denied that wealth marked the true test of civilization. He upheld the Old South aspiration to a nobility of conduct, "the mental, moral, political, economic education and the elevation of the population."[69]

Major Joseph B. Cumming, another of Augusta's premier orators, reminded

The Cowhorn Club gathered on a Summerville lawn on Augusta's Hill on a Sunday morning at the sound of the cowhorn to drink mint juleps and reminisce about old times. (Courtesy Reese Library, Augusta State University)

Colonel George W. Rains constructed and operated the Confederate Powderworks and was in charge of the Augusta Arsenal during the Civil War. (Courtesy Reese Library, Augusta State University)

Augusta's Clinch Rifles posed for a portrait before marching off to war. (Courtesy Reese Library, Augusta State University)

his listeners of the connection between slavery and chivalry in a speech in 1893. The South stood alone in its defense of its "peculiar institution," and in defending slavery spokesmen invoked the code of chivalry: "True chivalry was not sordid. It was not mean. It was not low. It was not commercial. It was high-minded. It was generous. It scorned unfairness. It lived in an atmosphere other than that of the mart. . . . To it stainless honor was a precious jewel. True deference to woman was its sacred duty and its graceful ornament."[70] It distressed the major, as it did the colonel, that there was so little talk about chivalry in the New South.

Northern histories of the recent war attacked southern leaders, particularly the planter class, for various wrongdoings, principal among them the defense of slavery. These attacks from the North and the commercialism of the New South caused some of the defenders of the Confederacy to organize and fight back. The United Confederate Veterans meeting in Houston in 1891 established a history committee and charged it with the task of redeeming the good name of the South. The Sons and Daughters of the Confederacy took up the cause with enthusiasm, appointing oversight committees in each state to supervise the contents of school texts.[71]

Augusta had two capable historians who wrote textbooks for schools. Professor Joseph Derry, a former Confederate officer whose school in Augusta young Woodrow Wilson attended, wrote that the southerner "never asked for more than protection to himself in the right to carry with him into the common territories of the Union any property that he might possess, including slaves." A younger writer named Lawton B. Evans, the son of Confederate General Clement A. Evans, explained that "the South maintained that the North was distinctly hostile to slavery, which was a right protected by the Constitution." Because southerners believed that the election of Lincoln marked "a triumph of anti-slavery feeling," they chose to secede.[72] While insisting on constitutional rights, neither author tried to conceal that the right in question was the transporting of slavery into territories. However, the general trend in the newer histories was to emphasize the Constitution and minimize mention of slavery.

Typical of the trend was the Georgia historian Thadeus K. Oglesby in his *A Vindication of the South Against the "Encyclopedia Britannica" and Other Maligners*, published in 1903. Oglesby omitted any reference to slavery as a cause of the war, explaining, "The people of eleven of these States numbering about 5,000,000, having found that, under that government their safety and happiness, their peace and tranquility were constantly, and seriously threatened, and disturbed instead of being secured, decided to institute a new government, one that to them seemed more likely than the existing one, to affect their safety and happiness." The historian of the United Daughters of the Confederacy adopted Oglesby's interpretation. Mildred Lewis Rutherford stated her position in her 1915 report to the annual meeting of the United Daughters: "The Southern States withdrew for better protection which the government was not giving as guaranteed by the Constitution."[73] Corresponding to the deemphasis on slavery, less was said about the mission of the Confederacy to build a higher civilization.

Also characteristic of the newer histories was a darker view of Reconstruction. Herbert Spencer's application of natural selection to human society, much in vogue at the turn of the century, fueled racial attitudes. Social Darwinism seemed to support the antebellum plantation philosophy. A textbook produced for McDuffie County schools by the Ida Evans Chapter of the United Daughters illustrates the trend. "That the Negro was happy under slavery cannot be denied," the authors stated; "as a race they possessed characteristics which enabled them to submit to slavery." The writers went on to describe how, after the war, "Negro rule" caused bad government and increasing debt. They concluded that "two races cannot rule in the same country, one or the other must be supreme, naturally the white race was the one to rule in the South, and the Southern people would not give over the supremacy to the inferior race without a struggle."[74]

Teachers who did not conform to a sufficiently patriotic style of teaching were criticized by local historical commissions. Professor William E. Dodd, a North Carolina native who taught at Randolph-Macon College, objected to what he called the campaign against any books that did not come up to the standards of local patriotism. He published an article in the *South Atlantic Quarterly* about the increasingly difficult task of teaching history in the South. The Virginia Veterans History Committee called for his resignation. Dodd left of his own accord for a faculty position in a northern college. Professor Enoch M. Banks of the University of Florida wrote an article stating that the North was relatively in the right regarding the abolition of slavery and the South relatively in the wrong. The United Daughters of Florida protested to the governor, and state legislators threatened the university's funding. Banks resigned in midsemester.[75]

The revisionist movement achieved a climax in the historical novels of Thomas Dixon, an ordained Baptist minister. His trilogy on the Reconstruction era, *The Leopard's Spots*, *The Clansman*, and *The Traitor*, was a best seller during the first decade of the century and made a profound impact on the thinking of the day. Dixon portrayed a South victimized by brutal troops and rapacious blacks. Dixon's blacks were inherently incapable of achieving equality with whites. According to Dixon's biographer, the novelist treated the African American as a brute, not a citizen, whose primary goal was sexual union with any convenient white woman: "Every description, action and conversation in the novel, made the Negro appear obnoxious."[76]

Dixon converted *The Clansman* into a play, featuring hooded heroes of the Ku Klux Klan riding real horses across the stage. It made marvelous theater and caused a sensation wherever it showed; two companies toured the country for three years, making a fortune for Dixon. Coincidental with the stage presentation, race relations underwent a marked deterioration: lynchings increased in frequency, and new segregationist legislation was enacted. In Atlanta in 1906 whites rioted through black neighborhoods, destroying property. In 1907 Georgia adopted legislation disfranchising blacks. The play was a symptom of the age.

Thomas Dixon collaborated with D. W. Griffiths in producing a motion picture version of *The Clansman* entitled *The Birth of a Nation*. Generally regarded as a triumph of cinematography, the film made a lasting impression on millions of Americans. Its depiction of dim-witted blacks in the legislature, voting for every extravagance, and evil black militia at war against whites represented the historic actuality for many. Colonel William Simmons of Atlanta viewed the film and organized a new KKK atop Stone Mountain in 1915.

Old Confederates lamented the direction of events. Major Joseph Cumming repudiated Dixon's version of the Reconstruction period. The drama, he said, was "not only nasty, but fiendish and cowardly, because it seeks to incite more violence against a helpless segment of our society"; not many spoke out so boldly. William J. White of Augusta, founder of Augusta Baptist Institute (later Morehouse College) and editor of the *Georgia Baptist*, tried to stem the segregationist tide. In an editorial in the September 6, 1900, issue, he made the point: "Six prosperous Negro physicians, three successful drug stores, hundreds of grocers, shoemakers, carpenters and other business establishments in a population of fifteen thousand Negroes, make talk about inferiority cheap." White, a man with a distinguished career of moderate leadership in race relations, was hunted down by a mob because of an article from a northern paper placed in his newspaper by an assistant. White had to leave Augusta for a time. When John Hope, president of Morehouse College, thought back to his Augusta childhood, he deplored the change: "When I think of the stupid, virulent and violent racial prejudice that has sprung up in the South since my boyhood, I am amazed."[77]

One of Augusta's achievements during the earlier era of flexible race relations was the establishment of a high school for black youth, Ware High School. After seventeen years of operation the board of education closed Ware. Augusta's leading black citizens brought a lawsuit against the board, claiming discrimination under the Fourteenth Amendment. The United States Supreme Court, in a landmark decision in 1899, ruled that states might deal separately with white and black schools, setting a policy that prevailed until the epochal *Brown v. Board of Education* decision in 1954. There followed a drastic lowering of standards in public schools for black students (though private schools such as Lucy Laney's Haines Institute maintained rigorous standards). Judge William T. Gary of Augusta expressed the new attitude in his charge to the grand jury in 1903: "If it spoils good farm hands and brings to our cities men who can find no occupation, creating need for stringent vagrancy laws, then I say the education of the Negro is a danger." He went on to criticize the effort to produce lawyers, judges, physicians, and other professionals when there were no opportunities for them and, he added, "there never would be as long as the white race maintains its supremacy." The jury could think of no better response than to assure the judge that the public schools were giving black children "merely the rudiments of education that would prepare them for such tasks as they might realistically perform." Thus the judge and jury were able to ignore seventeen graduating classes of Ware High School, whose alumni had, in fact, gone on to become doctors, lawyers, businessmen, and college presidents. The Augusta lawyer Judson Lyons served in the McKinley administration as the register of the treasury, the highest-ranking black person in the government.[78]

The turn-of-century texts, which conveyed to school children a history of victimization, helped form the mindset for much of the twentieth century. The Republican Party virtually disappeared. In Augusta the Cracker Party controlled politics by means of the white primary, adopted by the Democratic Party in 1900. When in 1946 reformers criticized Cracker Party election frauds, and there were many, party spokesmen defended the primaries as the "means used by the old Confederate veterans to wrest control of this state from carpetbaggers, scalawags and negroes."[79] The Cracker Party thus maintained its power by basing its stance on the revisionist histories earlier in the century. No one publicly pointed to the fact that the old Confederates actively solicited black votes and the white primary was adopted by those who shunted aside the old Confederates. Never in its colorful history did Cracker Party leaders call for a higher civilization or promote excellence. The thought would have made them laugh.

The members of the 1956 Georgia legislature, who substituted the battle flag of the Confederacy for the official Confederate emblem in the Georgia state flag, based their understanding of history on the turn-of-the-century texts. The legislators were as defiant as the most ardent secessionist, but they did not attach the same significance to the flag as did Alexander Stephens or Jefferson Davis or Father Abram Ryan. Father Ryan, the "poet priest of the Confederacy," served at Augusta's Catholic church during the Reconstruction period. His poems, particularly "The Conquered Banner," glorified the flag and its cause.[80] None of the frenetic speeches of the 1956 legislative session were about building a better society, or improving civilization, or elevating behavior, much less about nobility and what used to be called chivalry.

Historians are now far enough removed from legalized segregation to recognize that it incorporated the worst feature of the old plantation ideal, the relegation of a race to an inferior status, without adding the countervailing element, the responsibility to act decently and honorably for the common cause. At least since the 1960s, paternalism has been out of favor. The word *elite*, as used by social scientists, carries a pejorative connotation. *Excellence* sounds undemocratic. So it is that, as the twentieth century ends, some people find themselves in the same frame of mind as the old Confederates at the end of the nineteenth. Thadeus Oglesby's observation takes on a modern relevance: "Those old ideals were the grace and glory of a day that is dead and will never come back to us." Major Joseph Cumming saw something precious in the old ways when he spoke of them as "a rule of conduct and a living force . . . which raises love, friendship, honor, faith to the realm of sacred things."[81]

The angry writers of the letters to the editor, who have forgotten about slavery, have also forgotten the grace and the glory, the better things that were part of the Confederate vision.

Today, two of the formative influences are as powerful as ever. Augustans are as eager to make money as the first Carolina deerskin traders who moved across the river to avoid paying Carolina license fees. The influence of the Great Awakening is strong. Augustans, black and white, attend churches in impressive numbers. The third influence, that of the Virginia plantation, is crippled by its association with slavery and by the burlesque posturing of some of its antebellum champions. Paradoxically, and despite the critical comments in the preceding pages, the public weal would likely benefit from an infusion of the positive elements of paternalism. Walker Percy, the novelist, would have agreed. His hero in *Lancelot* finally refuses to abide by the shallowness of his age: "I can't stand the way things are," he says. "I cannot tolerate this age. What is more, I won't. That was my discovery: that I didn't have to." It is Percy's discovery that in his past there is an alternative lifestyle to that of the present. He will resurrect the values of an age that was scorned after Freud and forgotten after Dewey. He has Lance Andrews explain that he yearns for a society in which "one will work and take care of one's own, live and let live, and behave with a decent respect toward others. . . . there will be a tight-lipped courtesy between men. And chivalry toward women."[82] Symbolically, Lance Andrews returns to Virginia to begin the reformation of society.

Ironically, the controversy over the Confederate flag may revive some of the positive elements of paternalism. The antebellum defenders of slavery had to stress the values of the plantation system in order to justify the "peculiar institution." So, too, the defenders of the Confederate emblem in the Georgia flag must search their souls for vestiges of the better qualities they identify with flag and heritage, while denying that the flag represents racism, hatred, or anything ignoble. The emotional defense of the flag, the intense current interest in Civil War publications, the popularity of reenactments, all may indicate deep stirrings in the southern psyche and presage the revival of the Virginia tradition.

Notes

1. Coleman, *Colonial Georgia*, 20.

2. Boorstin, *The Americans*, 71; Gallay, *Planter Elite*, 62–64.

3. Ellis to Board of Trade, March 15, 1759, in *Colonial Records*, ed. Candler, 28(1):192–93; E. Cashin, *Colonial Augusta*, 29–35.

4. W. Harris and Mosteller, *Georgia's First Continuing Baptist Church*; E. Cashin, *Old Springfield*.

5. There is a brilliant chapter on the influence of the philosophy of Peter Ramus in Miller, *The New England Mind*, 117.

6. "It wasn't intended for a man with the smell of the land in him to live in a mill in Augusta. Maybe it's all right for some people to do that, but God never meant for me to do it." Caldwell, *Tobacco Road*, 117.

7. Kierner, "Hospitality, Sociability, and Gender," 480.

8. Milfort, *Memoirs*, 86–89; Milfort refers to some of the rough backcountry people as "Crakeurs" and "Gougeurs," the latter term referring to those who let their nails grow long, the better to gouge out opponents' eyes.

9. Hammond to John Lewis Gervais, June 22, 1777, in *Hammond Family*, ed. Tillman and Woodson, 4.

10. Gilmer, *Sketches*, 112.

11. Ibid., 114.

12. Freeman, *George Washington*, 1:79.

13. Philip Fithian, the visitor, exclaimed, "A Phenomenon, Mrs. Carter without stays!" Quoted in Morgan, *Virginians at Home*, 43.

14. Clinton, *Plantation Mistress*, 16–35, and "Southern Dishonor," 57, 68.

15. Fox-Genovese, *Within the Plantation Household*, 145; S. Abbott, *Womenfolks*, 102.

16. Greene, *Landon Carter*, 90–92.

17. Extract from Clarke's letter in William Campbell to William Preston, December 12, 1780, in "Preston Papers," 314–16; O'Donnell, *Southern Indians*, 119.

18. W. Harris, "Daniel Marshall"; W. Harris and Mosteller, *Georgia's First Continuing Baptist Church*, 257; Robertson, *History of St. Paul's*.

19. Pringle, *Prayer*; Brooks, "Silver Bluff Church," 172–75.

20. The views of Frazier, Blasingame, Stucky, and Joyner are in P. Johnson, *African-American Christianity*; see also E. Cashin, *Old Springfield*, 15.

21. Drayton to Francis Salvador, July 24, 1776, in *Documentary History*, ed. Gibbes, 2:28–30.

22. "Petition of the Inhabitants," 181.

23. Galphin to Willie Jones, October 26, 1776, in *American Archives*, ed. Force, 3:648.

24. J[ames] H[abersham] to Thomas Brown, in Thomas Brown to Vincente Manuel de Zespedes, December 20, 1785, microfilm, East Florida Papers, P. K. Yonge Library, University of Florida, Gainesville.

25. The argument that western land was a major factor in Georgia's ratification of the Constitution is in E. Cashin, "Georgia."

26. Coulter, *Georgia*, 197–98; speculation mania is treated in the *Augusta Chronicle*, September 29, 1798.

27. A description of the Yazoo legislation is in the *Augusta Chronicle*, February 7, 1795; repercussions, *Augusta Chronicle*, March 14, 1795; nullification, *Augusta Chronicle*, February 27, 1796; for a full account see Magrath, *Yazoo*.

28. Gilmer, *Sketches*, 189.

29. *Augusta Chronicle*, March 17, 1787, June 26, 1802 (the newspaper went through several name changes during the early years; I will use its most frequently used and final name); Lamplugh, "Importance of Being Truculent."

30. Lane, *Rambler in Georgia*, 25, 96, 110, 144.

31. E. Cashin, *Story of Augusta*, 62; Dillman, *Southern Women*, 9.

32. Diary of Emmaline Eve Smith, Southern Historical Collection, University of North Carolina, Chapel Hill.

33. *Augusta Chronicle*, April 18, 1801.

34. Journal of Susan Nye Hutchinson, Southern Historical Collection, University of North Carolina, Chapel Hill.

35. *Augusta Chronicle*, May 27, 1818.

36. Longstreet, *Georgia Scenes*, 135.

37. Ibid., 115–16.

38. Boatwright, *Status of Women*, 68.

39. Craven, "Portrait of Octavia."

40. Craven, "Portrait of Emily Tubman," 5–9.

41. Burr, *Secret Eye*, 122, 144.

42. J. Cashin, *Our Common Affairs*, 10; the introduction is a comprehensive review of historical writing about southern women.

43. Memminger quoted in Scott, *Southern Lady*, 16–17; James Henry Hammond to Marcus C. M. Hammond, August 25, 1858, in *Hammonds of Redcliffe*, ed. Bleser, 48–50.

44. *Augusta Chronicle*, July 7, 1850.

45. *Augusta Chronicle*, January 2, 1845, October 1, 1850, September 27, 1841.

46. Mitchell, *William Gregg*, 24–25, 60.

47. E. Cashin, *Story of Augusta*, 96.

48. *Augusta Chronicle*, October 1, 1850.

49. Percy, *Lancelot*, 157.

50. *Augusta Chronicle*, May 11, 1799.

51. *Augusta Chronicle*, March 2, 1811.

52. *Augusta Chronicle*, August 10, 1805, June 25, 1828, June 28, 1828, June 20, 1834.

53. *Augusta Chronicle*, October 26, 1829.

54. *Augusta Chronicle*, October 24, 1859, December 16, 1829, October 24, 1859.

55. Tax Digest, 1818, Probate Records, Richmond County Courthouse.

56. Woodson, "Free Negro Owners"; Johnson and Roark, "Strategies of Survival," 101.

57. Ibid., 92, 97.

58. Lane, *Rambler in Georgia*, 184–85.

59. E. Cashin, *Old Springfield*, 20–25.

60. Lane, *Rambler in Georgia*, 147.

61. *Augusta Chronicle*, January 7, February 26, 1860.

62. *Augusta Chronicle*, December 19, 30, 1997.

63. Stephens's speech was reported in the *Augusta Chronicle*, February 12, 1861.

64. Davis's proclamation is in E. Jordan, *Black Confederates*, 319–20.

65. Grant, *The Way It Was*, 106.

66. African American Eugene Smith recited to interviewers the words the soldiers chanted: "Don't you see the lightning? Don't you hear the thunder? It isn't the lightning; it isn't the thunder. It's the buttons on the Negro uniforms!" in Rawick, *American Slave*, 4(4):348.

67. Burr, *Secret Eye*, 276–77.

68. *Augusta Chronicle*, October 17, 1883; Bailey, *American Spirit*, 2:547–48.

69. C. Jones, *Georgians During the War*, 24–25.

70. J. Cumming, *New Ideas*, 7.

71. In a perceptive article Fred Arthur Bailey traces the successful revisionism of the apologists for the Confederacy: F. Bailey, "Textbooks."

72. Derry, *Confederate State*, 104; Evans, *Essential Facts*, 363–64.

73. Oglesby, *Vindication*, 214; Rutherford, *Historical Sins*, 31.

74. McCommons and Stovall, *History of McDuffie County*, 220.

75. F. Bailey, "Textbooks," 517–19.

76. Cook, *Thomas Dixon*, 73.

77. *Augusta Chronicle*, October, 22, 1905; *Georgia Baptist*, September 6, 1900; Torrence, *Story of John Hope*, 44.

78. E. Cashin, *The Quest*, 35–42.

79. *Augusta Chronicle*, April 13, 1946.

80. Weaver, *Poems of Father Ryan*, 17–18.

81. Oglesby, *Some Truths of History*, 240; J. Cumming, *New Ideas*, 8.

82. Percy, *Lancelot*, 157–59; see also E. Cashin, "History as Mores."

From Household to Market:
Black and White Women at Work
in Augusta, 1790–1825

MICHELE GILLESPIE

ISTORIANS KNOW TOO LITTLE about the lives and work of ordinary people in the Old South. They know even less about the lives and work of ordinary women. Although the past two decades have witnessed an explosion of scholarship on women in the antebellum South, much of this work has focused on the status of plantation mistresses and their attitudes toward slavery. This body of literature suggests that although plantation mistresses lived in subordination to their husbands and could often empathize with slave women, they nonetheless reaped important benefits from their elite status. At the same time, equally exciting work has begun to appear on slave women. This scholarship not only identifies the multiple hardships and tragedies slave women endured, but shows how they established their own identities and autonomy in their relationships with their children, their slave communities, their masters and mistresses, and the society as a whole.[1]

Together, these two important waves of scholarship have placed gender and women's history, along with race, squarely in the center of antebellum southern studies. At the same time, however, this work demonstrates how little is known about women who were neither plantation mistresses or plantation slaves. It also begs the question of where class fits in relation to race and gender in this rewriting of the antebellum past, since ordinary women remain virtually ignored. Fortunately, new scholarship is beginning to address this lacuna. Suzanne Lebsock, in her pioneering book *Free Women of Petersburg*, examined the private and public lives of ordinary as well as elite women, white and black, slave and free, in one antebellum southern town. She argued that these women, despite social expectations about their limited roles, found ways to shape the public life of Petersburg. Stephanie McCurry, building on the work of Elizabeth Fox-Genovese, has shown that yeoman households in lowcountry South Carolina, like plantation households throughout the South, were the center of all social relations and economic production. She argues that while the wives and daughters of yeoman farmers were legally free, their husbands and fathers viewed them as dependents, and therefore as a kind of property akin to slaveholding.[2]

Betty Wood, Timothy J. Lockley, and Robert Olwell have each argued that despite the social confines women experienced in the Old South, the establishment of informal exchanges of goods and services offered ordinary women, whether white or black, slave or free, ways to secure personal and financial independence from both men and masters. The essays in Christie Anne Farnham's *Women of the American South* mark an important point of departure for recovering southern women's experiences, in all their variety.[3] But more research steeped in case studies and local history remains necessary before one can profile the varieties of work women performed as well as assess the significance of their experience for understanding antebellum southern culture as a whole.

This essay marks an effort to continue this work by examining ordinary women's working lives in Augusta in the decades after the American Revolution, when the Old South was first taking shape. The frequent absence of women, especially black women and ordinary white women, from the formal records of the past makes this task difficult.[4] Nonetheless, the sources that are available offer striking evidence that all women shared at least one thing— subordinate status because of their sex. At the same time, these sources indicate that women's experiences and opportunities were predicated as much on class and race as on gender. Even more important, the records show that some black and white women in Augusta found ways within these cultural constructs to secure independence and authority for themselves through their work. That Augusta women could claim this relative autonomy, which they manifested in a variety of ways, was a direct result of Augusta's rapid growth as a commercial center during the early Republic.

Augusta women were not alone in their subordinate status; most women in the slave South, even elite white women, were relegated to a kind of second-class citizenship that limited their actions and expectations. Southern households in the decades after the American Revolution were almost always headed by white property-holding men whose individual rights and authority over their dependents received support from the state. This system nurtured a paternalistic ideology that legitimated white male dominance over the household and, by extension, over society. In turn, this ideology helped perpetuate the notion that white men were more or less equals in a society filled with dependents—women, children, and slaves. This ideology, therefore, encouraged white men to think of themselves as superior both to white women and to black men and women, whether slave or free.[5]

Women's subordinate place within this social hierarchy was reinforced by expectations about gender roles and women's work in the household.[6] The social status of white men in Augusta, like that of all white men in the slave South, emanated in large part from the household, which sat at the intersection of class, race, and gender. Women's work contributed not only to the efficient functioning of the household but to the ultimate order of the slave South. The work of black women in the white household added to both the smooth functioning of the home and the social prestige that the household head and white family enjoyed. In this sense women's work, the bulk of which took place in the household, was an important symbol of men's power. Women's work offered both practical benefits and symbolic ones to individual male-headed households and southern society at large.

First and foremost, women's work improved a household's productive capacity. Most single young men were well aware of this fact, recognizing that the quality of their lives could be dramatically improved by marriage. "It may be justly observed," wrote Reuben King, a young Georgia tanner, in 1805, "that a Single man Seldom obtains property so fast as one married[,] allowing them to be equally Industrus." King actually blamed his lackluster business and finances on his single status.[7]

A. B. Longstreet, the Georgia educator, lawyer, politician, and humorist who was born in Augusta in 1790, penned a telling story about southern white women's roles entitled "The Charming Creature as a Wife," which was first published in the *States Rights Sentinel* in 1834 and later included in Longstreet's well-known collection, *Georgia Scenes.* The short story begins by extolling the virtues of the mother of the central character, George Baldwin. She was exceedingly well educated and well read and at the same time managed to maintain order and cleanliness in her household. She knew the exact amount of provisions in her larder and when more would be required. Her servants understood their duties, and she never needed to scold or berate them. In sum, she was pious, diligent, industrious, economical, and educated. Indeed, she was the perfect helpmeet. Her son George, a man of good character and some ambition, chose his wife with little care, however, despite his

The print of the "Charming Creature as Wife" is from A. B. Longstreet's *Georgia Scenes*. Evelina is shown spurning the welcoming approaches of one of George's friends. "Having no tact for turning off these things playfully, and as little disposition to do so," the author wrote, "she repelled them with a town dignity, which soon relieved her of these intrusions; and in less than a week, stopt the visits of George's first and warmest friends, to his father's house."

mother's shining example, marrying a young lady not for her mastery of domesticity and modest ways but for her beauty and good family. Unfortunately for George, he soon found all his professional prospects foiled again and again by his new wife's lack of industry, as well as her love of luxury, spendthrift ways, and bad cooking. The moral of the story is clear. A man should marry a woman who brings good domestic skills to the household, not just beauty and family connections, or he will face personal and professional ruin.[8]

Augusta in the Early Republic

White men in Augusta, like white men elsewhere in the South, implicitly embraced this view; like all white southern men, they hoped to establish well-run households of their own, which would enable them to promote their incomes, secure heirs, and cement their political and social status within their communities. The nature of Augusta's settlement patterns and economic growth during the early Republic made such ambitions viable. This upcountry community on the fall line of the Savannah River, situated on the Georgia border across from upcountry South Carolina, drew farmers eager to sell their harvests from around the region. Local merchants purchased their crops and then shipped them to Savannah and Charleston for distribution in Europe. The migration of agricultural men and their families to this Georgia upcountry was so great that by the 1790s upcountry Georgians far outnumbered their brethren in the much older lowcountry settlements along the Atlantic. Augusta benefited greatly from this transition, growing in physical size, population, and wealth throughout the 1790s and early 1800s. Scores of workshops and stores lined Broad Street, the nearly two-mile-long main thoroughfare through town. At the end of every harvest season, the street was thronged by dozens of horse- and oxen-drawn wagons loaded with corn, tobacco, and, with the invention of the gin, short-staple cotton. The crops were unloaded at one of several warehouses and wharves that lined the north side of the street along the river, where they were attended by dozens of draymen, boathands, and stevedores. The harvests were then sold and shipped downstream by flatboat.[9] Visitors condemned the thick, choking clouds of dust the traffic created on dry days and the axle-deep mud on rainy ones, but they agreed that the city's future looked especially bright. Trade was the lifeblood of Augusta. Adam Hodgson, a Liverpool businessman visiting Augusta in 1820 noted, "There you find yourself surrounded by . . . all 'the pomp and circumstance' of commerce; carts coming in from the country with cotton, and crowding the streets, or rather avenues, of this rural town; tradesmen and agents bustling about in different directions; wharves loaded with bales; and steam-boats darkening the air with their black exhalations."[10]

Money earned from the sale of crops quickly left the palms of farmers and planters to be exchanged for goods and supplies purchased from growing numbers of Augusta shopkeepers, merchants, and artisans. The booming local economy this trade created doubled the town's population, from about 1,100 residents in 1790 to 2,270 in 1800, just over half of whom were white. This growth brought new cultural amenities to Augusta, including a half dozen churches, competing newspapers, an academy, and even a popular theater. Horse racing was a popular social event. Many men belonged to fraternal organizations such as the Sons of Saint Tammany, the Augusta Mechanics Society, and the Freemasons.[11]

Population increase leveled off to 2,476 in 1810, as even city dwellers hastened to the countryside to plant cotton, leaving 1,109 whites, 1,321 slaves, and 46 free blacks to people the town. Unfortunately, Augusta was not distinguished from the rest of the county population in the 1820 U.S. Census. The total population for Richmond County was 8,608, including 3,667 whites, 4,831 slaves and 110 free blacks (almost all of whom were city dwellers).[12]

Between 1790 and 1820, white men in the city worked as merchants, lawyers, shopkeepers, craftsmen, mechanics, and laborers. Planters also resided in Augusta for certain parts of the year. Free black men worked as carpenters, barbers, millwrights, saddlers, blacksmiths, boathands, wagoners, and house servants. Slave men also performed some of these occupations but in addition did much of the heavy manual labor at the warehouses and wharves.[13]

This same demographic evidence indicates that white men outnumbered white women by roughly three to two in 1800 and 1810. In contrast, free black women were the majority of the free black population. These sex ratios suggest that white women in Augusta may have had some choice in marriage partners, since white men were the disproportionate majority. This evidence also suggests that white women had more opportunities to marry into a better social class than women in older. cities with more balanced sex ratios. White women in the surrounding county may also have looked to the city in search of mates by 1810, given the skewed sex ratios of the countryside. In 1800 the sex ratio for whites in the surrounding county mirrored that of the city, but by 1810 adult white women outnumbered adult white men in the county (excluding Augusta) by four to three, an indication that more and more young men were establishing businesses in town or migrating westward to buy cheaper land. Meanwhile, free black women in Augusta had fewer opportunities to marry free black men, since so few resided in the area; many chose instead not to marry at all or in some cases to marry slave men. In addition, some free black women seem to have been the mistresses of white men, a reflection of the unequal white sex ratio during this era and the power of white men, as evidence by the number of light-complected free black children recorded in the registries.[14]

Census figures for 1820 list 944 white households in Augusta. Slightly fewer than half (42 percent) of these households owned slaves. Of those 944 urban households, only 42 (4.5 percent) could be identified as female-headed. Only a quarter of these female-headed households (11) owned slaves.[15] This demographic evidence suggests that white female-headed households in Augusta were not only a tiny minority but far less likely to own slaves, and presumably less likely to benefit from slave labor and the wealth that slave labor and slave ownership represented, than white male-headed households.

The Household Economy

The vast majority of white women in Augusta, however, lived in male-headed households, and most of the work these women performed was within their households. Antebellum southerners, including city dwellers, understood that their social status and economic success derived at least in part from the structure of the household in which they lived, their position within that household, and its productivity. The multifaceted work of white women in these households, and especially the work of wives, was clearly critical to men's ambitions.

How did white women in Augusta households negotiate these societal expectations about their domestic, sexual, and reproductive roles? The virtual absence of personal letters, diaries, and journals written by these women during this period makes answering this question difficult, though not impossible. Fortunately, public records like newspaper announcements and advertisements, along with estate and probate records, reveal how crucial women's work was for sustaining both individual households and the larger community. These sources indicate that women were important historical actors in their own right. They frequently stretched the boundaries of their gendered work roles, more so than in rural households because the town economy offered far more opportunities. Sometimes this reality secured new status and authority for them. Most times it proved beneficial to their husbands, fathers, and children. As the Augusta historian Edward J. Cashin has observed of this period, "Though contradictory to the . . . way things were supposed to be, there were many women in Augusta who were the family breadwinners."[16]

White women in Augusta understood that marriage was a civil contract ostensibly agreed upon by the two parties who had entered into it. Any wealth a wife brought into the marriage, as long as the husband "reduced it to possession through coverture," was legally recognized as his. Any subsequent possessions or earnings she gained were his as well. Nonetheless, husbands were expected to support their wives, and in return wives were expected to take charge of household labor, which revolved around the perpetual production of food, clothing, and household items. Estate inventories and appraisements suggest that these living and working spaces were chock full of the tools needed to facilitate women's domestic responsibilities—crockery, kettles, pots and pans, and barrels of food.[17] Augusta wives also tended small garden plots, raised poultry and hogs and milked a cow or two, depending on the size of their town lots.[18] Unlike rural women, these wives did not spend time at the spinning wheel until the War of 1812. In fact, not a single Augusta household inventory examined listed a spinning wheel before 1810.[19] Instead of spinning and weaving, both of which were quite time-consuming activities, most women in Augusta apparently bought their material ready-made. They then cut and stitched into clothes and linens the fabrics they had purchased from local shopkeepers until an international embargo and sweeping support for the president and Congress compelled many Georgians to wear homespun. Nevertheless, even during the War of 1812, and following the state assembly's unanimous vote to attire themselves only in homespun, Augusta merchants regularly advertised the availability of cashmeres, Canton and Nanking silks, crepes, Irish linens, the "best Buckskin," cottons, and osnaburgs in the *Augusta Chronicle*, suggesting that a market for these goods, most of them imported, still existed.[20]

Thus, household consumption, in addition to housewifery, marked an important arena where Augusta women had a measure of authority. In some cases, their purchases actually had political implications. One wonders what men made of some Augusta women's apparent refusal to settle for homespun during a national crisis. Generally, however, women's consumption related to women's "sphere."[21] An Augusta storekeeper's account book from this period shows that although most of the customers were men of some wealth, who purchased spirits and tobacco almost exclusively, women of the same class purchased household luxuries like cloth, brown sugar, loaf sugar, tea, spices, coffee, and vinegar.[22]

Women's duties in Augusta households were not limited to housewifery and consumption; they also included reproduction. Motherhood was a mixed blessing, and oftentimes childbirth proved to be a horrific experience.[23] Hannah Longstreet wrote family members that she did not have in attendance the midwife she had hoped would deliver her baby because the woman lived twenty miles away and Hannah's labor was proceeding too rapidly. Instead, "I was obliged to have an old woman that I did not like, and [she] almost frightened me out of my senses." Indeed, the entire experience of delivering this child was not a happy memory for Hannah:

I was poorly indeed for a day and night before it [the baby] was born, and had a most bitter time. . . . I had no warming pan so was put into a cold bed, and it was a violent stormy night. The room was wet from one end to the other where rain beat in. . . . I thought I could not live till morning. . . . We sent for the doctor and he gave me something that eased me but I slept none that night. The thought of home, my mother, my friends, the situation myself and the family was in, and all among strangers was as much as I could bear, [and] threw me into histerics and I worryed the night out.[24]

Hannah had good cause to worry. Childbirth was a dangerous time for mother and child alike. Although Hannah and her baby survived, the twice-widowed and thrice-married Martin Angus, a miller in Augusta, appears to have lost two of his wives and their babies to complications from childbirth. Sarah Bray and her husband, Thomas, a clockmaker and silversmith by trade, publicly mourned the death of their infant son, John, in 1799.[25] Nor did children's survival mean women's work and worry lessened, of course. Mothers had primary responsibility for their small progeny, even when their children were old enough to run errands and learn tasks at their mother's knee or in their father's workshop or store. And Augusta was always rife with disease by summer's end, including the periodic but deadly yellow fever.

In addition to fulfilling the role of mother, housewife, and consumer, women also assisted in the family business. Such assistance seems to have been requisite in most Augusta houses, which were quite small, often less than twenty by forty feet in size. These tight spaces could contain a craftsman's workshop and tools or a front room filled with merchant goods. They also contained the housewife's kitchen equipment and linens, as well as modest furniture, like tables, chairs, and bedsteads. Add to this crowded area other relatives, including grandparents and children, and, in more well-to-do households, apprentices, journeymen, free blacks and slaves, and finally, customers during the day, and one gets a sense of the interaction and degree of crowding that was an everyday part of ordinary Augustans' lives.[26]

Additional household members who were not members of the family meant that women's work took on added significance. Not only were women expected to be industrious, they were to model and reinforce the properly subordinate relationship between household dependents and the household head. When comfortably well-off men like Joseph Stiles, a silversmith, and John Catlett, a tinsmith and silversmith, trained apprentices in their respective trades, employed skilled journeymen at workshop tasks, hired free blacks, and gave directions to several slaves, their wives were expected to provide everything from room and board to subtle lessons in deportment to these extended household members. The more extended and the wealthier the household, the more likely wives and daughters were assisted in these domestic tasks by slave women.[27]

Slave Women

Reliance on the work of female slaves was commonplace in Augusta during the early Republic. White women could clearly benefit from the household labor of a slave domestic or cook, as did Sarah Bray, the wife of the jeweler and silversmith Thomas Bray. At the same time Thomas Bray probably bought this servant girl as much to advertise his status as a newly arrived luxury craftsman able to afford the expense of a house slave as to aid Sarah in performing her household duties, for the Brays owned no other chattel. On the other hand, the mechanic Isaac Wingate's decision to hire a slave cook seems motivated by his desire to ease his wife's onerous house duties.[28]

Some one thousand slaves lived and worked in Augusta during this period. By 1810 slaves were the majority of the city's residents. They were a diverse lot. Close to seven thousand slaves obtained from either Africa or the West Indies had been imported to Georgia during the 1790s, many of whom had been brought to the burgeoning upcountry, as evidenced by numerous runaway advertisements listing "country marks" on runaway slaves' cheeks and their difficulty with English. In some cases the ads actually listed the runaway slave's country of origin, such as Angola or Guinea. In contrast, other runaway slaves were described as native-born, dressed in "finery" and sporting adopted "airs," or working and living in Augusta independent of their masters. The backbone of the local economy, both in the city and the surrounding countryside, the labor of these slaves, in all their diversity, made the new wealth of Augusta possible. Whether as dockworkers and draymen, domestics and washerwomen, or carpenters and blacksmiths, slaves were an everyday presence in the city. In many respects, whites lived uneasily in their midst. Although the last maroon colony had been disbanded by General James Jackson and the Georgia militia in 1786, white fears prevailed throughout the early Republic. The successful revolt of slaves in Saint Domingue only encouraged that fear. After 1793 local laws discouraged the immigration of West Indian planters and their slaves to the region, then culminated in a ban against slave importations to Georgia in 1798. The economy and the slave population had grown enormously in the postrevolutionary era. Whites encouraged both developments but feared the implications of the later. Interestingly, slave women were rarely suspected of plotting insurrection and for the most part are difficult to unearth from the historical record, though their work was clearly indispensable.[29]

Although it is difficult to describe Augusta slave women's work lives in great detail, advertisements in newspapers suggest that most slave women worked almost exclusively as domestics and children's caretakers in white households during the early Republic. The following ads are typical for this period:

> *For Sale.* A Negro Wench about 22 years of age. Good cook, washer, ironer. . . . Sold for no fault. Cash or cotton will be taken in payment.
> *For Hire.* Until the 1st of January next a Negro Girl about 16 years of age. An excellent House Servant.
> *Wanted to Hire or Purchase*, a good cook and steady, middle-aged woman, accustomed to the care of children.
> *Wanted.* A Good Female House Servant. Also a girl 10 or 12 years old to take care of a child. For such good wages will be paid.[30]

The absence of more detailed evidence discourages heavy speculation about these women, their lives, or the work they performed. Runaway advertisements, nonetheless, hint that Augusta slave women who were sold or moved to upcountry plantations were almost always unhappy with rural slave life. These runaway women were invariably thought by their masters to have returned to Augusta to rejoin friends and family and in some cases to pass themselves off as free black women. Owners in fact frequently presumed that free black women were harboring their runaways.

These same ads also indicate that urban slave women in Augusta took some care in how they dressed and owned more outfits made of more varieties of cloth than rural slave women. Historians are fortunate in that slave owners believed detailing a slave's attire could lead to better identification of their runaways and could even suggest something about their sense of style as well as their character. This was certainly true of female runaway advertisements placed in the *Augusta Chronicle*. John A. Williams noted in his ad that his runaway slave, named Amy, "generally dresses well," and Augustan Isaac Herbert stated that his runaway slave, Rose, wore homespun and a blue cotton handkerchief tied about her neck. Owner Richard Bathe last saw Dolly in a yellow calico gown but knew she had several other outfits, made of muslin, silk, cambric, and dimity. Carriagemaker Nicholas Delaigle thought his run-away slave, named Nancy, would be dressed in a blue calico wrapper with a white petticoat but noted she might be wearing one of her other dresses instead.[31]

Many Augusta slave women's wardrobes probably were a direct result of the work they performed outside their owners' homes. Women's historians have long noted that white women frequently gave their favorite female servants their cast-offs. Given the prosperity of Augusta during this period and the availability of many kinds of materials and even ready-made fashions from Europe and New York, this bestowing of "gifts" upon slave women was quite likely. Yet it also seems likely that Augusta slave women found ways to secure their own material, which they stitched into clothing for themselves. This presumption seems especially credible given the evidence contained in an interesting set of letters to the editor of the *Augusta Chronicle*. Although most slave women in Augusta worked inside white households, these letters document slave women pursuing livelihoods outside them as well.

In May 1802 an irritated white resident submitted a scathing editorial claiming that merchants' clerks throughout the city were engaged in informal trade and in some cases prostitution with slave women. This author contended that while most slave women were trading garden produce or eggs and meat, some clerks and slave women were trading sexual favors for merchandise. The number of replies to this editorial, responses protesting vehemently that *most* store clerks did not engage in such exchanges, confirms that slave women created opportunities for themselves that extended well beyond the white household. Whether bartering goods or selling their bodies, this work enabled them to better care for their families or set money aside for their freedom or simply for material from which to assemble their own wardrobes, an act of autonomy in its own right.[32]

Slave women in Augusta clearly established their own economic networks, through informal barter and trade in goods and produce as well as through paid sexual liaisons with young white men in a city where adult white men outnumbered adult white women three to one. That slave women in Augusta used these various trade networks to carve out this kind of independence for themselves, made visible on a daily basis by slave women's attire among other things, must have been difficult for their white mistresses to understand or countenance. Because white women in Augusta, like all wives and daughters in slaveholding societies, were almost always subordinate in status to their

husbands and fathers, they must have found it exceedingly difficult to enforce
the male head of household's authority. Hugh Magee, who ran a mill on Spirit
Creek just outside of Augusta, owned four slaves in 1795. He married five
years later. Less than three weeks after his marriage, two of Magee's chattel, a
married couple named Billy and Manta, ran away with another slave. Given
the timing, it would seem that the introduction of Mary, the new wife, to
Magee's household, and Mary's apparent mishandling of her new duties as
mistress of that household, must have prompted these slaves to take flight.
Following their departure, Magee cautioned Augusta's white residents "not
to trade with, or have any sort of dealings with, my negroes," who apparently
were pursuing their own informal economic exchanges.[33]

Augusta "Businesswomen"

White women in Augusta were expected to contribute to the efficiency and
prosperity of the household in any number of ways, from performing house-
wifely duties, to stepping in to complete craftwork or sell merchandise, to the
supervision of slaves. Some white women in Augusta also found themselves
stretching their roles beyond the household by delving into commercial ven-
tures. Although most white women worked behind the scenes and generally
did not establish businesses of their own, for to do so might have signaled that
their husbands were not capable of supporting them, some women were forced
to apply their skills in public ways to sustain or improve their household
economy. Although theirs was a society where plentiful land and slave labor,
along with the profits to be made from staple crops, allowed some white men
to grow rich from the profits to be made from the new cotton economy, other
men at certain points in their career struggled mightily. Women commonly
filled in the gaps when a household economy began to fail. The wife of the
Augusta mechanic Hiel Chatfield, a habitual debtor and tax defaulter, chose
to use her home as an informal shop from which to sell bonnets, plumes, shawls,
and muslins. Several other women advertised similar millinery efforts. Harriot
Bond offered "fancy articles," including bonnets of all types, ribbons, laces,
veils, silk and cotton trimmings, and feathers at her shop. Hannah A. Dickinson
owned a millinery shop near the market that carried the latest styles from New
York. A Mrs. Newton announced that she had just received "a handsome supply of hats" from New York and Charleston. Several of these ads indicate that
some women were not only running their own shops but were engaged in

merchant trade with wholesalers in other cities, displaying a degree of business acumen that many of their male shopkeeping colleagues had yet to adopt. Mrs. Sera, a milliner and mantua maker from Paris, who advertised her new shop in 1821, was an especially shrewd businesswoman, offering "to instruct a few young ladies in the business" in exchange for work performed. Most women, however, lacked the resources to secure credit and establish a business, even if they acquired continental sewing skills. Teaching needlework to girls in their own homes provided a number of women, most of them wives, many of them widowed, a respectable means of earning money without committing to extensive investment or debt.[34]

Hannah Randolph Longstreet, the wife of the famous Augusta mechanic, inventor, and politician William Longstreet and mother of A. B. Longstreet, relied on boarders to meet her household needs beginning in 1805. Five years earlier, her husband had moved his family, along with their ten slaves, to a South Carolina farm some fourteen miles from Augusta. This venture failed, forcing Longstreet to return with his family to Augusta, where he resumed his former mechanical and speculative pursuits. It appears that it was Hannah's initiative in establishing first a private and then a public boarding home that renewed their financial stability. Her efforts proved so fruitful that by 1809, four years later, William Longstreet's resources were valued at a respectable $5,000. Interestingly, Hannah was also named directress of the Female Augusta Asylum and charged with the guardianship of an orphan in 1816, two years after her husband's death.[35]

Many women besides Hannah Longstreet ran boarding houses to supplement their income. Augusta's role as a commercial town, with its influx of mostly male migrants, encouraged this occupation. A Mrs. Sandwich advertised a private boarding house in 1820. Tabitha I. Beal, after her husband's death and the sale of his estate, rented a house in Augusta to take in boarders, limiting them to young ladies and small boys in the interest of propriety.[36] These kinds of boarding establishments, almost all of which were private, relied on word of mouth and personal recommendation. Advertisements for them were rare. At the same time, such establishments, almost always run by women, began to experience competition from new public houses run by men. Jeff Vauxhall promoted his new boarding house with its livery stable, billiard room, and "private spaces for entertainment" in 1809, and Isaac Herbert ran numerous ads for his "Boarding House and House of Entertainment" in 1812.[37] Well-heeled boarders eager for games and drink, or a good stable for their

mounts, were far more likely to put themselves up at these latter establishments than at the modest homes of women.

Schooling young girls offered women another arena in which to support
themselves and their families. The English-born Mrs. Sandwich, the wife of
the cabinetmaker and musical instrument maker Thomas Sandwich, used her
education and eventually that of her husband to supplement their household
income by opening a "Ladies Academy" in 1795. Here she taught young girls
"reading and writing and arithmetic [as well as] the useful and ornamental
needle works," a skill she believed most young women were woefully ignorant
about. The Ladies Academy at Mount Salubrity, or Mount Health as she touted
her institution, prospered for more than twenty-five years, adding new teachers and new curricular offerings throughout this period. Her husband, a respectable Augusta artisan and citizen in the 1790s, eventually chose to tie his
fortunes to his wife's school instead of his craft. He was wise to do so, for the
former instrument-maker, whose property was limited to a town house and
lot and a slave in 1795, eventually owned four slaves, several town properties,
the Mount Salubrity building (constructed in 1800 on what would soon be
known as the prestigious "Hill"), and eighty-three upcountry acres twelve
years later, thanks to his wife's venture. By 1814, in fact, locals generally referred to him as "Lord Sandwich."[38]

Sandwich was not the only wife to augment her family's fortunes by establishing a young ladies academy. Eighteen other Augusta women either opened
academies of their own for young women or were employed in them between
1792 and 1820, a development that reflected the rise of a gentry class able to
afford education for its daughters. Like Sandwich's academy, these schools
offered a variety of courses, from scholastic subjects to embroidery and fine
needlework. A Mrs. Maclean, a seamstress and apparently a widow, opened a
school for young girls in her home with her four children in 1807. She offered
reading, writing, arithmetic and needlework. A Mrs. Macmillan announced
she was opening her school for "Young Females" in a rented building owned
by the carpenter Robert Cresswell. She believed her curriculum of "reading,
Writing, Arithmetic, English Grammar—etc. would impress upon [her students'] minds the importance of an early and sincere devotion to the practical
duties of religion." She also was prepared to take in three or four boarders.[39]

That a good livelihood was to be made from educating young ladies was
not necessarily guaranteed. Even the Sandwiches, whose Ladies' Academy
was well known by the early nineteenth century, advertised the inexpensive-

ness of their tuition compared to that of similar academies in Charleston. They also offered to take produce in lieu of cash payment. After the War of 1812, these academies proliferated so quickly that they began to boast about their latest curricular offerings to stave off their competitors. Moreover, these academies were increasingly owned and operated by men only or in some cases husband and wife teams rather than the earlier tradition of women-owned and managed female academies. While Mrs. Jull offered French as well as English language and literature, music, and needlework in 1821, Oliver Danforth's Female Seminary boasted "Latin, Greek, Languages, Geography with Globes and Maps, History, Rhetoric, Logic, Surveying, English Grammar and Composition," a curriculum unique for this time and place because it so resembled what young men were learning. Mr. and Mrs. Wayne offered a similar curriculum that included Logic, Rhetoric, Moral and Natural Philosophy, Latin and Greek. Benjamin Chambers' Yorkville Female Academy, which opened in 1823, presented the traditional female disciplines as well as "Natural Philosophy, Astronomy and the higher Mathematics."[40]

By the 1820s enterprising men appeared to be taking the education of "young ladies" out of the hands of genteel women. They were able to do so by taking advantage of local interest in educating young women in the sciences, Greek and Latin, and other subjects, like rhetoric and natural philosophy, once deemed exclusively male domain—subjects most adult women would not be able to teach since they had been educated in an earlier era when different girls' and boys' curriculums prevailed.[41]

Whether a woman ran a school or a boarding house, owned a shop or took in sewing, or worked solely at domestic tasks in her home, the death of a male household head not only brought many married women to the brink of financial disaster but forced them to assume a new work role: legal administrators of their husband's estate. Generally, notices seeking payment of debts owed the deceased man and information about debts the deceased man owed were placed in local newspapers by his wife and kin, who were invariably named administrators of the deceased's estate. These notices were placed after the administrators had registered with the Inferior Court. While historians have tended to view the courthouse as an arena where men alone congregated, exchanging political views, evidence in Augusta suggests women were also frequent visitors, whether registering their estates or seeking assistance.[42]

Because many Augusta businessmen carried heavy debts at the time of their deaths, their wives often found themselves offering up the contents of their entire households for public sale in order to settle with their husbands' creditors. Mary Dearmond, wife of the carpenter William Dearmond, advertised the public sale of her deceased husband's personal estate on January 18, 1800. The items to be sold included the Dearmonds' household and kitchen furniture, Mary's cooking and kitchen utensils, William's tools, and all their slaves, horses, and hogs. Likewise Sarah Bray, administrator for her silversmith husband's estate, was forced to turn over the contents of her household to an auctioneer on September 14, 1799. Mary Cook, administrator for the tailor John Cook's estate, surrendered her household possessions, along with the household's slaves, horses, cattle, and hogs, to public sale in 1802.[43]

This must have been an excruciating ordeal for these women. In the midst of their grief over the deaths of their spouses, they had to go to the courthouse and then submit their prized personal possessions, from their mirrors and a few silver teaspoons to such necessities as pots and pans and the kitchen table, not to mention their home and property, to the humiliation of a public sale. Not only did they face deprivation from the loss of these possessions but they also had to endure the shame that came with this symbolic announcement of their new status as widowed dependents bereft of not only their husband but all their resources.

Not all wives, however, were left to fend for themselves after their husbands died. More prosperous men provided for their wives in their wills (although the writing and recording of a will was still a relatively uncommon act at this time) by leaving them a home and lot in which to reside as well as a small income until their death, at which time the property would revert to their children. The miller Hugh Magee bequeathed to his wife Mary "350 acres of pineland, including a handsome site near two springs," which upon her death would become their son's property.[44] But Magee's provisions for his wife were more the exception than the rule.

The Richmond County Inferior Court minutes for the first two decades of the nineteenth century abound with white women paupers and their children seeking support payment and the lifting of tax requirements. Some of these female paupers, however, found a way to support themselves through an arrangement with the city that proved mutually beneficial. Augusta, until 1810, lacked an orphanage or charity home. In 1790 the court recorded that the poor were to report to the next court meeting for charity and children to be bound out. Poor women subsequently took on the care of orphan children and received money from the city for their efforts. Thus Ann Banks, for example, was due forty dollars by order of the Inferior Court for the care of "an orphan in her charge."[45] Ironically, even poor women's work contributed to the smooth functioning of this society. Female paupers were fortunate to have this option, and, one hopes, so were the orphans in their charge.

This arrangement was a relatively short-lived one, ending in 1818, at least in part because the Female Orphan Asylum had been established in Augusta in 1810. This orphanage, and the other reform institutions that followed, were run not by poor women but by Augusta's elite and may have contributed to the demise of the town's system.[46] On one hand, the institutionalizing of benevolent work benefited greater numbers of desperate people. On the other hand, the mutually beneficial arrangement among the city, female paupers, and orphans had encouraged a measure of self-sufficiency and pride for ordinary women that was lost when churches and elite women, both with social agendas, assumed charge.

In this respect, by the early 1820s elite women in Augusta had begun to resemble their sisters in the North. But poorer white women in Augusta bore little similarity to impoverished northern women. Poor women in the urban Northeast, for better or worse, found themselves sewing piecework for pennies.[47] By contrast, poor women in Augusta did not gravitate toward outwork created by the rise of small industries, because there was no such work to be had. The 1820 Manufacturing Census for Richmond County lists only sixteen manufactories in Augusta. All were small-scale establishments, little more than craftsmen's shops: three ink-making companies, six saddleries, a carriage-making company, a furniture-making company, a nail-making company, a button-making company, and three cloth- and thread-making companies. Only one of these establishments, a cloth and thread manufactory, employed women, and only four at that. During the early Republic, white women's work in Augusta was generally limited to the household, though Augusta's prosperity enabled some women to run boarding homes, dressmaking establishments, and even female academies, work that extended women's assumed household duties into more public space. Eventually, the arrival of textile factories would offer more women wage-earning opportunities, but in the decades after the Revolution through the 1820s, a period in which the Old South was beginning to take shape, wage-earning opportunities were exceedingly restricted.[48]

Poorer white women may have resorted to prostitution, as some slave women did, but the historical record provides little evidence to support this position.

It is clear that some white women chose to earn their livelihoods in the seamier side of town, where drinking and gambling prevailed. Several "tippling houses" were actually operated by women.[49] But we know little about their lives.

Free Black Women

Free black women at work in Augusta appear even less frequently in the historical record than white women or slave women. The 1819 Register of Free Persons of Color, which listed 117 names, indicates the free black community had grown by leaps and bounds over the past few decades, nearly tripling in size since 1800. Throughout the early Republic, however, women remained the disproportionate majority of the free black population. Free black men worked in any number of occupations, from boat pilot to carpenter (the most common occupations) to house servant to barber to millwright and planter. These men were generally born in the 1770s, 1780s, and 1790s in the upper South. Similarly, free black women, the majority of whom were born in the upper South but included several natives of Saint Domingue (four) and Africa (three), tended to congregate in occupations associated with cloth. There may be good reason for free black women's commitment to this kind of work. The 1819 Register of Free Persons of Color also indicates that free black women were intent upon securing as much independence in their working lives as possible. Free black women were highly unlikely to work in white households. They preferred instead to provide whites with services they could complete in their own home. Thus Polly and Betsy Keating, for example, a mother and daughter who had lived in Augusta as slaves since 1793, were freed by their merchant owner in 1812 and subsequently chose to make their living as independent seamstresses. Over and over again, the women in the registry identified themselves as washers, ironers, spinners, and seamstresses.[50] These occupations, all related to the production and care of clothing, must have given free black women, many of whom were former slaves like the Keatings, a significant measure of personal autonomy, a modicum of economic independence, and an important social space beyond the reach of white society. In effect, they had secured their *own* households.

Free black women's financial independence may also have allowed them to work to undermine the institution of slavery. One slaveowner, for instance, suspected that Flora Fithburne, a free black woman in Augusta, was harboring Judy, her niece and his runaway slave. Free black women could not always prevent their kin from being returned to slavery, but they could pursue an alternative means of protecting them that took substantial time and money. The Richmond County Tax Digest for 1818 lists twelve free women of color who owned slaves. Undoubtedly these women had managed to purchase family members to give them—in an ironic twist—their freedom.[51]

White Augustans and Georgians alike worked hard to limit free blacks' lives. In 1806 the Augusta City Council voted to forbid free blacks to hire slaves. In 1818 the Georgia General Assembly passed an act requiring not only that all free blacks be registered but that those who could not prove their freedom be banished from the state. Whites often blamed free blacks whenever suspicious fires or deaths occurred. The free black community was also suspected of inciting rebellious acts among Augusta slaves.[52]

In one unusual instance a mulatto woman named Phoebe apparently earned her livelihood by passing herself off as a slave, although she was allegedly free and the daughter of a white woman. Phoebe persuaded men to purchase her from her white male owner, but once they had paid for her she ran away to pull off the scam elsewhere until she was caught and jailed in Augusta in 1814.[53] It seems her white partner escaped capture. Free black women also had to confront social disapprobation and fears of miscegenation. A Mrs. Posner, a free woman of color who lived with her white husband just outside Augusta, operated a bathing house at Richmond Springs. John Mellish, a Scotsman traveling in Georgia, raved about the quality of the establishment's quarters, their cleanliness, the tastiness of the food, and the "re-establishment" of his health and the "recruitment" of his spirits after bathing in the waters and spending the night. Yet he observed, "This place . . . is neglected. Mrs. Posner is a woman of color, and is disliked by the Georgia ladies, who will not go to her house. Where the ladies will not go, the gentleman will not go, and so Mr. Posner does not get a proper reward for his exertions."[54] The fate of the Posners' business, which relied so heavily on Mrs. Posner's exertions, Mellish's words to the contrary, is unknown.

Conclusion

Women's work in Augusta took many different forms. Whether performed by ordinary white women or poor white women, free black women or slave women, it invariably supported the white southern social order in significant ways. Free black women, for example, had found an important niche for themselves as laundresses and seamstresses but could not challenge the racial order by running a boarding house, especially if they were married to white men. Slave women could find ways to acquire money and goods but could almost never free themselves from their masters' legal hold. The most skilled of white women, or those who inherited some property, could set themselves up as businesswomen, but only in work deemed appropriate for their sex. And in some cases male businessmen actually began to compete with women in the few occupations women had staked out for themselves.

White men's legitimacy as citizens in the slave South rested in large measure upon the productive capacity and the respectability of their households; the two went hand in hand. To assure their status as independent white men, they committed themselves to the racial order of slavery by hiring and buying black chattel for use in their shops, fields, and homes. They cemented their privileged place in this social order through a sexual as well as a racial division of labor that made women's work in their households and in their communities indispensable to white males' success. The work of most women, whether white or black, took place in the household or in places that represented an extension of women's households. It was at this nexus that men, women, and children, white and black, slave and free, learned and acted out the hierarchical set of roles assigned them by their race, class, and gender. At times both black and white women found themselves stretching and in some cases even redefining those roles—to salvage their households, to salvage their futures, and even perhaps to salvage their own identities. Women's work in all its variety in Augusta helped assure the perpetuation of the slave South and the privileged place that white men across their class differences held within it.

At the same time, black and white women alike found ways to use their work to secure a degree of autonomy. Slave women used informal economies to achieve a measure of self-determination within their bondage. Free black women, condemned because of their race and gender to quasi-freedom, used service work performed in their own homes to secure their own kind of independence. White women, constrained by their gender and in many cases their class, discovered that hardship could work in their favor, expanding their authority and dictating their own future through the new kinds of work roles they came to assume.

The past is often contradictory. As historians continue the difficult and often painful process of rewriting this past, it seems especially important to recognize that black and white women's work in one southern city both shaped and challenged the emerging economic order of the Old South.

Notes

1. The literature on southern plantation mistresses is a large one. See especially Clinton, *Plantation Mistress*; Friedman, *Enclosed Garden*; Fox-Genovese, *Within the Plantation Household*. For slave women, see White, *Ar'n't I a Woman?*; J. Jones, *Labor of Love*; Stevenson, *Life in Black and White*.

2. The classic work on women in the early South remains Julia Cherry Spruill's *Women's Life and Work in the Southern Colonies*, originally published in 1938. See especially Fox-Genovese, *Within the Plantation Household*, 9.

3. B. Wood, *Women's Work, Men's Work*; Lockley, "Struggle for Survival"; Olwell, "Loose, Idle, and Disorderly"; Farnham, *Women of the American South*.

4. For example, the early U.S. Census records are no longer available for Augusta. Research in this era is also hampered by water damage to, as well as the illegibility of, many of the city's inferior court records and estate and probate records. Fortunately, thanks to the Georgia Newspaper Project, spearheaded by the University of Georgia, many issues of the *Augusta Chronicle and State Gazette*, first a weekly and then a biweekly newspaper, have been preserved for this entire period.

5. Fox-Genovese, *Within the Plantation Household*, 57–58, 64.

6. Tilly and Scott, *Women, Work, and Family*, provides a classic account of women's work in the preindustrial households of early modern France and England, which in some but obviously not all respects bears a striking resemblance to ordinary women's work in antebellum southern households.

7. V. Wood and R. Wood, *Collections*, 15:98.

8. Longstreet, "The Charming Creature as a Wife," in *Georgia Scenes*, 71–96; J. Wade, *Augustus Baldwin Longstreet*, 1–8.

9. Spalding, *Oglethorpe in America*, 22–23; E. Cashin, *Story of Augusta*, 42–43; C. Jones, *Memorial History*, 25; Federal Writers' Project, *Augusta*, 62–76; Dodd and Dodd, *Historical Statistics*, 18–21; Gilmer, *Sketches*, 5–9; Jones, *Memorial History*, 132–34; Dodd and Dodd, *Historical Statistics*, 148; Bonner, *History of Georgia Agriculture*, 32. A description of cotton economy's impact on Augusta is in Wade, *Augustus Baldwin Longstreet*, 17. In a decision reached by the Richmond County Superior Court in 1800, the grand jury declared that cotton was now the principle staple of Georgia; C. Jones, *Memorial History*, 165.

10. George Walton, "A Note on the Pine Land of Georgia," Augusta, May 1, 1793, manuscript, Georgia Historical Society, Savannah; Lane, *Rambler in Georgia*, xxiv, 25, 87; Georgia Writers Project, Augusta, Works Progress Administration, "An Historic Sketch of Augusta," by Hattie Courtney, manuscript, Hargrett Library, University of Georgia, Athens; Adam Hodgson's *Remarks During a Journey Through North America*, quoted in Lane, *Rambler in Georgia*, 53.

11. The population figures for 1790 are estimates from E. Cashin, *Story of Augusta*,

i. Richmond County census records for 1790 are no longer extant. The population figures for 1800 are from *Second Census of the U.S.*, 2N. For cultural amenities, see Jones, *Memorial History*, 144–48; for fraternal organizations, E. Cashin, *Story of Augusta*, 57.

12. *Aggregate Amount of Persons*, 80; *State of the Population*, 22. The *Augusta Chronicle* reported on April 4, 1822, that eighty-seven free persons of color lived in Augusta. There were thirty-three men and fifty-four women.

13. Gillespie, *Free Labor*, chap. 1; Register of Free Persons of Color, Richmond County, 1818, Inferior Court Records, 1819–47, Georgia Department of Archives and History; R. Wade, *Slavery in the Cities*.

14. Sex ratios based on population numbers for Augusta in *Second Census*, 2N; *Aggregate Amount of Persons*, 80. Figures for the free black population are based on the 1819 Register of Free Persons of Color for Richmond County, Georgia Department of Archives and History. *Adult* is herein defined as sixteen years or older to correspond to the age categorization in the U.S. Census records for Augusta and surrounding Richmond County.

15. Slaveholding numbers for Augusta were compared with those for the surrounding county, where just over half (55 percent) of all households owned slaves; U.S. Bureau of the Census, Population, 1820, Richmond County, Georgia Department of Archives and History. The figure for female-headed households in Augusta is at best an estimate, since the census records are difficult to read for Richmond County and contain many illegible names or only an initial for the first name. On the other hand, this figure cannot be too far from accurate, as female-headed households were determined by counting not only female first names but households containing adult women but no adult men.

16. E. Cashin, *Story of Augusta*, 84.

17. Boatwright, *Status of Women*, 50–52; Estate of John Cook, September 8, 1799, Estate of Thomas Bray, August 1, 1799, Estate of William Dearmond, January 24, 1790, Richmond County Estate Records, Inventories and Appraisements, 1799–1813, Georgia Department of Archives and History.

18. See the description of the carpenter Robert Cresswell's tenement, *Augusta Chronicle*, November 21, 1801.

19. Richmond County, Ordinary Estate Records, Inventories and Appraisements, Book A, 1799–1813. This seems especially curious given the apparent willingness of most Georgians to wear homespun during the War of 1812. Even more curious, the 1810 U.S. Manufacturing Census lists 626 spinning wheels and 162 looms in Richmond County but does not distinguish between Augusta and the surrounding countryside. However, preliminary and as yet unpublished research by Dale Couch, state archivist at the Georgia Department of History, has also found that inventories in Savannah and surrounding Chatham County failed to list spinning wheels. This suggests that the availability of manufactured cloth in stores and shops persuaded urban

women in Georgia to purchase material rather than produce it, whereas their rural sisters, who lacked access to stores and cash, continued to spin and weave. Travel accounts for the period abound with descriptions of rural women working at spinning wheels throughout the Georgia upcountry. For example, see John Mellish's observations in Lane, *Rambler in Georgia*, 33.

20. Lamar, *Compilation of Laws*, 119; *Augusta Chronicle*, June 14, 1802, August 16, 1808, September 22, 1810, September 17, 1813.

21. Women's so-called private sphere existed in respect to women's presumed authority over domesticity and piety. Women's historians have come to see that sphere as permeable in the nineteenth century. Not only were public/private distinctions less rigidly gendered than once argued, but women from all walks of life, including the middle class, challenged the ideology of separate spheres through their actions and beliefs. A voluminous literature exists on women's sphere in nineteenth-century America. The best starting points remain Welter, "Cult of True Womanhood"; and Cott, *Bonds of Womanhood*. Also see Hewitt, *Women's Activism*; and Ginzberg, *Women and Benevolence*.

22. Augusta Store Account Book, 1795–1796, microfilm, Georgia Department of Archives and History.

23. S. McMillen, *Motherhood*, 74–76.

24. Quoted in J. Wade, *Augustus Baldwin Longstreet*, 5–6.

25. For Angus, *Southern Centinel and Gazette of the State*, December 28, 1797; *Augusta Chronicle*, August 31, 1800, May 4, 1805, February 22, 1817, November 5, 1818. For Bray, *Augusta Chronicle*, September 7, 1799.

26. For a discussion of house size, see Soltow and Land, "Housing and Social Standing." On contents of Augusta households, see Richmond County Estate Records, Inventories and Appraisements, 1799–1813, Georgia Department of Archives and History. For example, Estate of John Cook, September 8, 1799; Estate of Thomas Bray, August 1, 1799; Estate of William Dearmond, January 24, 1790.

27. Stiles advertised for an apprentice in the *Augusta Chronicle*, May 26, 1792; Catlett sought a journeyman through a notice in the *Southern Centinel and Universal Gazette*, June 13, 1793.

28. *Augusta Chronicle*, August 17, 1799 (Bray); *Augusta Chronicle*, September 20, 1800 (Wingate).

29. For runaway advertisements attesting to the recent importation of African and West Indian slaves, see *Georgia State Gazette*, September 8, 1787, August 30, 1788, November 29, 1788, January 10, 1789, July 8, 1790, August 19, 1790. For runaway advertisements attesting to the relative autonomy and sophistication of some Augusta slaves, see *Georgia State Gazette*, May 24, 1788, June 14, 1788, March 17, 1789. On the slave trade see Wax, "New Negroes," 216–18. On white fears and resulting legislation see James Jackson to the Governor, Slave Rebellion Folder, Telamon Cuyler Collection, Hargrett Library, University of Georgia; Richmond County Superior Court,

Grand Jury, July 20, 1793, Telamon Cuyler Collection, Hargrett Library, University of Georgia; Horatio Marbury and William H. Crawford, *Digest of the Laws of the State of Georgia* (Savannah: Seymore, Woolhopter and Stebbins, 1802), 440–43.

30. *Augusta Chronicle,* January 14, 1809, August 20, 1813, February 18, 1821, January 21, 1822.

31. *Augusta Chronicle,* April 4, November 21, November 21, 1807.

32. *Augusta Chronicle,* May 15, May 22, May 29, June 12, 1802.

33. *Augusta Chronicle,* October 25, November 15, 1800, August 31, 1805.

34. *Columbian Sentinel,* October 4, 1806, from Museum of the Early Southern Decorative Arts Index, Research Files, Winston-Salem, N.C. On Hiel Chatfield's history of debt and default see *Augusta Chronicle,* October 1, 1791, November 24, 1804, July 19, 1806, November 21, 1807, May 27, 1809, February 1, 1821. For advertisements for these academies see the following: *Foreign Correspondent and Georgia Express* (Athens), March 17, 1810; *Augusta Chronicle,* June 2, 1792, December 4, 1794, May 9, 1801, May 23, 1801, August 6, 1803, October 8, 1803, May 4, 1805, March 28, 1807, March 12, 1813, May 27, 1814, July 2, 1817; *Augusta Herald,* August 17, 1803, January 12, 1809, November 28, 1811, December 14, 1815, May 5, 1820; *Anti-Monarchist* and *S.C. Advertiser* (Charleston), November 2, 1811; *Reflector* (Milledgeville, Ga.), December 9, 1817.

35. Jones, *Memorial History,* 146–47; J. Wade, *Augustus Baldwin Longstreet,* 10–14, 12–14, 20, 9.

36. *Augusta Chronicle,* December 25, 1820.

37. For these ads see *Augusta Chronicle,* May 27, 1809, January 10, 1812.

38. *Augusta Chronicle,* February 28, 1995; Augusta Tax Digests, 1794–1797, microfilm, and Richmond County Census, 1807, microfilm, Georgia Department of Archives and History; *Augusta Chronicle,* May 14, 1796, July 16, 1796, September 7, 1799, July 19, 1800; *Louisville Gazette,* May 16, 1801; *Augusta Chronicle,* January 7, 1809; *Charleston Courier,* January 29, 1811; *Augusta Chronicle,* April 23, 1817; *Savannah Republican,* January 3, 1818; *Augusta Herald,* December 5, 1817; *Georgia Journal,* October 5, 1819; M. Cumming, *Two Centuries of Augusta,* 26. See also E. Cashin, *Story of Augusta,* 59.

39. Academy statistics based on the Museum of Early Southern Decorative Arts Index for Richmond County, 1780–1820, Museum of Early Southern Decorative Arts, Winston-Salem, N.C. For Maclean, *Augusta Chronicle,* April 4, 1807; for Macmillan, *Augusta Chronicle,* March 19, 1813.

40. *Augusta Chronicle,* August 20, 1813, February 18, 1821, December 28, 1823.

41. Dorothy Orr, *Education in Georgia,* 22–30, notes that the course of study for girls in county academies in Georgia consisted of English, French, and needlework. Boatwright, *Status of Women,* 10–11, observes that academies in Georgia experienced their greatest growth between 1830 and 1840, a decade when the proportion of girls to boys increased dramatically. Augusta seems to have been ahead of this important trend

by at least a decade. On female curriculum change in the early Republic, see Kerber, *Women of the Republic*, chap. 6.

42. Mary Wingate was the administrator for the mechanic Isaac Wingate's estate, *Augusta Chronicle*, May 22, 1802; and Ann Pool administered the carpenter Baxter Pool's impoverished estate, *Augusta Chronicle*, October 15, 1808. See the public announcement about the carpenter Peter Fontaine's debts at the time of his death, *Augusta Chronicle*, December 19, 1789. For an interesting discussion of women and courthouse business see Gundersen, "Kith and Kin."

43. *Augusta Chronicle*, January 18, 1800, August 17, 1799, January 1, 1802.

44. Will of the Augusta shoemaker Francis Vallotton, dated July 22, 1807, and the will of the carpenter Robert Cresswell, dated May 17, 1814, Richmond County Ordinary Estate Records, Wills, 1789–1853, Books A–B, microfilm, Georgia Department of Archives and History. Will of Hugh Magee, dated September 8, 1812, Richmond County Ordinary Estate Records, Wills, 1798–1853, Books A–B, microfilm, Georgia Department of Archives and History.

45. Richmond County Inferior Court Minutes, Book B (1805–19), Book I (1790–94), p. 25, Book B (1805–19), microfilm, Georgia Department of Archives and History; Federal Writers Project, *Augusta*, 75. The city also distributed food to the poor; see *Augusta Chronicle*, October 22, 1810.

46. *Augusta Chronicle*, June 11, 1813, February 24, 1819; E. Cashin, *Story of Augusta*, 84. An article on Sunday schools in the September 17, 1816, edition of the *Augusta Chronicle* notes that two benevolent institutions existed in the city, attended by "some of our most venerable and respectable matrons."

47. Stansell, *City of Women*, 33–42.

48. U.S. Bureau of the Census, Manufacturing Schedules, Richmond County, 1820, microfilm, Georgia Department of Archives and History.

49. Boatwright, *Status of Women*, 83.

50. W. Johnson, "Free Blacks," 12; Schweninger, "Property-Owning Free African-American Women."

51. *Augusta Chronicle*, November 4, 1809; E. Cashin, *Story of Augusta*, 65.

52. City council resolution printed in *Augusta Chronicle*, September 13, 1806; act published in *Augusta Chronicle*, February 24, 1819; incitement incident described in the lead editorial in the *Augusta Chronicle*, May 10, 1819.

53. *Augusta Chronicle*, August 5, 1814.

54. Mellish quoted in Mills, *Rambler in Georgia*, 24.

Paternalism and Protest in Augusta's Cotton Mills: What's Gender Got to Do with It?

LEEANN WHITES

WITH THE PUBLICATION in 1921 of his classic work *The Rise of the Cotton Mills*, the historian Broadus Mitchell set the framework for discussions of the nature of the mill workforce and the mill owner in the southern textile industry. According to Mitchell, the development of that industry in the late nineteenth century was benign and benevolent. The white southerners who established mills wanted to promote the betterment of their communities and ameliorate the condition of the growing ranks of the rural and urban poor created by the economic decline of southern agriculture. In establishing textile mills, local capitalists were empowered to offer these less fortunate white members of the community remunerative employment when their farms failed. They often supplied improved housing, started schools for children, and helped to finance mill churches. Altogether, Mitchell concluded, mill owners behaved more like fathers than like employers to "their" mill people, and the workers responded with gratitude and intense loyalty to the men who had created a better way of life for them. It was unfortunately true that these mill owners paid workers miserable wages and worked them long hours, while making handsome profits from their employees' labor. However, since the profit motive was basically secondary to the mill owners' desire to promote class relations that would mirror those found in a happy family, Mitchell expressed his hope that this one blight on the industry would soon be eliminated.[1]

Of course, this "one blight" on the industry, the exploitative nature of labor-capitalist relations, was not eliminated. Revisionist historians have taken Mitchell to task for his failure to recognize the centrality of the profit motive among mill owners and have criticized him for his assumption that millworkers were active and happy participants in the myth of paternalism.[2] Perhaps the most telling evidence for the revisionist critique is the bitter and protracted series of strikes that racked the late-nineteenth-century southern textile industry, first in 1886 and again in 1898. Centered in Augusta, where the largest concentration of southern millworkers was employed during much of the period, the strikes demonstrated the divergent interests of capital and labor.[3] Standing united as a group in the 1886 strike, three thousand workers in the Augusta cotton mills joined the union en masse in resistance to wage cuts and long hours. They persisted in their protest against deteriorating labor conditions despite months of lockouts, threatened and actual eviction from their homes, life in tents in the dead of winter, the threat of their replacement by black labor, and the failure of national union support. In their determination to secure a just wage and decent working conditions, these workers demonstrated a solidarity and a level of resistance to the overwhelming power of the employing class arrayed against them that seems diametrically opposed to Mitchell's picture of the dependent and grateful worker. In their stiff-necked determination to strike for their rights, these workers appear instead to exemplify what historians understand to be the legacy of their rural, yeoman heritage, much as their fathers had as common soldiers in the long and bloody Civil War a generation earlier.[4]

But can these strikes really be taken as evidence of a separate, class-based culture among millworkers? Unlike their counterparts in northern industry, southern textile workers never succeeded in organizing permanent union structures in the nineteenth century. Even in Augusta, the center of class conflict and union organization in the southern textile industry, one could argue that two strikes, however bitter, over a sixty-year period did not necessarily undermine the mill owners' basic position as benevolent paternalists in the workplace. In a more recent history of southern textile workers, appropriately entitled *Like a Family*, Jacquelyn Hall and her coauthors have refocused the question of class politics away from workplace organization and returned to the centrality of the family as the critical basis for worker autonomy and cultural integrity. They argue that although workers were largely unable to alter their position in the cotton mills through labor organization during the nineteenth century, they were able to turn to their families for self expression and survival. While the mill owners may have viewed their workers as docile and dependent members of one big mill family, that is, *their* mill family, workers themselves maintained their autonomy as a group through their experience of family as discrete and separate from that of the mill owner. Thus Hall and her coauthors believe the workers' families created not the basis for labor's acquiescence, as Mitchell thought, but the bedrock of labor's separate interests as a class.[5]

The arguments of Hall and her coauthors concerning the cultural significance of the family bear a striking resemblance to those advanced by historians of slavery. Historians point out that although the slaveowner may have envisioned the slave plantation as his or her "family, black and white," slaves in actuality took refuge in their own kin structures and used them to create the basis for a culture independent of planter domination. Historians of slave culture have demonstrated that despite the power of the owner, slave men acted as fathers to their families—they undertook to provide for and protect their wives, children, and larger kin networks.[6] Similarly, revisionist historians of millworkers, who have taken issue with the mill owners' claims to paternalism, have been intent upon proving that mill-working men undertook to protect and provide for their own. These historians cite the independent labor organization of the millworkers, and their militant action in strikes, as evidence for their position. Melton McLaurin entitled his book on the textile industry *Paternalism and Protest* because his discussion of labor relations centered on this issue. He described the factory owner as the purported "paternalist" and the factory worker as the "protestor" of the hegemony of the mill owner.[7]

In McLaurin's account both the paternalists and the protestors are assumed to be men. However, if one examines the phenomenon of mill paternalism more closely, one discovers that not all its adherents in fact were men. The "benevolent" activities generally attributed to mill paternalists, such as the establishment of mission churches, schools for mill children, day care, and hospitals, were actually much more likely to be the work of their wives, daughters, or the women of their class. While mill-owning men may have financed the initial costs of church or school structures, it was frequently their women who engaged in the daily work of "maternalism." Similarly an analysis of the "typical" millworker and striker reveals that they were usually women or children. Not only was the workforce composed largely of women and children, but a sizeable percentage of mill households were headed by women as well. In Augusta, before 1880, statistics indicate that more than 40 percent of all mill households were headed by women. Even this number underestimates the extent to which mill households were headed by women, because female-headed families, being generally less well off than male-headed families, were much more likely to board in a larger household than to live by themselves.[8]

Lewis Hine made this portrait of a mill family, with wages written at the bottom. (Courtesy Hargrett Library, University of Georgia)

Although he was not allowed to photograph these children at Augusta's King Mill, Lewis Hine waited until the noon break to take their picture, January 1909. (Courtesy University of Maryland, Baltimore County)

So if women in Augusta played critical roles, both as "paternalists" and as "protestors," then why has this question of middle-class benevolence and working-class militancy been framed by so many historians of the textile industry in such male terms? Perhaps millworkers have been routinely presented by historians as though they were all men because acknowledging the role of women would serve to dilute the case for the "manhood" of mill-working men. Again the history of antebellum slave studies is instructive. In much the same fashion, some historians of slavery have focused their energies on rehabilitating the "fatherhood" of the male slave, a fatherhood that takes as its paradigmatic model the gender roles of the slaveholding planter class. It is this underlying commitment to the elite white model of both fatherhood and motherhood that leads historians to turn a blind eye to the range of contributions that slave women made to their households. Similarly, the role of women both in the textile workforce and as heads of their own households is ignored because it is counterproductive to historians' efforts to make a case for the manhood of mill-working men patterned after the gender roles of mill-owning men.[9]

Thus for all the focus on paternalism—who has it, who doesn't—there is still no real history of manhood as a historical category of analysis capable of changing its form and meaning with the changing race and class order that the development of the urban industrial world of the textile mills created. When Broadus Mitchell argues that the mill owners were like paternalistic slaveholders, and when Melton McLaurin counters with the mill-working men "resisting" as protestors, or even when Hall paints a comforting picture of the mill family united like the fingers on a hand, none of them directly confronts the question if mill-owning men took up the "paternalistic" legacy of slaveholders in their role as mill employers, what or where did that leave mill-working men? Indeed, historians seem to assume that despite the widening class divisions of industrial society, where mill-working men now had nothing but their labor to sell and mill-owning and -managing men were left as the sole "heads" of the business, mill-working men could still somehow occupy the "paternal" role, as defined by a single standard set by the experience of elite white property-holding men.

Although historians of southern textiles have focused on the concept of "father," manhood is not a fixed entity that they can somehow prove belonged to all men irrespective of their class or race location in the social order. Manhood, like womanhood, was constructed out of particular historical contexts. The move toward an urban, industrial society that the textile industry spearheaded in the South, and in Augusta in particular, can therefore be understood as creating a state of flux and uncertainty in preexisting definitions of manhood. It is instructive to examine whether mill-working men continued to view themselves as men in the preindustrial sense of the term after becoming "hands" in another man's operation. In the context of the antebellum South, this would have placed them in a permanently dependent position like that of women and slaves. From this perspective, the outbreak of militant labor organizing and strikes in Augusta in the 1880s and 1890s can be understood as part of a larger process of renegotiation of what it meant to be a free white man in late-nineteenth-century Georgia.[10]

Millworkers in the Old South

The discussion of this process starts with the origins of the mills in Augusta and the question, What does gender have to do with it? If being a mill "hand" was so antithetical to what southern white men understood to be their proper place as "heads" of their own economically independent households, how did the mills get started in antebellum Augusta in the first place? The construction of the mills occurred because they reinforced the larger patriarchal social order. Mill owners provided employment to women and children, especially rural widows and their children, who had no adult male heads of household to work the family farm. These women came to Augusta in the hope of finding labor for themselves or their children, or public support from the benevolent resources of the city's churches and government. What they found in antebellum Augusta, especially before the construction of the first textile mill in 1847, was not very encouraging. The main form of employment for women throughout the nineteenth century was domestic labor. In the South white women found this avenue of employment generally closed to them, because it was regarded as the province of black women, either slave or free. Without education or capital, white southern women found that they could not take up schoolteaching, enter into a small business like a grocery, or keep a boardinghouse, the other main forms of employment for white women in the town. That left the possibility of sewing for a living, which, given the limited alternatives for remunerative employment for women of this class and station, created a surplus of needlewomen and low wages.[11]

Catherine Rowland, the wife of a prominent Augusta cotton factor, described the plight of one widowed woman and her daughter who were reduced to the support that sewing could provide. "I went this afternoon to see

Harriet Tyndall, poor girl. . . . What a sad life is hers having to support herself
and her mother by her needle and her mother in a perfectly helpless condition being both blind and palsied."[12] No amount of "plying her needle" could
compensate for the structural position in which women like the Tyndalls found
themselves in the rural, patriarchal, slave-based economy of antebellum Georgia. Nevertheless, the migration of women and children to the city did open
the way for the eventual amelioration of their condition through the establishment, in 1847, of Augusta's first cotton mill. As the price of cotton declined in
the 1840s, it shook loose the most economically marginal of rural families from
their land. They moved to town, which undercut the economic health of the
town in general, as profits from cotton factoring fell off and rural demand for
the town's goods declined. This economic slump was further compounded
by the extension of the railroad to factoring towns farther west, particularly to
Macon, which also reduced Augusta's rural trade.[13]

The destitution in the ranks of the poor, especially women and children,
combined with sluggish rural demand and low prices for cotton, motivated
several prominent men to consider establishing a textile factory. By making
cotton profitable even in unprofitable times, a mill would bolster the sagging
urban economy, employ the destitute, and make a profit for the investors. Although Augusta was located on the Savannah River, the establishment of such
a mill required the construction of a canal to improve water power. The actual
construction of the Augusta Factory in 1847 represented a new opportunity
for destitute women and children, a more profitable investment outlet for the
town's merchants and businessmen, and an incentive toward a wholesale program of urban improvement.

This convergence of charitable benevolence, public improvement, and private profit is a marvelous example of the configuration of forces that Broadus
Mitchell's analysis would lead one to expect. That is, it created the structural
space for the position of the paternalistic mill owner, "father" to his dependent millworkers on the one hand, powerful male profit maker on the other. It
was, however, precisely the logic of antebellum, white, rural gender relations
embedded in a slave-based, cotton producing economy that enabled patriarchal benevolence and capitalist industrial development to go hand in hand. It
might seem that the establishment of such a mill would violate the commitment of slaveholders and yeoman farmers alike to an autonomous existence
grounded in their status as independent producers. But it was precisely the
underside of this male autonomy and independence, the dependent position
of women and children within these male-headed households, that formed

the structural basis for the paternalistic nature of labor relations within the mills. As long as the industry remained marginal, as it did in the antebellum period, as long as the work experience of women and children remained subordinate and marginal to the work experience of most white men, then the mills, rather than violating the antebellum understanding of what it meant to be a free man, actually served to reinforce it.

What happened to the harmonious and apparently benevolent nature of labor relations when the textile industry, rather than representing a marginal spin-off of the predominantly rural, patriarchal family structure of the antebellum economy, moved to the center of the economic life of the town? During the Civil War, when this first began to happen, events served to intensify the convergence of profitability, benevolence, and community promotion. The larger economic and social forces that had created the space for the mill owner as paternalistic figure, and that had fostered the construction of the Augusta Factory, intensified. Wartime conditions increased the demand for textile goods dramatically, improved the profitability of the industry, and enlarged the supply of women and children in the town looking for some kind of work to replace the labor of their fathers and husbands who were at the front. As a result, the Augusta Factory became, according to its postbellum president, John Phinizy, a virtual "gold mine." At the same time it enhanced its benevolent reputation by offering employment to household members of men who were at the front.[14] The initial period of antebellum mill construction was one of "father lack." The war, a period of massive expansion of textile production intimately connected to "hyper–father lack," increased the numbers of women and children pouring into Augusta, especially in the last two years of the war, as they searched for some form of employment or charity to compensate for their absent brothers, husbands, and sons.

After the war, high prices for textiles and the persistence of a surplus of eager hands allowed the mill to pay dividends beginning with a high of 20 percent per annum in 1865. It paid this rate until 1873, when it lowered its dividends to 12 percent, which it paid throughout the remainder of the decade.[15] At the same time the persistence, in fact the slight increase, of widowed women and their children in the workforce and the community allowed mill owners and mangers to boast of their good working conditions and harmonious labor relations. As one Augusta capitalist described the situation of female textile workers to the Senate Investigatory Committee on Relations between Labor and Capital in 1883, "You take a girl and put her into a sewing house here and she has got to work very hard to make 50 cents a day, and

Lewis Hine photographed a group of young workers at the Enterprise Mill in Augusta. The small boy in the bottom row center had been working in the mill for four years at the time of the picture. (Courtesy University of Maryland, Baltimore County)

The Enterprise Mill (1876) was the first to take advantage of the increased water power of the enlarged canal. (Courtesy Augusta Museum of History)

many of them cannot do that. . . . A woman can make $1.00 to $1.25 a day and you cannot put an ordinary woman at any work outside a factory at which she can make that much."[16]

What constituted good wages for a woman constituted poor wages for a man. In the logic of a patriarchal social order, this was reasonable. Men's wages were pegged to the cost of supporting a household, at least in theory, while women's wages were considered to be additional supplements to that of the male head of household. The smooth functioning of the mills was in this logic intimately connected with the replication in the factory of the larger social order of gendered dominance and subordination, wherein the men held the skilled and supervisory roles and only the women and the children actually functioned as "hands" under someone else's direction. As one Augusta capitalist explained to the Senate committee, "The worst thing in a factory is a sixteen year old boy; he will give more trouble than anybody else. . . . I make it a rule to put a woman to every loom where I can, but I am obliged to have men to fix the looms and put in the beams and various other things. However, if I could, I would not have a man in the weaving room except those that do the heavy labor. . . . the women do a great deal better."[17] As the president of the Augusta Factory concluded, "The men really do very little work except to watch the others and take care of the labor of the machinery. The actual operatives are nearly all female."[18]

Even as these mill men spoke, however, forces were at work that would lead to the rapid conversion of white men into mill operatives. Declining prices for cotton combined with the high profits of the Augusta Factory provided the incentive for yet another major expansion of the textile industry in Augusta in the late 1870s. The resultant expansion of the Augusta Factory and the construction of six new mills increased the total mill workforce dramatically, from some seven hundred employed in the mid-1870s to close to three thousand by the mid-1880s. The construction of these mills was made possible by the enterprise of local townsmen in the face of declining cotton prices and by the simultaneous development of a largely new form of surplus labor created by the increased incidence of economic failure among hinterland yeoman farmers. As a result, migrants to the city included an ever increasing proportion of male-headed households. The gender composition of the mill workforce and of the typical mill family began to shift dramatically. The total employment of men in the town's mills increased from 23 percent in 1880 to 39 percent in 1890, while the percentage of women declined from 52 to 43 and the percentage of children employed also declined from 25 to 18.[19] This gender shift was

also apparent in the larger mill community as the percentage of mill households headed by women began to decline, from 43 in 1880 to 27 in 1900.[20]

Although the Augusta Factory persisted in its policy of hiring only white
women and children as operatives, the newer mills had to accept more men.
The president of one of these newly established mills, William Sibley, was
inclined to put a good face on the increased employment of adult white men
in his mill. In his testimony before the Senate committee, he asserted that the
increased employment of entire families, that is, male-headed households,
actually contributed to the "reliability" of his labor force.[21] This increased
reliability resulted from the greater stability of these men who, according to
Sibley, were more likely to persist in the mill workforce than those who were
single. The familial position of men, as heads of households, rather than as
footloose sixteen-year-old boys, made their increased participation in the mill
workforce desirable.

The Knights of Labor

It was this familial status of the new male operatives, however, that contributed to the formation of the town's first textile union, Knights of Labor Local
5030, in 1884 and to the outbreak of labor militancy in the strike of 1886. Although historians have considered the role of several factors in this emergence
of autonomous organization among Augusta's workers, including the mills'
concentrated urban location and the depressed economic conditions that then
prevailed, no one has considered the contribution that the increased participation of men in the mill workforce or in the mill family might have made to
labor organization and labor militancy.[22] Even a brief consideration of the
politics of the Knights local and the course of the 1886 strike it mounted makes
the role that larger gender structures played in the conflict apparent.

First, the name of the organization, the *Knights* of Labor, makes one think
of *men* as the honorable defenders of labor. They were prepared to do battle.
Of course, the Knights were originally named not by southern textile workers
but by northern workers. But for southern white men the image of the chival-
rous knight protecting his own was probably even more powerful than it was
in the North. These laboring men called themselves knights at the same time
the rural world of horse-riding men passed away. Indeed, the organization
itself has been understood by labor historians as a last-gasp effort on the part
of the skilled worker and the small farmer to hang on to their preindustrial
position in the face of the spread of urban industrial capitalism in the late
nineteenth century.[23]

Not every adult white man was destined to be economically independent, as was largely the case in preindustrial, rural Georgia, but the advent of large-scale industrial production did not necessarily signal the end of this old form of manly independence. According to the Knights, by joining together the workers could hope to combine their own capital, form cooperatives, and continue to own the means of production, albeit collectively. In the Knights' vision the textile workers in Augusta would have to pool their resources together to eventually own and run one of the town's textile mills.

Much has been made of the unrealistic nature of this vision and its connection to the decline of the Knights of Labor. In particular, historians have pointed to the way the national organizations' commitment to the cooperative vision ran into conflict with the rank and file's desire to eat. The Knights aimed at a general reform of industrial capitalism that would reestablish them as relatively economically independent, but the immediate pressures to provide sufficient wages to support their households demanded their attention. The Knights of Labor faced a dilemma. On the one hand they hoped to retain or reestablish their old position of authority as men who ran their own business and households. On the other hand they needed to make a living through the new economic forms that were emerging, if only to support those households.

In the particular context of the textile industry, the Knights also had to make common cause with the rank and file of the textile workforce, the unskilled women and child laborers. This proved problematic. In Augusta an attempt to form Local 5080 in 1884 was defeated. In 1886 membership increased for a time because of a walkout by the entire mill workforce of three thousand. The organized skilled workmen of the mill community found themselves confronted with the challenge of protecting their own positions in the workplace and their own dependent family members while simultaneously shouldering responsibility for the needs of the entire mill community. They did, indeed, find themselves like knights on the battlefield arrayed against the men of the mill-owning class. The question was, Who could play the "manly" role? Who could really protect and provide?

The demand for union recognition precipitated the strike. The mill owners were determined to reject this demand because it affronted their property rights as capitalists, and it cut to the very heart of the traditional structure of labor relations grounded in the dependent familial status to which female and child employees were subject. Knights Local 5030 had the temerity to suggest that the union, not the mill owner, represented the larger interests of mill-working women and children—that the union, not the mill owner would stand as the father figure of mill-working families. Implicitly repudiating the pater-

nalistic and benevolent claims of the mill owners, these adult male trade union-
ists issued demands that would explicitly enhance their own familial roles.
They called for a wage increase and for concessions that specifically recognized their independence and autonomy, such as the abolition of the pass
system that, according to the union, "lower[ed] the dignity of manhood." By
promoting their own individual autonomy, millworkers hoped to improve the
position of mill-working women and children and advance the interests of
their entire class.[24]

When the union was initially formed, Augusta's capitalists tried simply to
ignore it. The issuance of the union demands in January 1886 and the walkout
of the most skilled male operatives in July of that year, which halted production, forced mill owners to act. They formed their own organization, the Southern Manufacturers' Association, and responded to the militancy of the workers by locking out the entire mill workforce in early August. From the capitalists'
perspective, this action was intended to force workers to recognize their dependent relationship to the mills, and by extension to their "paternalistic"
employers, and to see the foolhardiness of seeking class autonomy through
the union. As one prominent textile capitalist advised Augusta mill owners:
"Crush the Knights beyond resurrection, they present a greater threat to the
mills than the depression of the last two or three years, or any threat in the last
twenty years. . . . Stamp out the Knights then and now, and make it amongst
the operatives discreditable for one to admit that they even belonged to the
organization. When they get good and starved and utterly ruined, they will
turn upon and murder [J. S.] Meynardie and the other leaders of the organization."[25]

Women, especially widows, and their children were expected to be the
union's weakest link. Shortly after the general lockout, the local paper sent a
reporter down to the mill neighborhood to inquire into the attitudes of the
women in the community. "Will the women support the strike?" the reporter
asked one male worker. "Yes, they will be the last to give in," he replied.[26] The
union's ability to support its members, however, was becoming increasingly
precarious. The strikers, especially widows and their children, were dependent upon the support of the national organization to put bread on their tables.
When the national decided to cut off this support at the end of August, the
Augusta local sent one last desperate plea to the organization: "Do for God's
sake render us such assistance as will hush the bitter wails of hungry children
and poor, ill-treated widows and thin little orphan children—General Master
Workman, you may think this an overdrawn picture, but God knows 'the half
is not told.' "[27]

A stalemate ensued. Despite the increasing misery in their ranks, the workers would not capitulate, and the capitalists would not acknowledge their right to organize. At this point local union forces were in shambles, deserted by the national organization, and suffering ever more intensely with the deepening winter chill. Finally, in early November, the capitalists agreed to negotiate. The workers failed to win any of their demands, and the union collapsed shortly thereafter. The capitalists had addressed their biggest grievance, and at least tacitly acknowledged their autonomy, when they recognized the union's right to exist. The local paper advised the workers to "go back to work and accept the settlement. There is honor in defeat, remember those who are dependent upon you."[28]

Male operatives learned they had entered into a new kind of the dependent status as hands in someone else's workplace. Their very resistance, unionizing, and striking constituted a vehicle for the internalization of this knowledge. This lesson in "feminization," which women learned in childhood, many of these men found bitterly galling. Their previous experience as yeomen farmers and independent household heads expected to be masters of their own fate stood in sharp contrast to their new situation. At the same time, capitalists were forced to recognize that this influx of adult male operatives had altered their relationship to the mill community. Indeed, while the increased presence of adult male wage earners represented a degradation of their own individual relationship to production, it simultaneously enhanced the prospects for independence and autonomy for the working-class community as a whole. For mill-working women and children were now increasingly empowered by their very dependence upon the men of their own families, a dependence that finally allowed them at least a modicum of liberation from the harsher and more exploitative life they could expect when they stood in direct relationship to mill employment and the mill owner alone.

Notes

1. For a later expansion of Mitchell's argument, see Cash, *Mind of the South*.

2. Melton McLaurin takes this position in *Paternalism and Protest*, as does Bess Beatty, "Textile Labor."

3. The story of these strikes has been told in several places. See McLaurin, *Paternalism and Protest*; Reed, "Augusta Textile Mills"; German, "Augusta Strike."

4. Two studies of Augusta's hinterlands, source for most of the town's operatives, describe yeoman farmers in these terms; see J. Harris, *Plain Folk*; and Burton, *My Father's House*. In fact, Augusta's hinterlands provided the most concentrated support for the Populist Party in Georgia in the 1890s, as Shaw, *Wool-Hat Boys*, has dem-

onstrated. Augusta's textile workers were also militant supporters of the movement and of Tom Watson in particular; Woodward, *Tom Watson.*

5. Hall et al., *Like a Family*; Hall, Korstad, and Leloudis, "Cotton Mill People."

6. See, for example, Blassingame, *Slave Community*; Gutman, *Black Family*; and Genovese, *Roll, Jordan, Roll.*

7. McLaurin, *Paternalism and Protest*, 41–61.

8. These findings are based on a study of all households that included at least one millworker in the Augusta manuscript census. For a more extended discussion of the analysis, see Whites, "Southern Ladies and Millhands," chap. 4.

9. For a further discussion of historians' treatment of black manhood, see White, *Ar'n't I a Woman?* Elizabeth Fox-Genovese has perhaps carried this assumption that white gender roles are the only gender roles further than any other historian, arguing that under slavery black women had no gender; see *Within the Plantation Household.*

10. For a further discussion of changes that were occurring in the social construction of male gender roles, see Ownby, *Subduing Satan*; Rotundo, *American Manhood*; Bederman, *Manliness and Civilization.*

11. For a further discussion of the limited occupational options for women in the town, see "Occupations of Women," *Augusta Daily Constitutionalist*, August 26, 1860. Although the relationship among the situation of widowed rural women, gendered migration to urban centers, and pressure for the development of new forms of industry to employ these women in towns where they congregated has received scant attention in the case of the South, Alice Kessler-Harris discusses the situation in rural New England in similar terms in *Out to Work*, 17–23.

12. Catherine Barnes Rowland, Diary, entry for November 4, 1863, Georgia State Archives, Atlanta.

13. For a further discussion of the factors behind the establishment of this mill, see Griffen, "Augusta Manufacturing Company," and "Origins of the Industrial Revolution." Also, see Detreville, "Little New South."

14. The reference to the mill as a "gold mine" during the war was made by its president, John Phinizy, while he was being interviewed about the mill years later; U.S. Senate, *Capital and Labor*, 4:697. For a discussion of the benevolence and patriotism of the mill during the war itself, see *Augusta Chronicle*, April 24, 1863, October 28, 1863, October 29, 1863, November 3, 1863.

15. U.S. Senate, *Capital and Labor*, 5:697.

16. Ibid., 741.

17. Ibid.

18. Ibid., 699.

19. One Augusta capitalist, Hamilton Hickman, described this annual migration out of the countryside: "Every fall, especially when there have been poor crops, we have a number of country people who have been broken up on their farms and who

come into Graniteville with their families to put them in the mill, and in many cases the children have to support the parents"; U.S. Senate, *Capital and Labor*, 5:740. In his study of Augusta's hinterlands, J. William Harris found that in 1860, 14–24 percent of all farm operators were renters. Conditions had deteriorated by 1880, and renters had increased to 26–30 percent of all farms in the counties he studied; J. Harris, *Plain Folk and Gentry*. The next step was to give up altogether and move to the mill, a process that Gavin Wright describes as a "sorting mechanism, in which families with the fewest resources and poorest prospects in agriculture found that the family unit could do better in the mill village"; Wright, *Old South, New South*, 138. The process was similar to the one described earlier for the antebellum period, except that male-headed households were being squeezed out to a much greater extent as the countryside was increasingly subordinated to the dictates of urban market forces.

20. Here I rely upon officially compiled statistics for the Augusta mill workforce rather than my own research, which is based on the manuscript census in order to be consistent with the 1890 returns, available only in this form. U.S. Census Office, *Tenth Censuses*, 2:383, 379, 19(2):163; *Eleventh Censuses*, 6(2):44–49; *Twelfth Census*, 8(2):992–93, 9(3):32.

21. Wright, *Old South, New South*, 138–39, gives general figures for the shifting gender and age composition of the southern textile workforce that reflect the same pattern as that of Augusta, although at a somewhat later date. He finds a decline from 57.2 percent female in 1880 to 44.3 percent female in 1900 to 36.7 percent female in 1920. Wright is inclined to dismiss the role of gender in structuring the mill workforce, especially the role of Civil War widows, as he finds the predominance of females in the 1880 mill workforce to be concentrated in the age bracket between sixteen and twenty-four. In the Augusta case, however, the majority of those single females were daughters of widowed women who were of an age to have been widowed during the war.

22. U.S. Senate, *Capital and Labor*, 795.

23. Although the relationship between the influx of women into previously male-dominated areas of the workforce and the development of labor militancy in an effort to preserve laboring conditions has been discussed in several places for this period, perhaps most notably in the case of the turn-of-the-century garment industry, scant attention has been paid to the reverse case, where men entered a previously female-dominated industry. On women entering male domains, see Jensen and Davidson, *Needle, Bobbin, Strike*; Milkman, *Women, Work, and Protest*; and Baron, *Work Engendered*.

24. For a further discussion of the Knights, see Voss, *Making of American Exceptionalism*; Fink, *Workingmen's Democracy*; Grob, *Workers and Utopia*; and McLaurin, *Knights of Labor*.

25. Along with the demand for the abolition of the pass system and a general wage increase, the Knights also demanded an increase in machinists' wages, an end to "over-working," May 1 as a holiday, the understanding that no Knight would be required to

replace a discharged Knight without investigation, and agreement that the employer would discuss hirings with the Knights; *Augusta Chronicle*, January 7, 1886. This local was also responsible for the first petition for child labor legislation that was presented to the Georgia legislature. The politics of promoting the position of male heads of household is particularly apparent here, as the Knights hoped to improve male wages by eliminating competition from children. McLaurin, *Paternalism and Protest*, discusses the Augusta Knights' role in promoting child labor legislation.

26. McLaurin, *Paternalism and Protest*, 105.

27. *Augusta Chronicle*, August 10, 1886.

28. McLaurin, *Paternalism and Protest*, 106.

Paternalism among Augusta's Methodists:
Black, White, and Colored

GLENN T. ESKEW

ATERNALISTIC INTERRACIAL COOPERATION characterized biracial Methodism in Augusta throughout the nineteenth century. Close ties developed among the white and black ministers and members of the Methodist Church. These personal associations encouraged the growth of the denomination and influenced the outcome of religious reconstruction. Indeed, the antebellum paternalism espoused by the white leaders of the Methodist Episcopal Church, South (MECS) led directly to the postbellum creation of the Colored Methodist Episcopal Church (CME) by black leaders. Some scholars have suggested the MECS created the CME Church to hinder the political efforts of the northern and independent African Methodist churches on behalf of the freedmen. Others argue the black members of the MECS acquiesced to the formation of the CME in order to retain church property.[1] Perhaps elements of both arguments are true, but the story is more complicated than simply issues of property or politics. By looking at the actions of black Methodists in Augusta from the bottom up instead of the top down, as favored by historians of black religious institutions and of reconstruction, a different picture emerges. Through an analysis of Methodist denomination building, it becomes apparent that agency belonged to the freedmen and freedwomen in Augusta.

A contradiction of seemingly minor importance led to the initial inquiry into this history of black Methodism in Augusta. With religious reconstruction, Trinity Church, the MECS mission to the slave and free black population of the city, had the opportunity to affiliate with either of the black independent denominations, the African Methodist Episcopal Church (AME) or the African Methodist Episcopal Zion Church (AMEZ), or the overwhelmingly white branch of the northern Methodist Episcopal Church; but the congregation in Augusta remained in the fold of southern Methodism and organized the CME Church in Georgia. Historians have been inaccurate or unclear on this affiliation, however, and the following analysis attempts to clarify the inconsistencies. The confusion began with the Reverend James Walker Hood's account of the denominational struggles over Trinity Church in his *One Hundred Years of the African Methodist Episcopal Zion Church*. Hood acknowledges that the Trinity congregation joined the AMEZ Church but then abruptly left, an event that he argues cost the denomination a foothold in Georgia. Harry V. Richardson, in his influential history of black Methodism, *Dark Salvation*, closely recounted Hood's analysis but adds that Trinity not only left the AMEZ Church but returned to the Methodist Episcopal Church, *North*. Edmond Drago, in his otherwise excellent study of reconstruction in Georgia, confuses the issue all the more by suggesting the AME Church gained Trinity. Since this particular congregation was noted for its historic role in the founding of the CME Church, the contradictions in this denominational alphabet soup demand clarification.[2]

Many studies of African American Methodism in the postbellum period are plagued by partisan beliefs and bitter recriminations resulting from decades of denominational strife. To understand what actually occurred, one must cut through the rhetoric of emotional church leaders and their historical followers and get to the few records that exist on the local level. Through a careful reconstruction of the history of the three major black Methodist denominations in Augusta, one can see how the congregations formed. As Trinity began as a mission to the slaves, its history stretches back into the antebellum period. Consequently, long-standing ties existed between black and white Methodists in Augusta. This study builds on the work of two previous historians, George G. Smith Jr., a Methodist minister in the North Georgia Conference who in 1898 wrote *A Hundred Years of Methodism in Augusta*; and George E. Clary Jr., a Methodist minister and professor emeritus of Paine College who coined the phrase "interracial cooperation" to describe the close association of black and white Methodist leaders in the founding of that school. The essay expands on Clary's work by adding the idea of paternalism to describe the particular nature of interracial cooperation.[3]

Never based on issues of equality, paternalistic interracial cooperation instead emphasized the personal relationships that had developed among black

and white Methodists as a result of slavery, kinship, and evangelicalism. Social, political, and economic concerns were secondary to spiritual ones among
many of these Methodists, who shared a sense of reciprocal duties and mutual obligations growing out of Christian charity. A paradox, paternalism both
hindered and helped African Americans. As Edward J. Cashin observes in his
history of Springfield Baptist Church, paternalism harmed African Americans by inhibiting individual initiative. And yet, as is apparent in the Methodist example, paternalism also led to the creation of important institutions
in black Augusta. It was this very ambiguity that allowed paternalistic interracial cooperation both to develop and to underdevelop the African American
community.[4]

Augusta's Methodist Awakening

Methodism in Augusta found its origin in a young white student named Stith
Mead, who joined his father's slaves in evangelical worship during the first
Great Awakening. The interracial religious experience disturbed Mead's soul.
While attending college in Virginia, he converted to Methodism. Upon his
return to Augusta in 1798, he found four thousand black and white inhabitants who were—for the most part—unchurched. The evangelical fanaticism
of his first sermon in the city so offended family members and friends that
Augusta might have remained unchurched had it not been for his persistent
labors and generous financial contributions. After his sermon, Mead organized a Methodist Society. On a Greene Street lot that he donated, he constructed a frame meeting house with a simple interior and slave gallery that
served Augusta's black and white Methodist congregation for the next half-
century. Ten years would pass before the Presbyterians built a church and
another ten before the Baptists did so. The first church in Augusta, Saint Paul's
Protestant Episcopal Church, initially built in 1749, had been abandoned by
the diocese and burned during the Revolution. Rebuilt in 1789, it served as a
nondenominational house of worship in which Methodist circuit riders and
other visiting clergy preached. Two years before the formal organization of a
Methodist society in Augusta, Bishop Francis Asbury had spoken there. On
the edge of town, slaves and free blacks held services as a congregation known
today as Springfield Baptist Church, the oldest black church in America. On
occasion, white and black evangelicals joined in services at Springfield, as
when Lorenzo Dow preached there in 1802.[5]

Stith Mead's labors prospered, for the Augusta society grew as a stop on the Methodist circuit, attracting the white and black of the laboring classes at first but in time becoming a more affluent congregation. For much of the nineteenth century, two men in particular managed the church as stewards: Ignatius P. Garvin, the son of the first minister, and John H. Mann, the son of another early Augusta Methodist. These two men would assist Augusta's black Methodists in organizing Trinity Church.[6]

Individuals decided whether to join an evangelical church, and the process of seeking membership in a congregation involved confession, conversion, and trial. Members guilty of grievous sins were often expelled by the congregation. During the first decade of the nineteenth century, membership in Augusta's Methodist church hovered around eighty white people and seventeen black. James O. Andrew arrived in Augusta in 1820, and his evangelism and that of Lovick Pierce increased the size of the church to three hundred black and white members by 1824. During the second Great Awakening the congregation grew quickly; many of the new converts were African American slaves. George Foster Pierce, the son of Lovick Pierce and a promising preacher in his own right, assisted Andrew at the Augusta Station in 1832. That year's General Conference of the Methodist Episcopal Church elected Andrew a bishop, an act that also elevated Pierce to the pastorate in Augusta. Later in the summer, the two ministers conducted a revival that increased Augusta's Methodists by another one hundred people.[7]

The antebellum growth of the Methodist station in Augusta led to the peaceful division of the biracial congregation into three churches. By the early 1840s there were nearly six hundred Methodists in Augusta, out of a total population of just over six thousand people. African Americans made up nearly half of the congregation. The church had outgrown the frame meeting house. To solve the space problem, the Methodist congregation followed a three-part solution. First, in 1842, it assisted its black members in organizing Trinity Church. Then, in 1844, it erected a new brick sanctuary on the original Greene Street site, the present day Saint John Church building. The black Springfield Baptist congregation bought the old meeting house and moved it to Reynolds Street, where it stands today as a parish hall. Finally, in 1855, Augusta's Methodists divided the white membership into two congregations. The original station remained Saint John and the new congregation became Saint James, the names taken from the brother disciples but also from the leaders of the two church congregations.[8]

In 1842 John Mann, I. P. Garvin, and other white trustees acquired from the city land on which to build a church for the black Methodists. By 1843 a building stood on Lot 46, bounded by Jackson (Eighth) Street to the west and Corduroy Alley to the east. This was a remarkable feat, for just two years earlier authorities had foiled an attempted slave insurrection in Augusta. Elsewhere in the South, white leaders responded to slave rebellions by passing laws to restrain the independent religious services of African Americans, in part because many of the insurrectionists, such as Nat Turner, were also exhorters of Christianity. Having just returned to the city, James Sewell, pastor of the Methodist church, described the 1841 insurrection to a friend: "Nothing material had transpired in my absence, except the discovery of a plot by some white *scamp* and a few negroes to murder & plunder the city. The trial of one of [the] blacks is now in progress: how it will eventuate, I know not." In their chronology of black Augusta, the Terrells note the conspiracy involved taking over the arsenal and burning the city. Authorities executed one black man for his involvement in the plot. White Methodist ministers kept an eye on the black Methodists by preaching at Trinity, owning the building, and working with the slave preachers under their charge. Yet a measure of independence developed among the black congregation.[9]

As this narrative suggests, the exact origins of Trinity Church within Saint John are obscure; yet evidence exists to explain the building of a separate church and the use of black preachers. The "1843" chiseled in the present church's cornerstone accurately dates the building of the first Trinity Church, although the members rebuilt the current structure in 1893 and again in 1921. Several black lay leaders served Trinity before the congregation had its first African American pastor. In the 1830s "two colored exhorters and eight class leaders" ministered to the black congregation. In his history of Augusta Methodism, George Smith described the church gallery as filled "with the leading colored people, and Ned West and Fortunatius Dugas and sundry other trusted servants of leading Augusta families were in their places." Smith's characterization was apt, for elite house slaves and free blacks of mixed-race ancestry constituted an important segment of the congregation. In 1850 members of Trinity bought the freedom of their first black preacher, James Harris, who was born a slave in Athens. Edward S. "Ned" West succeeded Harris and pastored the congregation through the turbulence of Civil War and Reconstruction. He died in 1887. The congregation buried both men in the churchyard, and although pollution has eroded the extensive inscription on Harris's marble marker, the brief epitaph is legible on West's tombstone: "Faithful Servant."[10]

Slavery and racism divided Methodism in America. Two black denomina-

tions split from the national church over issues of racial discrimination. The
AME Church formed in Philadelphia in 1816, and in New York the AMEZ Church
formed in 1822. These independent black denominations remained centered
in the North until after the Civil War. The father of Methodism, John Wesley,
had denounced the pernicious system of slavery; yet as Methodism spread
across the frontier, Wesley's followers overlooked his opposition to the peculiar institution. With the rise of abolitionism in antebellum America, the morality of slavery came into question. Southern Methodists argued that the Bible
justified slavery, and they buttressed their proslavery belief by conducting plantation missions to convert slaves to Christianity.[11] Northern Methodists condemned slavery as immoral, a charge that made the slaveholder immoral too.
According to that logic, one such immoral Methodist was Bishop James O.
Andrew. Rather than remain in fellowship with northern Methodists who
denounced their southern brethren as evil, the leaders of the church, meeting
in general conference in New York City in 1844, agreed to divide peacefully
into northern and southern ecclesiastical units. They followed the example
set fifty years before, when Methodist bishops representing the distinct pastoral charges, districts, and annual conferences of Canada separated from the
American church.

Augustus Baldwin Longstreet of Saint John Church wrote the declaration
of protest made by the southern delegates in response to abolitionism within
the Methodist church. James E. Evans and George Foster Pierce joined others in drafting a formal "Plan of Separation" that authorized the annual conferences in the slaveholding states to send their delegates to a special southern organizing conference. Gathered in Louisville, Kentucky, in 1845, these
delegates constituted themselves the Methodist Episcopal Church, South.
They retained the property the southern church had owned before division,
and they adopted, almost without change, the Methodist *Discipline*. In 1846
the MECS held its first general conference in Petersburg, Virginia, marking the
completion of the orderly separation. In 1848, however, northern Methodists
repudiated the division and attempted to reclaim southern church property.
They lost a subsequent challenge through the federal courts, and their hostile
actions staved off reunification for nearly a century. Thus the MECS was born
amidst the rapidly changing atmosphere of the sectional crisis. A similar division would occur among southern white and black Methodists during Reconstruction.[12]

In Augusta, the MECS used Trinity Church as a station on its plantation
missions circuit. The Methodist church moved its ministers around every two
years, and every time the bishops stationed a new pastor at Saint John, they

sent a new missionary to Trinity. Young white novices learned their trade by preaching to audiences of slaves and freedmen. The sermons of the white evangelists inculcated ideas of black subservience and stressed the mutual obligations and reciprocal duties of paternalism. One can only speculate on the receptiveness of the African Americans and what lessons of Christianity the white missionaries learned from their black charges. George Foster Pierce was a leading proslavery advocate, and after his consecration as bishop in the MECS, he stopped often in Augusta and preached at Trinity Church. Through public speaking, ministers like Pierce provided moral leadership for the black and white southern community.[13]

The Civil War disrupted paternalistic race relations in Augusta as the city's black population trebled through an influx of refugees. To maintain order, the city council increased slave patrols and strengthened the slave code. Likewise, Bishop Pierce preached on the virtues of paternalism, as when he addressed the Georgia General Assembly on March 27, 1863. Yet the war had strained the message and the resources of the MECS. The church quit supplying Trinity with white missionaries. Black exhorters and preachers like Ned West quickly filled the void.[14]

An event in late 1864 underscored the brutality always lurking behind the paternalism. By this time in the war, Augusta bordered on anarchy, as refugees pushed civil order to the breaking point. One night the slave patrol stumbled upon a large group of African Americans apparently violating the pass system. The paddy rollers started whipping the alleged offenders. Yet the crowd contained many members of a black congregation—perhaps Trinity Church—that had just concluded services. Reflecting the reciprocal nature of paternalism, several black witnesses reported the incident to Pierce. In defense of the African American Christians, the Methodist bishop wrote a letter to Governor Joseph E. Brown criticizing the slave patrol's interference in ecclesiastical matters; but Pierce soon recanted, for, as he explained in a letter to the Augusta *Daily Chronicle and Sentinel*, the white "worthy citizens" of the slave patrol had only whipped the black people who "were visiting about in the neighboring houses without passes, and were liable under the law." It was all an "accidental coincidence." As a good paternalist, Pierce justified the need for discipline, but the members of Trinity Church could have lived without that aspect of paternalistic interracial cooperation. Indeed, as one Methodist observer noted about the congregation by war's end, "the colored people wished to be independent, and now were allowed to control their own affairs."[15]

With Confederate defeat, the white leaders of the MECS recognized that they could no longer control black Methodists in the region, so they prepared for an orderly separation of the congregations still under their charge. At the New Orleans General Conference of 1866, the bishops addressed the question, "What shall be done to promote the Religious Interests of the Colored People?" Under the careful direction of James E. Evans, pastor of Saint John in Augusta, the church recommended the peaceful separation of the minority black members from the majority white body by building, from the bottom up, a new African American denomination, what would become the CME Church. The separation conformed to the wishes of many black Methodists still in the southern white church who wanted the CME to be the mirror image of its parent body, the MECS. Evans, Pierce, Andrew, and others at the general conference arranged the same orderly route to separation they themselves had followed in 1845; yet then the MECS already had the pastoral charges, districts, annual charges, and general conferences that the black church lacked in 1866. As in the previous division, the churches arranged the legal transfer of property from the one to the other. Having Christianized these black Methodists, members of the MECS felt obligated to assist them in setting up their own institution. Out of a belief in paternalistic interracial cooperation, that commitment remained strong among many black and white Methodists even after they had completed the separation of the churches.[16]

As white Methodist leaders developed plans for division, black Methodists in Augusta confronted new opportunities for worship led by missionaries from the African denominations and the northern church. Already a black Methodist congregation independent of the MECS operated in Augusta: Bethel Methodist Protestant Church. During Reconstruction, the African Methodist Episcopal Zion Church organized Mount Zion AMEZ Church, and the northern white Methodist Episcopal Church started an integrated mission (although it attracted an all-black congregation), which in 1881 became Saint Mark's. Thus Augusta boasted a variety of Methodist churches, with Saint John, Saint James, and a mission to millworkers serving the white community, and Trinity, Bethel, Mount Zion, and Saint Mark's serving the black community.[17]

Bethel African Methodist Episcopal Church

With freedom, the congregation of Bethel Methodist Protestant Church affiliated with the AME Church. Bethel's pastor, Samuel W. Drayton—a native of Africa—had been a popular preacher among black and white evangelicals in antebellum Augusta. When AME Bishop Daniel Alexander Payne returned to Charleston in May 1865, Drayton traveled down to meet him. The AME Church admitted Drayton to the itinerancy and sent him back to Augusta. The denomination expressed overt political objectives. James Lynch, a northern black missionary in the AME Church who had recruited congregations on the Sea Islands during the war, spoke before Augusta's freed people on the Fourth of July 1865. Frequent visits by Henry McNeal Turner, a fiery preacher and radical politician, secured the AME foothold. Yet the very radicalism of the AME Church probably limited its appeal among some black Methodists. The church hurt its missionary efforts in Augusta when, in late 1866, it sent Drayton to Savannah after the minister there—Tunis Campbell—defected from the AME Church for the AMEZ Church. Drayton's replacement in Augusta, Richard Vanderhorst, defected from the AME Church for the CME Church in 1868. The ease with which black Methodist ministers moved from denomination to denomination suggests a weakness of institutional support.[18]

Despite the ministerial setbacks, Bethel AME won many converts among Augusta's black working class. The congregation first worshiped in a structure on Campbell (Ninth) Street in the integrated Dublin community of Augusta. In May 1867 the Georgia Conference of the AME Church stationed C. L. Bradwell at Bethel. By 1869 Sunday school attendance averaged 670 pupils. The AME Church sent the itinerant preacher, Andrew W. Lowe, to Bethel in 1870, and under his leadership the congregation purchased a plot of land on Campbell Street in 1871. By this time a church building already stood on the lot. Bethel AME trustees Thomas Payne, Henry Pemberton, Nathaniel Burdell, Patrick Gould, and John Joshua purchased the property for two dollars from prominent white Augustans, suggesting paternalistic interracial cooperation extended to this independent congregation of African Methodists. The trustees typified urban African American workers: Joshua and Pemberton were laborers, Payne was a gardener, Gould was a hostler, and Burdell was a painter. No identifiable member of Bethel AME came out of the Trinity congregation.[19]

Like the white Methodist churches, the AME Church moved its ministers in and out of Bethel, stationing there, among others, E. P. Holmes in 1874 and Daniel McGhee in 1877; yet through it all Bethel benefited from the loyal service of its treasurer, H. D. Paschal. With Lowe back as pastor again, and with Paschal as the head of the building committee, Bethel AME Church constructed an impressive brick sanctuary on the original church lot in 1888, a testimony to the dedication of its membership. The building easily accommodated the rather large congregation of mostly common black laborers whose tithes paid for the eighty-five-hundred-dollar cost of construction. Of the church's trustees, only two were listed in the city directory, H. D. Paschal and Thomas Williams; both men were shoemakers.[20]

Mount Zion African Methodist Episcopal Zion Church

Common black laborers also constituted the membership of Mount Zion AMEZ Church, organized in Augusta in 1866. In its early years the Reverend Willie Harris served Mount Zion, which worshiped in a sanctuary on Fenwick Street. Under the leadership of Henry Thomas, the AMEZ congregation moved the church to its present location off Twiggs Road some time before 1877. Two of Mount Zion's trustees, Simpson Ferguson and George Green, served during the period. As was typical of many African Americans in Augusta, both men were laborers, and neither could sign his name. Both men lived on Turknett Spring Road, near the church, in the Augusta area known as the Terri. Two of Mount Zion's trustees appear to have had ties to Trinity Church: Joseph Childs, a carpenter, and Abram Washington, a farmer who also lived in the Terri.[21]

Trinity Colored Methodist Episcopal Church

By comparing the trustees of Trinity Church to those of Bethel AME and Mount Zion AMEZ, one can see how class differences within the African-American community of Augusta influenced the composition and character of the different Methodist congregations. All nine of Trinity's stewards who signed the property deed for the church in 1874 were listed in the city directory as artisans, craftsmen, and service workers. The most recognizable, Charles A. Ladeveze, functioned as church superintendent. A mixed-race descendant of refugees from Santo Domingo, Ladeveze operated a fashionable art supply store on Reynolds Street. Of the nine, only he was a free black in 1863. The names of two draymen, George C. Driscoll and Henry C. Simpkins, and two carpenters, Henry Oakman and George Edwards, appear on the deed. One must wonder if Oakman, an employee of the William H. Goodrich Company, helped make the exceptional window shutters and sashes in the beautiful Cotton Exchange Building. Three men worked in service capacities: Abel C. Wright as a porter for the Georgia Rail Road and Banking Company, Austin George as a barber, and Frank Brown as a waiter. The city directories include the final name twice. One Thomas Porter ran a grocery store on Centre Street, and the other made shoes. It is unclear which one attended Trinity Church, but either Porter fits the pattern established here. Though not wealthy compared to Augusta's white elite, these gentlemen represented Augusta's colored elite.[22]

Class differences divided Augusta's black community much in the same way class differences divided the white community. Both groups of elites created their own private institutions that served themselves and their children. While elite white children attended Richmond Academy and Tubman Girls High, elite black children attended Fourth Ward Grammar School and Ware High. Social clubs and churches performed similar functions. Perhaps because of these shared interests in exclusion, paternalistic interracial cooperation worked best among elite white and black people. In her analysis of black Augusta, Diane Harvey found the African American community divided between aristocrats of color, who descended from house slaves, and everyone else, who came from common field-hand stock. A faculty member at Paine College, Harvey deplored the "racial disunity" that resulted from class differences within the black community. As Thomas Holt and others have argued, class differences among African Americans influenced the outcome of Reconstruction.[23]

With freedom, Trinity Church participated in Reconstruction. When black Augustans celebrated the Emancipation Proclamation for the first time as freed people on January 1, 1866, the Reverend Ned West of Trinity gave the benediction at the event. At the podium with West stood Samuel Drayton of Bethel AME Church. Springfield Baptist Church and its pastor, Henry Watts, hosted the affair. Out of the pulpit thundered the voice of Henry McNeal Turner. It was a stirring occasion, and Trinity Church played a part.[24]

Likewise, when the American Missionary Association organized freedmen schools in Augusta, the congregation allowed its building to be used as the Trinity Free School, which had 167 pupils and was directed by a white northern schoolteacher, Mrs. M. C. F. Smith. The Freedmen's Bureau's superintendent of education in Georgia, G. L. Eberhart, spoke at Trinity on March 5, 1866, in a public meeting of the Richmond County chapter of the Georgia Equal Rights Association, the radical organization that demanded the franchise for freedmen. No account of this meeting is apparently extant, but if it was anything like the meeting held the Friday night before at Springfield Baptist, then Trinity was in the thick of it all. After Eberhart spoke that night, the black school children gave orations, recited scripture, and then sang the "Battle Cry of Freedom." In what the northern white schoolmarms later described as an act of "patriotism" but what southern white Augustans interpreted as an act of provocation, the children concluded by whipping out American flags, waving them wildly, and shouting "Down with the traitors! Up with the stars!" Such dissension boded ill for paternalistic interracial cooperation.[25]

An analysis of the *Loyal Georgian*, the mouthpiece of Reconstruction in Augusta, edited by the carpetbagger and racial egalitarian John Emory Bryant, reveals that some members of Trinity's congregation supported the Georgia

Equal Rights Association, but others apparently did not. Charles Ladeveze frequently advertised his business in the newspaper. Ned West announced weddings held in Trinity Church. Yet only Austin George's name appeared on the list of members in the Summer Convivial Association, which raised funds for the *Loyal Georgian* by performing in a tableaux. The more radical the newspaper became, the less the names appeared. By 1868 the *Loyal Georgian* carried mostly national wire copy and advertisements, with very little local information.[26]

In July 1867 the *Loyal Georgian* reported that the Trinity congregation had affiliated with the AMEZ Church, breaking its ties to the MECS. Within months however, Trinity appeared back in the fold of southern Methodism. This peculiar waffling deserves analysis. The little evidence that exists sketches out the following scenario.[27]

Of the three northern Methodist churches, the AMEZ was the smallest, with the least money to spend on missions. In 1860 the denomination claimed only forty-six hundred members compared to the nearly twenty thousand in the AME Church. Nonetheless, Zionists engaged in the postwar effort to proselytize to freedmen. In 1867 AMEZ Bishop J. J. Clinton toured the South organizing conferences for the denomination. In some states, such as Alabama and North Carolina, AMEZ missionaries had successfully cultivated black Methodist congregations before affiliation, but in other states, such as Georgia, the conferences were little more than paper creations.[28]

Bishop Clinton convened the South Carolina Conference in March 1867 and the Alabama Conference in May. In June he traveled between the two to Augusta to organize a Georgia conference. To help with the work, Clinton brought with him powerful AMEZ evangelists like Wilbur G. Strong of Alabama. A delegation from the AMEZ North Carolina Conference, headed by the future bishop James Walker Hood, attended. The AMEZ missionary in Savannah, Tunis Campbell, played an active role in the proceedings, as did Presiding Elder Adam Palmer of Warrenton. At the time of the organizational meeting, the AMEZ Church had two small congregations in Augusta, Mount Zion and Social Chapel; but outside the city little AMEZ churches were scattered across the countryside of eastern Georgia and western South Carolina in such places as Red Hill, Fair Haven, Hamburg, and Beech Island. Augusta served these communities as a regional center, and it was a logical place for Bishop Clinton to convene the conference. Furthermore, by claiming the independent Trinity Church with its 1,160 members, the AMEZ could double its size in Georgia.[29]

Few black Methodists in Augusta actually played a role in the proceedings, as AMEZ delegates from Alabama and North Carolina dominated the committees. Bishop Clinton called the conference to order in Trinity Church on June 15, 1867. Yet, as was typical of the day, subsidiary meetings were held in Springfield Baptist and other area churches. Indeed, the entire conference reflected the culture of the southern evangelical community. Springfield's Henry Watts was made an honorary member. Republicans Robert Kent and Simeon Beard of Springfield also participated, as did the "Baptist Sisters" who prepared lunch for the delegates. Following the pattern Bishop Clinton had established in South Carolina and Alabama, the Georgia annual conference spent five days staffing various committees and debating numerous resolutions; yet this busy work was created from the top down, as the members of committees came from the neighboring states. Little, if anything, was indigenous to Augusta.[30]

On the first day Bishop Clinton authorized Ned West and Robert Brown of Trinity Church to consult with Henry F. Russell and R. H. May, white Methodist laymen, about receiving the blessing of the MECS. Both Russell and May were stewards at Saint John, and both had served as mayors of Augusta. In response to the request, Russell and May announced their willingness to attend the undertaking, for "if the colored people were not ashamed of *them*, they were not ashamed of them." At the same time the AMEZ meeting took place at Trinity, Saint John held its quarterly conference, and the subject of Trinity's affiliation with the AMEZ Church received official recognition. In response, the AMEZ conference adopted a resolution thanking Saint John for its assistance and "for the sympathy expressed for Zion Connection."[31]

Since emancipation Saint John's leadership had respected the wishes of the black congregation and left Trinity Church to its own devices. The *Yearbooks of the North Georgia Conference* from 1867 on demonstrate that from the perspective of white Methodists in Augusta, the black church was basically independent. The minutes of these difficult postbellum years do show the MECS rebuilding after the war. A lack of interest forced the conference to close Asbury Mission to Augusta's white millworkers in 1869, but in 1873 it reopened as Saint Luke MECS. The conference struggled to fund an orphanage for victims of the war. The minutes also show a steady decline in the number of "colored charges," black preachers and black Methodists in the MECS. This decline corresponds with what the church historian Othal Lakey described as "the rise of colored Methodism."[32]

No sooner had Trinity connected with the AMEZ Church than the congregation bolted from the black independent denomination from the North in order to build a new colored independent denomination in the South. Perhaps the affiliation had all been a misunderstanding exaggerated by John Emory Bryant, for Trinity's role as host had been in keeping with southern evangelical tradition. Perhaps the radical politics of Tunis Campbell concerned the more conservative members of the congregation, for Campbell was deeply involved in state affairs. Perhaps getting the title to the church property worried the congregation, although in its annual report the Augusta district of the MECS no longer listed the Trinity building among its possessions. Perhaps the AMEZ Church failed to follow through with its promise of institutional support, for its presiding elder in Warrenton, Adam Palmer, soon defected from the AMEZ for the northern Methodist Episcopal Church. Whatever the reason, Trinity rejected the AMEZ denomination and accepted the ecclesiastical authority of the MECS. The congregation would later memorialize West as the founder of Trinity CME Church.[33]

It is clear that in July 1867 the *Southern Christian Advocate*, the church newspaper of the MECS in Georgia, announced that, in accordance with the general conference of 1866, the MECS in Memphis and Nashville had ordained African American deacons, named African American presiding elders, and formed an annual conference of African American charges in Tennessee. Through paternalistic interracial cooperation, the black and white southern Methodists had begun to build a new black church from the bottom up by naming pastoral charges and districts. The newspaper recommended, "Our Presiding Elders in Georgia, South Carolina and Florida should be studying this subject with a view to future and perhaps early action in this direction." It is also clear that Ned West, Robert Brown, and others at Trinity called Richard Vanderhorst to pastor the congregation in 1868. He had just defected from Bethel AME Church, and he worked with West and Brown to build colored Methodism in Georgia.[34]

Bishop George Foster Pierce had not abandoned his African American charges after the war, and he continued to preach paternalism from the pulpits of the South. With the collapse of the Confederacy, Pierce ordered his subordinates to minister "both among whites and blacks." During the military occupation of Augusta, he joined John Emory Bryant and other Republicans on the rostrum at a mass meeting on May 27, 1865. Gathered on the parade grounds known today as May Park, some five thousand freedpeople listened to the chaplain of the United States Army and frequently interrupted his speech with applause. He told the newly freed slaves that "in all cases where they were not treated with cruelty or manifest injustice, that they should remain with their former masters." Bishop Pierce could not have said it better. Episcopal visitations to the West detained Pierce in 1867, but by 1868 he had returned to the South and actively assisted black Methodists in organizing the CME church in Georgia.[35]

Across the state black exhorters and itinerant clergymen such as Ned West and Lucius Henry Holsey preached under the authority of the MECS. Bishop Pierce called sixty of them to report to Augusta on January 4, 1869. That day in Trinity Church he assembled the first meeting of the Georgia Colored Conference of the MECS. Pierce ordained African American ministers and appointed them to colored charges. West stayed in Augusta, but Holsey went to Savannah, where he confronted denominational strife among black Methodists.[36]

After the war the different Methodist denominations competed over the freedpeople by promoting factions within the congregations and by claiming church property. The possession of a sanctuary gave one group an advantage over others. When Holsey arrived in Savannah to pastor the old MECS mission of Andrew's Chapel, he found it occupied by an AME-supported faction. Months before, the AME missionary Henry McNeal Turner had arrived in the city, aligned with members of the congregation, and seized the building. The white trustees of the MECS in Savannah allowed the remaining black Methodists to meet with Holsey in the library of Trinity MECS until they had repossessed Andrew's Chapel for this loyal black congregation. As the MECS still owned the missions property used by its black members, it was logical that it would hold this property for the new CME congregation. Paternalistic interracial cooperation required it to do so. In time, the CME took possession of Andrew's Chapel in Savannah, while the AME faction organized Saint Phillip's and built a new sanctuary. Although some scholars have suggested a similar turn of events occurred in Augusta, there appears to be no evidence to suggest that factions splintered Trinity Church or that Saint John ever repossessed the property.[37]

Bishop Pierce convened the second meeting of the Georgia Colored Conference in Macon on December 15, 1869. He ordained Holsey and Vanderhorst as presiding elders. The conference elected the two men as delegates to the organizational meeting of colored Methodism. In Macon, Holsey chaired the committee on education, and it requested the MECS to establish "a school for the training of our colored preachers and teachers." As Holsey later explained, "We could not see any reason why the people of color should not be taught by southern white Christian people." He believed in paternalistic interracial cooperation and, despite opposition from many white and black people, his dream of a school for freedmen sponsored by biracial southern Methodists found fruition twenty years later as Paine Institute.[38]

Shortly after its own quadrennial general conference in Memphis in 1870, the MECS convened in nearby Jackson, Tennessee, the organizing conference of the Colored Methodist Episcopal Church in America. Four years had passed since the white bishops had adopted a plan of separation in New Orleans. The division had been an orderly process. With the assistance of the MECS, black Methodists across the South had formed the pastoral charges, districts, and conferences that, like Georgia's, sent delegates to the meeting. These colored delegates chose the name of their new denomination, adopted with minor changes the *Discipline* of the MECS, and expressed appreciation for the paternalistic interracial cooperation that had made the new church possible.[39]

On December 21, 1870, Bishop Robert Paine of the MECS consecrated William Henry Miles and Richard Vanderhorst the first bishops of the CME Church. The death of Vanderhorst in 1872 necessitated an extraordinary general conference of the CME Church for the election of his successor. The delegates gathered in Trinity Church in Augusta, where Holsey had preached since 1871. Old MECS friends Pierce and Evans joined the colored Methodists in the historic occasion on March 23, 1873, when the delegates elected Holsey and two other men as bishops in the CME Church. The next morning, white Bishop Pierce preached the ordination sermon and joined black Bishop Miles in the laying on of hands. The act symbolized more than just establishing ecclesiastical authority, for it reflected the paternalistic interracial cooperation that had given rise to the southern black Methodist denomination.[40]

Paternalistic interracial cooperation among black and white Methodists in Augusta continued after Reconstruction. The Trinity Church property passed from the hands of John H. Mann, Ignatius P. Garvin, and other trustees of Saint John MECS into the hands of Ned West, Charles A. Ladeveze, and the trustees of Trinity CME Church in 1874. Trinity prospered along with the growth of the CME denomination leading to the formation of congregations and the building of churches.[41]

A new congregation of African American Methodists led by Robert Brown of Trinity formed in the Summerville community as Rock of Ages CME Church in 1878. That year, William W. Montgomery Jr., a wealthy white attorney and landowner in the exclusive village, sold the congregation a lot adjacent to the Summerville cemetery for twenty-five dollars. In 1880 Montgomery sold a similar lot to the Richmond County Board of Education for ten times that

The congregation of Trinity Church in Augusta had to abandon the building in 1998 because of ground pollution caused by a nearby gas works. (Courtesy Mark Albertin)

Bishop Lucius Henry Holsey (1842–1920), a leader in the CME Church and founder of Augusta's Paine College, worked to improve race relations but became disillusioned at the onset of segregation. (Courtesy Glenn Eskew)

amount. The latter was used by the Summerville Academy, and the former was used by Rock of Ages. Paternalistic interracial cooperation accounts for the difference in price. Harriett Montgomery—one of Montgomery's slaves, who had reared him and his children as the mammy of the household—had helped found the church and served as a trustee. When she died at the age of seventy-seven in 1888, the Rock of Ages congregation buried her in the churchyard, and the Montgomery family marked the grave with a marble stone that read: "For us the children whom she reared, her love was unselfish, her devotion unswerving and profound." A nearby black congregation of Baptists experienced a similar paternalistic relationship with the Cumming family.[42]

The black and white southerners who founded Paine Institute saw it as a shining example of paternalistic interracial cooperation. After his Macon address in 1869, Bishop Holsey of the CME Church had never stopped asking white members of the MECS for educational assistance for colored people. On several occasions he attended the general conferences of the MECS, and in 1882 he addressed the body of white Methodists convened in Nashville. His speech appealed to a shared belief in paternalism. Holsey received help from the Reverend Atticus Green Haygood of the MECS, who in his 1881 book, *Our Brother in Black*, echoed Holsey's sentiments. The two men succeeded in establishing a unique new school that used southern white professors and ministers to train southern black teachers and preachers. They organized Paine Institute in 1882, began classes in rented rooms on Broad Street in 1884, and in 1886 bought land for a campus in the Woodlawn area of Augusta. After the death of

Haygood, Holsey traveled the South raising money for the construction of a main hall to be named in his memory. Completed in 1898, Haygood Hall stood as a landmark in Augusta until 1968, when it burned. A replacement was built and suitably christened Haygood-Holsey Hall. Many of the buildings on Paine College's campus bear the names of the black and white southern Methodists who served the institution out of a belief in paternalistic interracial cooperation.[43]

Quick to condemn southern Methodism because of its plantation missions, many historians of the African American church and religious reconstruction ascribe the actions of MECS and CME Church members to cynical motives. Yet, when considered in the context of paternalistic interracial cooperation, the concerns of these biracial southern Methodists go beyond issues of property and politics and enter the realm of interpersonal associations that can only be understood through a careful analysis of place and time. By giving African Americans agency, one can see how they used reciprocal duties to their own advantage. Despite today's dislike of paternalism, one must acknowledge the sincerity of these black, white, and colored Methodists in Augusta and respect their accomplishments.

Notes

1. Northern black and white Methodist missionaries in the postbellum period assumed that southern black Methodists would want to leave the MECS and would logically join one of the northern independent churches. Some southern black Methodists contradicted this arrogant assumption by forming the CME Church. In response, missionaries then and many historians since then, refusing to acknowledge the choice made by these freed people, have denounced the CME Church as a conspiracy of the former slaveholders. Arguments over politics are most often posited, because of the denominational struggles among black Methodists during the postbellum period. For a contemporaneous account see Gaines, *African Methodism*, 21–22; for a more modern account see Walker, *Rock*, 98–99, 103–7; for struggles to achieve ecclesiastical equality see Dvorak, *African-American Exodus*; for issues of property see Gravely, "Social, Political and Religious Significance." Two studies have considered paternalism as important but not the major reason for the founding of the church: Lakey, *History of the CME Church* (Lakey is a bishop in the church); and Hildebrand, *Times Were Strange*, 3–27. Hildebrand acknowledges the paternalism but disregards the sincerity behind the belief. For an insightful analysis of religious reconstruction that places postwar Methodism in the context of the Baptist and Presbyterian struggles, see Stowell, *Rebuilding Zion*. For a thoughtful history of southern Methodism see Owen, *Sacred Flame of Love*.

2. Hood, *One Hundred Years*, 365; Richardson, *Dark Salvation*, 210; Drago, *Black Politicians*, 19; and Lakey, *History of the* CME *Church*, 227. Lakey argues, "Trinity was another of those churches that had been taken over by the A.M.E.s, repossessed by white Methodists, and deeded to the Colored M.E. Church." A search of Richmond County Courthouse records has uncovered no account of repossession.

3. G. Smith, *Hundred Years of Methodism*; and Clary, "Founding of Paine College." See also Clary, "Origins of Methodism." For a general history see Hammond, *Methodist Episcopal Church*.

4. For a discussion of antebellum paternalism, see Genovese, *Roll, Jordan, Roll*, 3–7, and *From Rebellion to Revolution*, 4–6; and E. Cashin, *Story of Augusta*, 57, 113. In this, the best general history of Augusta, various language is used to describe paternalism: "Virginia attitudes," "Virginia plantation tradition," and the "Virginia theory." The essay "The Myth of the Plantation" in Cashin's *General Sherman's Girl Friend*, 42–56, analyzes the effects of paternalism on white and black people. See also E. Cashin, *Old Springfield*. For a feminist critique of paternalism described as "social fathering," see Whites, *Civil War*. For a theoretical analysis of how hegemonic ideologies such as paternalism function, see the writings of Antonio Gramsci, as in *Antonio Gramsci Reader*, ed. Forgacs, 234–38.

5. G. Smith, *History of Methodism*, 416–18; Clark, *Journal of Asbury*, 3:80; E. Cashin, *Old Springfield*, 1–15; Strickland, *Religion and the State*, 92, 158–59, 168–72; and Dow, *History of Cosmopolite*, 127.

6. G. Smith, *History of Methodism*, 418–19; the Reverend John Garvin had been a missionary to Africa.

7. *Chronicle of Christian Stewardship*, 435; and G. Smith, *Life of Andrew*, 113–15, 218–39.

8. In 1840 Augusta's population stood at 6,254, with 3,205 whites, 2,900 slaves, and 149 free persons of color. See *Augusta Directory & City Advertiser, 1841* (1841; reprint, Augusta Ice and Coal, 1943); and G. Smith, *History of Methodism*, 438–39. The congregation leaders were John H. Mann and the Reverend James E. Evans.

9. Richmond County Realty Book 3-C (1874), 218–21, Superior Court Clerk's Office, Richmond County Courthouse, Augusta; James Sewell to William Wightman, February 9, 1841, Methodist Leaders Papers, MS41, Special Collections Department, Robert W. Woodruff Library, Emory University, Atlanta; Terrell and Terrell, *Blacks in Augusta*, 2.

10. Cornerstone of building and tombstones in churchyard, Trinity CME Church, 818 Eighth St., Augusta, Ga., 30901; *Century of Stewardship*, 20 and passim; G. Smith, *Hundred Years of Methodism*, 33, 38, and comments on 40–41; Terrell and Terrell, *Blacks in Augusta*, 3. Harris's son, Jacob Walker Harris, married Elizabeth Johnson Harris in the Church of the Good Shepherd on July 5, 1883. The use of the white Episcopal church by the black Methodists reflected paternalistic interracial cooperation, for the bride attended the colored Sunday school, and her grandfather, Peter Stewart, served the parish as sexton. She noted in her 1922 memoir that "the church

was filled to its capacity by colored and white friends." See Elizabeth Johnson Harris, unpublished memoir, Special Collections, Duke University, Durham, N.C., 31–32.

11. For a good account of the separations, see Richardson, *Dark Salvation*, 76–147. For the best analysis of the proslavery ideology, see Jenkins, *Proslavery Thought*.

12. Three accounts of the schism that vary in perspective include Mathews, *Slavery and Methodism*; Holland N. McTyeire, *History of Methodism*, 618–51; and Norwood, *Schism*, 96–100. See also Alexander, *History of the Methodist Church*. There were 327,284 white and 124,811 black Methodists in the newly formed MECS. On the topic of hostility to the MECS, see the *Journal of the General Conference, 1848* of the Methodist Episcopal Church (North), 16–22.

13. The white evangelists were Robert Bingham (1845), J. B. Smith (1849), Lewis J. Davies (1851), James M. Armstrong (1856), and R. A. Connor (1858), according to G. Smith, *Hundred Years of Methodism*. For a history of the MECS missions, see Harrison, *Gospel Among the Slaves*.

14. Corley, *Confederate City*, 70–75, 78–83; Harvey, "The Terri." Pierce's address can be found in G. Smith, *Life of Pierce*, 465–77.

15. *Augusta Daily Chronicle and Sentinel*, September 3, 1864; G. Smith, *Hundred Years of Methodism*, 50. Corley notes that by 1864 civil order was on the verge of collapse in Augusta; hence the breakdown in paternalism and the use of violent force; see *Confederate City*, 78.

16. Coverage of the 1866 general conference can be found in the special New Orleans newspaper edition, *Christian Advocate: General Conference Daily*, April 1866, copies in the Pitts Theology Library, Emory University, Atlanta. Similar coverage is found in J. Brawley, *Two Centuries*, 411–12. In their report the bishops complimented the church on its unwavering support for the plantation missions that had promoted the "salvation and improvement" of the slaves: "It is grateful to our own feelings to know that if the colored people do not remain under our pastoral care, their departure reflects no discredit upon our labors in their behalf, and is necessitated by no indifference on our part to their welfare. Many of them will probably unite with the African M.E. Church, some of them with the Northern Methodist Church, while others, not withstanding extraneous influences and unkind misrepresentations of our church, will remain with us." Indeed, many had stayed with the MECS, for of the 200,000 black Methodists before the war, nearly 40 percent remained in the church after the war (207,766 in 1860 and 78,742 in 1866). See McTyeire, *History of Methodism*, 666–71.

17. For a general history of the period see McCoy, "Historical Sketch"; see also Richmond County Realty Book 3-L, 75–77; and V. Miller, "United Methodism." On the problems of the northern Methodist Church in Georgia see Stowell, "Negroes," 65–90.

18. On Drayton see E. Cashin, *Old Springfield*, 27, 37; and C. Smith, *African Methodist Episcopal Church*, 67–68, 89; Campbell, *Songs of Zion*, 54–59; Lynch, "Mission of the Republic"; Gaines, *African Methodism*, 9–12, 291. On Turner see Angell, *Bishop*

Henry McNeal Turner, 67–72. For Turner's speech see the *Colored American* (Augusta), January 13, 1866; Duncan, *Freedom's Shore*, 45, 64. Duncan neglects to explain Campbell's change in denomination; see Drago, *Black Politicians*, 24–25; and Currie-McDaniel, *Carpetbagger of Conscience*, 56–58.

19. Richmond County Realty Book 2-Y (1871), 710–11; *Loyal Georgian* (Augusta), July 6, 1867, March 10, 1866; Gaines, *African Methodism*, 15.

20. Richmond County Realty Book 3-Y (1888), 162–65; Gaines, *African Methodism*, 23–24. In the extant city directories Bethel is first listed in 1874, as is Paschal. See *Hooper's Augusta City Directory*, 31. The cornerstone of Bethel AME Church on Ninth Street lists the trustees at the time of construction in 1888, yet only Paschal and Williams appear in the directories. In the 1980s the congregation abandoned the old Bethel AME Church rather than finance extensive renovations and built a new structure across town on Crawford Avenue.

21. Washington, "Eight Nineteenth Century Documents"; in the appendix is a brief history of Mount Zion by member Mamie L. Bostic. See also *Loyal Georgian* (Augusta), July 6, 1867; and *Sholes' Directory*, 1877, 42. Ferguson, Green, Washington, and Childs are listed in this directory. All of the Mount Zion AMEZ Church trustees in 1884 were illiterate. See Harvey, "The Terri," 69; and *Loyal Georgian* (Augusta), June 15, 1867.

22. For a general reference, see Rowland, *Index to City Directories*; *Haddock's Directory*; *Hooper's Augusta City Directory*, 1874; *Sholes' Directory*, 1877; *Sholes' Directory*, 1879; and E. Cashin, *Old Springfield*, 78–79. Goodrich attended Saint John MECS, and several of his black employees were Methodists, although they attended different churches: Burdell the painter attended Bethel AME, Childs the carpenter attended Mount Zion AMEZ, and Oakman the carpenter attended Trinity CME. On Goodrich and the Augusta Exchange Building, see E. Cashin, *Story of Augusta*, 96, 149.

23. Edward Cashin tells an anecdote that captures the class differences nicely. In 1844 Henry Clay visited Augusta. "A carriage drew up at the Planters Hotel to take Clay to the banquet in his honor. A few minutes later, another carriage arrived to take Clay's black servant to a banquet prepared by black Augustans," *Old Springfield*, 23. See also E. Cashin, *Story of Augusta*, 93, 108–9, 113, 164, 184; Gatewood, *Aristocrats of Color*, 90–91; Leslie, *Woman of Color*, 110–12; and Harvey, "The Terri," 66. Harvey says that "the Black bourgeois or 'house niggers' imitated what they considered to be white, and therefore right. They arrogated authority and set themselves up as leaders of the black masses or simply attempted to ignore or isolate themselves from the so-called 'field niggers.'" The black educator Lucy Laney taught elite black pupils, such as John Hope and Channing Tobias, at Fourth Ward. See Cottingham, "Burden," 27; and E. Cashin, *The Quest*, 15–20, 36. See also Torrence, *Story of John Hope*; Holt, *Black over White*. Other members of the colored elite left Springfield Baptist Church in 1879 to organize Union Baptist Church. Their endeavors received assistance from the white First Baptist Church and the Augusta Board of Education. See Minnie B.

Harper's unpublished memoir, on file at Historic Augusta, Augusta.

24. *Colored American* (Augusta), December 30, 1865, January 13, 1866. On black participation in reconstruction in Augusta, see E. Cashin, *Old Springfield*, 44–62.

25. *Loyal Georgian* (Augusta), January 27, 1866, March 10, 1866. On AMA teaching experiences, see J. Jones, *Soldiers of Light and Love*, 109–39.

26. For announcements see *Loyal Georgian* (Augusta), March 10 and March 17, 1866; for politics and national wire see May 16, July 6, and August 10, 1867. See also Currie-McDaniel, *Carpetbagger of Conscience*, 90, 100, 105.

27. *Loyal Georgian* (Augusta), July 6 1867.

28. Richardson, *Dark Salvation*, 146–47; Hood, *One Hundred Years*, 364–65. In contrast, the MECS claimed 207,766 black Methodists as members.

29. Richardson, *Dark Salvation*, 208–10. On p. 210 Richardson gives the figure for Trinity as 1,160 and says the AMEZ Church in Georgia had 2,032 members in 1868 but only 4,317 in 1878. The *Loyal Georgian*, July 6, 1867, lists twenty-four AMEZ churches in Georgia with a total membership of 3,369.

30. *Loyal Georgian*, July 6, 1867.

31. *Loyal Georgian*, July 6, 1867. On Saint John Quarterly Conference, see the *Augusta Constitutionalist*, June 16, 1867, and the *Southern Christian Advocate*, July 19, 1867. The AMEZ also adopted a resolution that called on "the members of Trinity Church to carry out in good faith all arrangements made for this year with the brethren of the M. E. Church South and thus show their appreciation of kind acts, past and present of those brethren, and the resolutions passed by them as a body in relation to the transfer of church property."

32. *Yearbook of the North Georgia Conference*, 1867–72, microfilm, Pitts Theological Library, Emory University, Atlanta. According to the minutes, in 1869 Saint John had 344 members; Saint James, 345; the city mission, none; and Asbury, 300. Trinity was no longer listed as an MECS Church. In the conference in 1869, there were 395 white and 6 black preachers, and 42,127 white and 851 black members of the MECS. By 1872 there were 412 white and 1 black preacher, and 46,447 white and 176 black members of the MECS. See Lakey, *Rise of "Colored Methodism."*

33. It is possible that the editor, John Emory Bryant, took liberties in his reporting and made up some of the information in his account. See Duncan, *Freedom's Shore*, 46–54. In July 1867 Campbell attended the Republican state convention. He participated in the constitutional convention and then was elected to the state senate, becoming one of the expelled black members in 1868. Yet one might question politics as the reason, for the congregation was aware of his participation in the Georgia Republican Party, as evidenced in the coverage of the *Loyal Georgian*, May 10, 1867, and other issues. The *Yearbook of the North Georgia Conference in 1867* leaves blanks next to Trinity's name where numbers on membership, property value, and donations were listed for the other churches. In 1869 Trinity was dropped altogether. See Inscoe, *Georgia in Black and White*, 81. The full inscription on the tombstone in Trinity CME

churchyard reads, "Rev. Ned West / Born 1816 / Died 1887 / Founder of / Trinity CME Church / Faithful Servant."

34. *Southern Christian Advocate,* July 5, 1867; Harris and Craig, *Christian Methodist Episcopal Church,* 17; Angell, *Bishop Henry McNeal Turner,* 70, 103. Angell believes the MECS formed the CME Church as a conservative rival to the AME Church and Turner's radicalism. He notes that with competition, fewer African American Methodists joined the AME Church after 1869 than before. It is also possible that the AME Church had recruited its logical membership by that time, and that those African American Methodists who were not AME had not joined the denomination for other reasons. Angell argues that "AME Church records showed an overwhelming loss of members in the Augusta region, the area of greatest strength for the CME Church," an interesting suggestion given the nature of CME development in the area. In contrast to Angell, Campbell, in *Songs of Zion,* 56, identifies Augusta as one of the cities in Georgia where the AME experienced its "greatest harvest." The Reverend James Evans attended the annual meeting of the Georgia General Conference of the AME Church in 1869 to inform the delegates of the plans made by the MECS on behalf of its black members. As Evans explained, the MECS organized the CME as an "independent body" and not "for the purposes of engendering strife" with the AME, because the MECS "did not propose to disturb our [AME] congregations and would not affiliate with a minority of our congregations for that purpose." See Gaines, *African Methodism,* 20. Gaines failed to appreciate Evans's comment.

35. *Augusta Daily Chronicle and Sentinel,* May 28, 1865; *Southern Christian Advocate,* August 31, 1865, quoted in Hildebrand, *Times Were Strange,* 135 n. 17. On Pierce in the West, see his microfilmed correspondence in the George Foster Pierce Papers, Special Collections Department, Robert W. Woodruff Library, Emory University, Atlanta; G. Smith, *Life of Pierce,* 499–530.

36. Holsey, *Autobiography,* 11–20. George E. Clary Jr. edited a reprint of the introduction to Holsey's autobiography in 1988, and it is available from Brier Creek Press, P.O. Box 5, Keysville, Ga. 30816. On Holsey, see also Cade, *Holsey;* and Eskew, "Black Elitism."

37. Holsey, *Autobiography,* 23; Bowden, *History of Savannah Methodism,* 129–30, 139–41; Gaines, *African Methodism,* 14, 30. Lakey suggests the MECS repossessed Trinity; *History of the* CME *Church,* 227. The discovery of toxic coal tar seeping into the churchyard from an adjacent industrial plant forced the congregation to abandon its historic sanctuary in 1998. Under the leadership of the Reverend J. Ronzell Maness, Trinity CME Church joined several local residents in a class-action lawsuit filed by attorney Duncan D. Wheale against the Atlanta Gas Light Company, which owned a nearby manufactured-gas plant that had cooked coal to produce gas for domestic consumption and had buried a coal tar residual in pits on the site. Although the plant was decommissioned decades ago, Atlanta Gas Light left behind industrial waste con-

taining carcinogens, which bubbled up throughout the African American neighborhood. Atlanta Gas Light finally admitted its responsibility for cleaning up the site but
refused to compensate the residents harmed by the pollution. Rather than spend
money to remove the contamination, the company hired lawyers to fight the lawsuit.
Forced into an out-of-court settlement in May 1997, Atlanta Gas Light presented its
case before a court-appointed umpire, Percy J. Blount, who considered the "intrinsic
value, historic meaning, denominational impact, and replacement cost" of the church
and awarded Trinity nearly $3 million as compensation. Much is made of corporate
paternalism today, but the absence of any real sense of duty to the community or
willing acceptance of restitution to those wronged by Atlanta Gas Light suggests that
outside welfare capitalism, the dehumanized corporate world is incapable of true paternalism.

   38. Lakey, *Rise of Colored Methodism*, 76–77; Cade, *Holsey*, 50, 80–81; and Eskew,
"Black Elitism."

   39. Summers, *Journal of the General Conference*, 168; and Phillips, *Colored Methodist Episcopal Church*, 56–64.

   40. With this apostolic succession, Holsey could write that the CME was "the only
Negro Methodism whose episcopal ordination is perfectly correct and legitimate, and
whose records and history are clear and unquestionable. Its organization was regular,
consistent, and free from those agitative and chaotic ebulliations that give others birth."
See Cade, *Holsey*, 142; Phillips, *Colored Methodist Episcopal Church*, 61. See also Lakey,
History of the CME *Church*, 36, 126, 220. For a copy of the proceedings of the 1873
general conference, see Williams, "Inquiry," 6–13.

   41. Richmond County Realty Book 3-C (1874), 218–21.

   42. Richmond County Realty Book 3-H (1878), 82–83, and 3-T (1880), 683. On
William Montgomery, see Jones and Dutcher, *Memorial History*, 338, 344; and E.
Cashin, *The Quest*, 15, 19–20. James Gardner Montgomery reputedly kept two photo-
graphs on the mantel of his room, one of his mother and the other of his mammy;
Erick Montgomery to the author, March 26, 1996, in the possession of the author. On
Cumming Grove Baptist Church, see E. Cashin, "Summerville," 59; and Callahan,
Augusta, 59.

   43. Clary, "Founding of Paine College, " 143–51; "Speech Delivered Before Several
Conferences of the M. E. Church, South," in Holsey, *Autobiography*, 239–48. Holsey
raised eight thousand dollars for the building of Haygood Hall. See Phillips, *Colored
Methodist Episcopal Church*, 217; and Haygood, *Our Brother in Black*, 144–57. On
Paine College see Richmond County Realty Book 3-T (1886), 137. Another example
of paternalistic interracial cooperation as expressed in campus architecture is Gil-
bert-Lambuth Chapel, named after John Wesley Gilbert, Paine's black educator and
a CME Church member, and Bishop W. R. Lambuth of the MECS, two men who traveled together as missionaries in Africa.

No Middle Ground: Elite African Americans in
Augusta and the Coming of Jim Crow

KENT ANDERSON LESLIE

T HE ERECTION OF THE COLOR LINE at the close of the nineteenth century ended the practice of treating elite African Americans as different from the black masses. George Washington Cable described the division within the black community best when he rhetorically asked, "Then tell us gentlemen, which are you really for: the color line, or the line of character, intelligence, and property that divides those who have and those who have not the 'right to rule'?" In *Gender and Jim Crow*, Glenda Gilmore argues that "white supremacy entailed more than violence and the denial of economic opportunities and political rights. It forced African-Americans to endure an excruciating assault on their hopes and dreams." In Augusta that "excruciating assault" eventually made it perilous for elite African Americans to act like others of their class and exercise the "right to rule" in the public sphere. Indeed, segregation made it impossible for elite African Americans to rise above the black masses and thus remove themselves from public humiliation.[1]

Augusta's African American elite reacted to the dramatic change in its status as an exception to the rule in various ways. Amanda America Dickson, who inherited a fortune worth approximately five hundred thousand dollars from her white father, sought to protect herself from racism by retreating into a world of private privilege. Bishop Lucius Henry Holsey of the Colored Methodist Episcopal Church abandoned his strategy of accommodation with whites and advocated the creation of a separate black state. The members of the Ladeveze and Harper families at first relied on their extraordinary talents and extended connections among white Augustans to secure special treatment. Ultimately they confronted the white power structure through the law, and when they lost their struggle for racial justice in the courts, they either retired from public life in Augusta or passed into the white world elsewhere. Rather than relying on the pretense of ladyhood, the indomitable Lucy Craft Laney endured by developing a separatist strategy of service to black Augusta through Haines Institute.

Immediately after the Civil War, Georgia's most popular African American leaders, Tunis Campbell and Henry McNeal Turner, articulated a vision among freedmen of a world based on racial equality. Turner went so far as to advise those "on freedom's shore" to "love whites," and "soon their prejudice would melt away." By 1872 Reconstruction had failed in Georgia, and with its demise dimmed the bright hopes of these and other African Americans who had chosen to enter the public realm through the struggle for equal rights. The historian Horace Wingo described the era in race relations as one of inconsistency: "Alternatives clearly existed, and Negroes and whites alike exercised them on occasion without incident. . . . From 1872 to 1891, white Georgians frequently spoke on behalf of the Negro, protected him against violent racism, and promised him a better day." The distinguished president of Morehouse College and Atlanta University, John Hope, described this period in Augusta's history as a time when young African Americans could "aspire to the heights and receive encouragement from whites to do so." H. L. Walker, the principal of Ware High School, found Augusta a place where the "two races of people [are] living in such accord and sympathy as are no where else to be found in all the southland." Professor Channing Tobias of Paine College commented, "There was something in the atmosphere. I cannot say just what it was. John Hope and I used to talk about it at times. We did not know how it came about." Years later John Hope would lament, "When I think of the stupid, virulent, and violent racial prejudice that has sprung up in the South since my boyhood I am amazed."[2]

Sherman and his marauding troops had spared both the downtown business district of Augusta and the industries that had flourished there during the war. These resources, coupled with Augusta's location at the headwaters of the Savannah River and at the crossroads of the railroads, resulted in a postwar boom. Augusta became "a gateway through which passed most of the agricultural products of several Southern states." Its population increased from 12,000 in 1860 to approximately 40,000 in 1900, when Augusta was the third largest city in Georgia, surpassed only by Atlanta, with 65,533 people, and Savannah, with 43,189.[3]

In 1886 Augusta boasted six banks, including the Georgia Railroad and

Banking Company with assets of $4.2 million. Municipal works included the new Augusta Canal, which had cost the city $1 million to build in 1873, a trolley car system, and "enough water to turn a million spindles." Indeed, the city was succeeding in "bringing the factory to the field." Six cotton mills operated in Augusta, employing 5,264 white workers who operated 89,464 spindles. The work force included 3,381 males over the age of sixteen, 1,340 females over the age of sixteen, and 543 children; in aggregate, this working class represented a third of the white population of the city in 1890.[4]

The rapid urbanization and industrialization that Augusta underwent during the postwar period produced tensions in the city's population. City services were archaic and deteriorated in the 1880s and 1890s, especially in the white factory settlements and in the poor black section south of Gwinnett Street, known as "the Territories." In these working-class sections of town, hollow-log water pipes broke open, and green scum and foul odors bubbled to the surface of septic fields. The citizens complained about the problems but to no avail. From 1880 to 1890, factory wages for white workers declined. At the Sibley Mill workers' annual wages dropped from $216 in 1880 to $181 in 1900. The same trend prevailed in the King Mill, where annual wages dropped from $242 to $225. The declining standard of living for white workers increased racial tensions in Augusta.[5]

In 1886 the Knights of Labor strike erupted, constituting the first large confrontation between capitalists and workers in Augusta and the first attempt by the Knights to unionize in southern mill towns. The struggle was bitter and ultimately futile. Early in the strike, mill owners acting in concert posted eviction notices on houses rented by strikers, leaving them "stunned, shocked and bewildered" in the streets while new mill hands and their families moved into the striking workers' homes.[6] The collapse of the strike left few members of the Knights of Labor in Augusta after 1890, as the white upper class retained control of the city.

Amanda America Dickson

When Amanda America Dickson arrived in Augusta five days before the Knights of Labor strike, she found a relatively cosmopolitan Southern town. Gas lights illuminated the major thoroughfares, and as many as four rows of trees on the main streets provided a grand promenade and relief from the heat. Citizens could purchase ice from the Arctic Ice Company, ready-made clothes, cut flowers, "fine" French wine and pastry, a newspaper edited by a black editor, or a newspaper edited by a white editor. They could also take a ride on an integrated streetcar. Augusta was not a residentially segregated city. Amanda Dickson's factor, W. H. Howard, lived seven blocks down from the house she purchased at 452 Telfair Street. Howard acted as her white male emissary in Augusta. Most important, Dickson, the "richest black woman in the South,"[7] could buy a large and expensive house in the most fashionable section of the city and live there comfortably despite her notoriety as the illegitimate mulatto daughter of the "prince of Georgia farmers," David Dickson. Her status as an exotic afforded her limited protection by the white community, for when her health failed, she obtained medical care from distinguished professors at the Medical College of Georgia.

As Dickson discovered, race relations in the public sphere were in flux. Two hospitals served the critically ill, the City Hospital for whites and the Freedman's Hospital for blacks. The city directory listed the majority of the community's churches and cemeteries as either white or colored. Of fifteen Baptist churches listed, the directory designated four as white and eleven as colored. The Christian, Jewish, Lutheran, and Catholic churches were all listed as single congregations with no racial designation, as were the Presbyterian and Episcopal churches.[8] The ten Methodist churches included five white and five colored congregations. Segregation existed in both the public and private schools in Augusta. African American schools included Ware High School, which was Georgia's only publicly supported high school for blacks, and Paine College. However, neither public transportation nor public accommodations were legally segregated.

With the exception of the relief and benevolent societies, social organizations in Augusta included racial designations in their advertisements. Six Masonic societies were white; the A. Y. M. Benneker Lodge Number 3 was black. The Independent Order of Odd Fellows listed two white lodges, and there were two black lodges as well, the Boaz Lodge and the Star of Bethlehem Lodge. In this era Augusta still housed racially separate military units, for of the seven militia groups two were colored, the Douglas Infantry and the Augusta Light Infantry. Since its inception in the 1880s, the Woman's Christian Temperance Union (WCTU) had segregated its unions in Georgia, for, as one administrator noted, "our colored people wish to do their work as an independent organization, and not as an auxiliary to our state W.C.T.U."[9]

In 1886 black Augustans worked in limited numbers as artisans and professionals. African Americans dominated the trades of barbering, blacksmithing, carpentering, huckstering, junk dealing, and food services. Black businessmen managed half of Augusta's undertaking establishments. Several African Americans worked only with white clients. George Walton practiced the trade of barbering at the fashionable Augusta Hotel on Broad Street, and John C. Ladeveze sold art supplies at 315 Reynolds Street. Ladeveze's cousin Robert A. Harper, the only African American piano tuner in Georgia, also sold pianos in the art store. One black lawyer, Judson W. Lyons, a graduate of Howard Law School, practiced in Augusta in 1886, and one black physician, E. H. Mayer, practiced medicine at 928 Walker Street, five blocks from Amanda Dickson's house.[10]

Several of Augusta's black citizens were wealthy in 1890. Nora Butterfield paid taxes on property valued at $1,000. L. Henson owned a restaurant business worth $18,500. Mary Butts paid taxes on property valued at $11,800. Mary J. Ladeveze and Mary F. Harper each claimed $17,500 worth of property. The merchant Henry Osborne had $8,650 in taxable goods, and the mortician Mary Skinfield claimed $7,850 in property. In 1890, 37 percent of all black Georgians worth more than $6,000 had inherited wealth. By 1915, only 1 percent of the same demographic group had inherited wealth.[11]

The elite black community of Augusta based status on more than money—whether earned or inherited—for community position depended on a constellation of attributes including color, status before the Civil War, education, manners, family connections, and wealth.[12] Given these standards for judgment, Amanda Dickson, as a mulatto and specifically a quadroon, held an enviable position in the elite black community of Augusta.[13] Although she had not been legally free before the Civil War, Dickson enjoyed material advantages other African Americans listed in the Hancock County *Register* as free could not. She was literate, could play the piano, and dressed with impeccable taste, as was expected of any proper lady, black or white. After the war she attended Atlanta University for two years. Before Dickson came to Augusta, her African American family connections were not aristocratic; however, her children by her first marriage, to a white Civil War veteran named Charles Eubanks, soon married into two of the city's most prominent black families, the Holsey and the Walton clans. Her wealth became her crowning attribute. She displayed that wealth by choosing to live in an elite neighborhood and by opulently furnishing her home.[14]

Amanda America Dickson's residence at 452 Telfair Street was located in a multiracial neighborhood. Elite whites and blacks lived on the streets, running east and west, and whites and blacks of meager means lived in houses on the numbered avenues, running north and south. Yet exceptions to this gen-

Amanda America Dickson's residence on Augusta's Telfair Street was situated in a fashionable neighborhood. (Courtesy Mark Albertin)

Amanda America Dickson's monument at her gravesite is in Augusta's Cedar Grove Cemetery. (Courtesy Mark Albertin)

eral rule existed. The black barber George Walton lived at 831 Telfair Street, while Nora Butterfield lived at 307 Walker Street. Mary J. Ladeveze, Mary F. Harper, John C. Ladeveze, and Henry Osborne all lived in the three hundred block of Reynolds Street, which was located across Broad Street beyond the main business district.[15]

According to John M. Crowley, one of Dickson's white neighbors and a manager of the Western Union Telegraph, the eclectic neighborhood held the Dickson family in high regard. When asked to describe the wealth, refinement, intelligence, and lifestyle of Amanda Dickson, Crowley replied: "It was common report that she was worth $100,000. My family held her family in very high esteem and would exchange little neighborly acts. I have never heard a word of slander or anything of that nature against them." Crowley continued in what appears to be a matter-of-fact tone, "The general reputation of the Dickson family in the neighborhood is very good. From the reported wealth of the Dickson family they made no ostentatious show nor did they push themselves forward or out of their way. Whilst they had every comfort, I never observed any excess of comfort." Dickson displayed what William S. McFeely has described in his biography of Frederick Douglass as "bourgeois values maintained with the staunchest respectability."[16]

When a reporter from the *Atlanta Constitution* attempted to arrange an interview with Dickson through Howard and Company, which was "attending to" her business affairs, the firm's employees informed the reporter that she had been advised not to talk to members of the press. Nevertheless, when the determined correspondent knocked on the door at 452 Telfair Street, Dickson herself answered the door. "She was," he said, "an unassuming, intelligent mulatto and does not seem at all 'set up' by her singular good fortune. She would not be noticed in the streets from hundreds of other colored women by any display or show of dress." He continued, "She states that as yet she has no idea what she will do or where she will live in [the] future, but I understand that she has been advised to move north."[17]

These were not peaceful years for black Georgians who lived outside the world of private privilege. After the Civil War, a legal code based on the segregation of the races evolved in Georgia, as race relations deteriorated from a climate of measured hope during Reconstruction, to inconsistency before the turn of the century, to apartheid as the new age dawned.

During the 1890s the federal government abandoned African Americans to home rule and states rights in the South. Southerners took the cue to "ostracize, segregate and disfranchise" all "Negroes regardless of individual achievement and worth." With the withdrawal of federal troops in 1877 and the repeal of the Civil Rights Act of 1875, black Georgians lost their legal right to equal treatment in public transportation, in accommodations, in places of entertainment, in churches, in cemeteries, and in the public schools. With the defeat of the Lodge Bill in 1890, which called for federal troops to return to the South to supervise national elections, black citizens were left with no federal protection of their civil rights.[18]

As a consequence, Georgia began the process of establishing legal apartheid by racially segregating the schools. In 1887 a representative introduced in the Georgia General Assembly a bill making it a crime for any teacher to educate a white and "colored" child together in the same institution. State Superintendent of Education G. R. Glenn explained that "it is the settled policy of this State, as inherited from our fathers, and as imbedded in our constitution, that the two races shall run parallel, but separate courses. They shall be as two streams, which flow alongside of each other, each with equal privileges, and equal rights, but inexorably forbidden to commingle." Glenn believed "social chaos" would result from the commingling of the races, and he warned that "if the co-education of the races is permitted in Georgia, all the intelligence of this State cannot save the public school system from instant destruction." In 1891 the Georgia General Assembly passed a statute segregating all railroad passenger cars except Pullman sleeping cars. The law also urged streetcar conductors to separate the races "as far as possible." By 1898 white Georgians had succeeded in segregating first-class sleeping cars as well. As white southerners were encoding the rules of segregation into law, they resorted to the most violent form of extralegal social control, lynching. The peak years for such vigilante violence in the United States occurred from 1889 to 1893, a period described as the "nadir" for black citizens but the "Gilded Age" and "Age of Innocence" for white citizens.[19]

While white Georgians established segregation as the ruling social order, Dickson went on with her private life. On July 14, 1892, she married Nathan Toomer of Perry, Georgia. Like Amanda America, Toomer was a "wealthy and highly educated" mulatto. The *Houston Home Journal*, a Perry newspaper, wrote that Toomer, "the esteemed colored farmer," had married the "richest Negress in Georgia" and that he "has many white friends in Houston County who will cordially congratulate him." Born in 1839 near the Haw River in Chatham County, North Carolina, Nathan Toomer began life as a slave of Richard Pilkinson. Pilkinson sold Nathan to John Toomer, who subsequently moved the child and his family from North Carolina to Houston County, Georgia. When John Toomer died in 1859, his brother, "Colonel" Henry Toomer, purchased Nathan's mother, Kit, and seven of her children from the estate. Nathan became Henry Toomer's body servant and in that position had the opportunity to learn the manners of gentility. Some time before 1869, Nathan married a mulatto woman named Harriet. They had four daughters: Theodosia, born in 1869; Fannie, born in 1871; Martha, born in 1872; and Mary, or "Mamie," born in 1879. Harriet died intestate on August 17, 1891, and the Henry Toomer plantation, which she had purchased and mortgaged in her own name, reverted to the grantor.[20]

Eleven months after his first wife died, Nathan Toomer married Amanda America Dickson at her home in Augusta. The Reverend R. S. Williams of Trinity CME Church presided over the ceremony. At fifty-three years old and over six feet tall, Toomer appeared "well nourished," for he weighed in at over two hundred pounds. Years later Jean Toomer, Nathan's son from another marriage who as a Harlem Renaissance author wrote *Cane*, described his father as a handsome, elegant man who had the "air of a Southern Aristocrat of the old stamp."[21] After their marriage, Toomer took up residence in his wife's house in Augusta. There the Toomers enjoyed all the luxury that money could buy, including a live-in maid.

However, Amanda's health was frail and she was afflicted with an assortment of ailments that required the constant attention of her family physician and neighbor, Dr. Thomas D. Coleman. A prominent doctor in Augusta, Coleman had graduated from the University of the City of New York and held a position as professor of physiology at the Medical College of Georgia. Coleman described Amanda as "a woman of delicate constitution" who suffered from chronic bronchitis, uterine trouble, premature menopause, wandering pains, catarrh of the stomach, and muscular rheumatism.[22]

By May 1893 Amanda America's health had improved to the point that her symptoms had "practically disappeared." Unfortunately, at about the same time, a family tragedy erupted. Charles Dickson, her twenty-three-year-old son by Charles Eubanks, who had married Kate Holsey, the daughter of Bishop Holsey, became infatuated with Nathan's twelve-year-old daughter, "Mamie" Toomer. The ensuing turmoil contributed to a general decline in Amanda's health. She died on June 11 at her home on Telfair Street. Her death certificate listed the cause as "complications of diseases."[23]

Haggie Brothers Funeral Home prepared the body for burial. They embalmed her corpse and dressed it in the wedding gown that she had worn when she married Toomer. They then placed the body in an expensive copper-lined casket with rose-colored plush cushioning. The *Milledgeville Union Recorder* described it as the "handsomest casket ever brought into [Augusta]." Toomer and the family ordered one hearse and six carriages from Haggie Brothers for the funeral.[24]

Amanda America Dickson Toomer's funeral took place in Trinity CME Church. According to a tribute written for the *Augusta Chronicle*, "a very large and respectful gathering of friends and acquaintances" attended the funeral. Three ministers of the gospel "officiated," paying tribute to her "Christian life and character, her exemplary worth, her unostentatious charities, and the beauty of her home life." They read passages that she had marked in her own Bible, and the service ended with the singing of the hymn she had requested for the occasion, "Shall We Meet Beyond the River," which "moved to tears almost the entire audience." The family buried the body in Augusta in the Toomer plot of the Colored Cedar Grove Cemetery, located behind Magnolia Cemetery for whites.[25]

The Amanda Dickson Toomer of the obituaries was a fiction similar to the myths of true womanhood and of the southern lady that were articulated in the nineteenth century for white "ladies." The *Atlanta Constitution* described her as a "modest, generous, and benevolent" woman who enjoyed her fortune" while "others shared her pleasure." It noted that she "was kind-hearted and in no way pompous or assuming on account of her wealth." In this era, "ladies" were socialized to accept purity, piety, domesticity, and submissiveness as ideal behavior patterns. Amanda Toomer's obituaries mentioned all these attributes except purity. In the nineteenth century southern ladies were also described as physically weak, timid, modest, beautiful, graceful, innocent, and self-denying. Although Toomer was not described as beautiful, graceful, innocent, or self-denying, she was described as physically weak, respectful, and uncomplaining and as "a devoted and loyal wife, a loving mother and a dutiful child."[26]

If one compares the idealized Amanda America Dickson Toomer of the obituaries to expressed ideals for the behavior of African American "ladies" of the late nineteenth century, then another important imperative is missing: racial uplift. It was not unusual for colored elite women to aspire to the cult of true womanhood in this era. But these women were also encouraged by the ideals of their community to step outside the domestic sphere and engage in community building and racial uplift. The Amanda America Dickson Toomer of these obituaries, with her quiet charities and attention to the needy, appears to have no racial identification, no influence outside the limited sphere of an attractively disabled "lady." Indeed, she may have escaped the prevailing white myths about being a degraded female Negro only to be partially trapped by a myth of the proper role of an elite white woman.[27]

Bishop Lucius Henry Holsey

Bishop Lucius Henry Holsey's career represents a concerted effort not to challenge the white power structure but to cooperate with it in a struggle to obtain some middle ground. Born a slave in 1845, Lucius Holsey described his white father, James Holsey, as "a gentleman of classical education" and remembered his black mother, Louisa, as a "pious and exemplary" woman of "pure African descent." Years later the bishop commented that "the way amalgamation has been brought about in the Southern States is enough to make the bushman in the wild jungles blush with shame."[28] Upon the death of his father, Lucius became the property of T. L. Wynn of Hancock County, whom he served until 1857. As Wynn died of fever, he asked Lucius to select his next master. The young body servant chose Richard Malcolm Johnston, a planter and schoolmaster of Rockby Academy.

In 1862 Holsey married Harriet A. Turner, a slave on the neighboring plantation owned by Bishop George Foster Pierce of the Methodist Episcopal Church, South. The Holseys had fourteen children, six of whom survived to maturity. In 1868, the Methodist church licensed Holsey to preach the gospel. Bishop Pierce assigned him to Ebenezer Church, which black Methodists in Sparta had recently organized. As part of the MECS plan to set up a separate black Methodist conference, Pierce called Georgia's black Methodist ministers to Augusta and assisted them in creating the Colored Methodist Episcopal Church in 1869. Holsey attended as the delegate from Hancock County. Henceforth the history of the CME Church and the life of Holsey became so intertwined that "the history of either must include much of the history of the other."[29] In 1873 the CME Church elected Holsey bishop of Texas, Arkansas, Alabama, and Tennessee. When not traveling to these states, the bishop lived in Augusta. Because of his generosity to others, the Holsey family never gained wealth, and its material circumstances sometimes appeared desperate.

Holsey joined other elite African Americans in an effort to procure higher public education for black children. In 1879 the Augusta Baptist Institute moved to Atlanta, leaving a vacuum in black education in Augusta. Holsey accompanied William J. White (cofounder of the institute), James S. Harper,

Alonzo McClennan (Augusta's first black physician), and Elbert Rogers to a meeting of the Augusta Board of Education. The elite colored men "respectfully and earnestly" asked the board for positive action on a petition filed in 1880 that requested the 1872 law requiring equal educational facilities for blacks and whites be implemented. The chairman of the school board, William H. Fleming, commented, "To grant the petition of the colored people would be only an act of tardy justice."[30] Soon Ware High School opened as the state's only publicly funded black high school.

In 1882 Bishop Holsey made an "eloquent" appeal to the MECS General Conference that resulted in the endowment of Paine College, an institution established to train ministers. Holsey pleaded: "We ask your sympathy, aid, and cooperation in redeeming your friends and former slaves from the long night of darkness and degradation. Who will come to the rescue? Who will hear the cries of the children of Ham?" In this nationally recognized interracial endeavor to establish a college to train African American ministers, Bishop Holsey became well acquainted with prominent white southern Methodists, including Morgan Calloway, Atticus Haygood, and Warren Candler. Holsey made the first monetary contribution to the college and worked vigorously to expand its physical plant. In the face of "antagonism," he agreed to hire only white teachers. According to A. B. Caldwell in *History of the American Negro*, Holsey believed that "nothing could be more vital than the establishment of harmonious understanding regarding color differences between preachers of the same Church engaged alike in bringing the gospel to all people. He [Holsey] has ever felt that the right-thinking white man is the Negro's best friend and that the poorly trained ministers of his Church needed the help they could give."[31]

Holsey served as a bishop of the CME Church for forty-seven years, twenty of which he spent as the secretary responsible for keeping the minutes of meetings and conducting all official correspondence. Holsey's long and productive career reflected an effort to court white citizens seen as helpful to "their brothers in black." Holsey waged a struggle for equality for African Americans until he could no longer realistically believe in the "plantation mission ideology of paternalism." During the decade of the 1890s, southerners created a legal caste system that no longer recognized class differences among African Americans in the public sphere. As white Georgians adopted segregation ordinances and carried out other demeaning acts of racial discrimination, Holsey promoted a separate state for African Americans in the western territories. He wanted as citizens in his utopia only the colored elite, those with "reputable character, some degree of education, and perhaps a competency for one year's support."[32]

Ladeveze-Harper Families

The Ladevezes and Harpers, members of an extended family with kinship ties among the white elite, employed another strategy for survival in Jim Crow Augusta. They had long been recognized for their talents as artistic cabinetmakers and piano tuners. The patriarch of the family was a white man of Scottish and Irish descent, Robert Augustus Harper Sr., who worked as a musician and book dealer in Augusta. He married Elizabeth "Betsey" Keating, a woman of color and a native of Santo Domingo, who was listed as free in 1830. She held property in her own name before her marriage. In 1823 or 1824 they had a son, Robert Augustus Harper Jr. The 1850 Register of Free Persons of Color in Augusta listed him as a twenty-seven-year-old mulatto piano tuner who owned one thousand dollars' worth of real estate. The 1860 Register of Free Persons of Color listed him as a thirty-six-year-old mulatto piano tuner who was worth two thousand dollars in real estate and also owned his own home. After receiving a musical education in Boston and New York, Robert Harper Jr. returned to Augusta and married Laura Ladeveze, the mulatto sister of Charles A. Ladeveze and daughter of the white Haitian refugee Raymond Ladeveze. Laura attended the white Saint John Methodist Church until its black members, including her husband, Robert, and her brother Charles, formed Trinity as a mission church. Augusta's prominent white citizens held Robert Harper Jr. in high regard, as illustrated by an incident that occurred just before the Civil War. Extremists in the Georgia legislature passed a bill authorizing city recorders to sell free persons of color into slavery on suspicion of misconduct. When the Augusta City Council discussed the matter, Councilman Henry H. Cumming asked a rhetorical question: Should a man like Robert Augustus Harper Jr. be sold into slavery? Councilman William Gibson replied, "Let him go. There are plenty of white piano tuners to take his place."[33]

In the aftermath of Civil War, Robert A. Harper Jr. recognized an opportunity to gain public services for African Americans. The Augusta historian Ed Cashin describes Harper as one of the African Americans who addressed the issue of public education for black children. The question centered on whether white Augustans would allow their tax dollars to be spent in support of public schools for black Augustans. Harper believed that the "whites could be trusted to do what was right." In the interim Harper promoted private education in the black community by placing a boxcar in his backyard for use as a schoolroom. It served as the chrysalis for the Augusta Baptist Institute, which, after it moved to Atlanta, became Morehouse College. In 1869 Republicans appointed him the register for municipal elections. In the private sphere, he played the organ for the Springfield community and organized the Oglethorpe Band, a group of upper-class white musicians who played in the homes of upper-class African Americans.[34]

When Robert Augustus Harper Jr. died in March 1876, he left his son, James S. Harper, to continue the family tradition of public advocacy for African Americans. By 1897 James had served as a trustee for Atlanta University, treasurer of Trinity Church, and the president of the first black bank in Georgia, the Workingman's Loan and Building Association. Like his father before him, James advocated black education in Augusta. In 1879 he joined William Jefferson White, Lucius Henry Holsey, Alonzo McClennan, and Elbert Rogers in petitioning the Richmond County Board of Education to "respectfully and earnestly" comply with the 1872 law authorizing a public black high school in Augusta. The board voted unanimously to approve the request and build the school. Classes began at Springfield Baptist Church. The black leaders named the facility Ware High School after the white president of Atlanta University, Edmund Asa Ware, a former official of the Freedman's Bureau. They hired as the first principal Richard R. Wright, the valedictorian of the first graduating class from Atlanta University and Lucy Laney's close friend.[35]

Yet in 1897 the Richmond County Board of Education voted by a margin of twenty-three to three to close Ware High School and to use the money to expand elementary education in Augusta by hiring four instructors to teach two hundred new black students. Immediately Augusta's colored elite filed a suit, *Joseph W. Cumming, James S. Harper, and John C. Ladeveze v. School Board of Richmond County*, in an effort to stop the action. Harper joined the case as a plaintiff requesting an injunction against the closing of the high school that had successfully educated sixty African Americans. The black elite hired the white elite as lawyers; on their behalf prominent attorneys Salem Dutcher Jr., Hamilton Phinizy, and Joseph S. Reynolds filed a companion case, *Albert S. Blodgett and Jerry M. Griffin v. School Board*, which asked the court to reopen Ware High School. On December 22, 1897, the Richmond County Superior Court ruled in favor of the plaintiffs, but the board of education appealed to the Georgia Supreme Court, which reversed the ruling by "granting the Board entirely unlimited discretion over high school." Augusta's com-

munity of color hired United States Senator George F. Edmunds to appeal
the *Cumming* case to the United States Supreme Court. Yet here too the court
ruled in favor of the Richmond County Board of Education. Justice John
Marshall Harlan wrote the opinion, which argued that, in order to sustain an
equal protection claim under the Fourteenth Amendment, the plaintiffs would
have to demonstrate that the board had proceeded in bad faith and was motivated by "hostility toward the colored population because of their race." The
historian Morgan J. Kousser asserts that the ruling established the premise
that "states could blatantly deny blacks equal protection as long as there was
no direct evidence that they did so because of racism." James S. Harper and
John C. Ladeveze shouldered a major portion of the financial burden of insti-
gating and appealing the case, and their defeat marked a terrible blow to race
relations in Augusta.[36]

The colored elite responded to the outcome of the *Cumming* case in different ways. James S. Harper stayed in Augusta, but one of his sons migrated to
the North and became a "militant" editor of the *Chicago Defender*. John
Ladeveze moved to Los Angeles in 1900 and passed as a white American. It is
said he "made a fortune" in California. Joseph Cumming moved to Philadelphia and also passed for white. Thus these two men chose the extreme survival strategy available to the colored elite in Augusta: they escaped the public
struggle over race by passing into the white world.[37]

Lucy Craft Laney

In contrast to her contemporaries in the colored elite who ultimately denied
their racial heritage, the African American educator Lucy Craft Laney emphasized racial pride. She opened a private school for black children in the
basement of the white Presbyterian church in 1883. She served the school as
its principal for fifty years, until her death on October 23, 1933. Unlike Amanda
America Dickson, Laney made no pretense to ladyhood in the ornamental
sense. Unlike the Ladeveze and Harper families, Laney had no elite white
kinsmen to appeal to for support. Unlike Bishop Holsey, who favored the
colored elite, Laney was "blacker than black" and never wavered in her role as
the educator of the black masses and the "mother of the children of her
people."[38]

Lucy Craft Laney was born in Macon, Georgia, on April 13, 1854, the sev-
enth of ten children of David Laney and his wife, Louisa. A skilled carpenter
during slavery, David Laney was a deeply religious man. After the Civil War

Left: Lucy Craft Laney (1854–1933) founded Augusta's Haines Institute. The nurses' training department at Haines later became the school of nursing at Augusta's University Hospital. (Courtesy Reese Library, Augusta State University)

Below: Lucy Laney's Haines Institute offered a classical education to several generations of Augustans. The Lucy Laney High School (1952) occupies the same location. (Courtesy Augusta Museum of History)

he became one of three African American preachers ordained by the northern Presbyterian Church, which founded the all-black John Knox Presbytery. The Campbells, a wealthy white family from Macon, had purchased Lucy Laney's mother from a wandering band of Native Americans. The mother knew nothing of her parents or how she came to live with the Indians, but she was about the same age as one of the Campbell daughters, and the two children established a lifelong relationship.[39]

Lucy Laney described her childhood to her good friend Helen Jackson McCrorey as being filled with sly pranks, generosity to those in need, and devotion to the Christian faith. "We always had enough to eat, we were always comfortable, had books to read and such fun we children had. Pa always said that there was enough to share with one more." By age four Laney had learned to read. She accompanied her mother to the Campbell house, and, while her mother worked, she would sit in the library reading. When her siblings complained to their father, Lucy would reply, "Pa, I just must finish reading this book." Laney inevitably responded, "Let her alone, I want her to finish the book."[40]

As a young woman Lucy Laney attended the Lewis School in Macon, which later became the Ballard Normal School, and she was selected as one of the first eighty-nine students to attend the newly organized Atlanta University. Since only men could matriculate in the classical program, she graduated from the Normal Training Department in 1873. Milledgeville offered Laney her first teaching post, but she left there for Macon, then Augusta, and finally Savannah. In 1883 she returned to Augusta at the invitation of black parents and the Board of Missions for Freedmen of the Presbyterian church. That year Laney opened her private school with five students. Enrollment rapidly grew, for she directed the education of seventy-five students by the end of the first year. In 1886 the state of Georgia accredited the institution, which she named Haines Normal and Industrial School after Mrs. T. E. H. Haines, a white friend, benefactor, and the president of the Women's Department of the northern Presbyterian Church U.S.A. Focusing on both elementary and secondary education, Laney took in young children, who saw her as "the only mother they ever knew." By 1913 Laney directed nine hundred students and a staff of thirty-four teachers.[41]

Laney opened Haines because she believed that through the private sector she could provide black students with an education broader than that offered to them in the public schools. She used tuition payments and funds from the northern Presbyterian church to educate the "heads, hands, and hearts" of her students. Laney refused to allow what she saw as a false dichotomy between classical and industrial pedagogy to limit her school. Rather, Haines evolved into a five-year high school program offering a classical New England education that included limited industrial training. Students at the school chose from Latin (often taught by Laney herself), Greek, and German courses. Eventually Negro Studies became a requirement for graduation. Laney maintained strict discipline and required daily devotional chapels. She administered corporal punishment, and her former students described her as capable of taking large teenage boys to the basement for a thrashing. Nevertheless, they also remembered Laney as balancing love with discipline. She lived in her school or on the grounds until her death. She sent graduates from Haines to Atlanta, Brown, Lincoln, and Yale Universities.[42]

Laney's interest in the welfare of Augusta's black community extended beyond Haines Normal and Industrial School. When the local black hospital, called the Pest House, burned, Laney made the school available for patients until the community built a new facility. In 1890 Laney organized Augusta's first kindergarten and persuaded Irene Smallwood Bowen, a trained white teacher from the North, to become its first instructor. In 1892 Laney organized the Lamar School of Nursing and persuaded a trained white teacher, Virginia Borden, to come from Canada to direct the effort. Laney selected ten of her female students to begin the program at Lamar. By 1927 African Americans directed the nursing school, which contained two hundred beds. Laney promoted biracial communication in Augusta. She served on the Augusta Interracial Committee, helped organize the local Urban League chapter, and joined the National Association for the Advancement of Colored People. The black Georgia Federation of Women's Clubs elected Laney its fifth statewide president. She epitomized the slogan "Lifting as We Climb," for she worked to improve municipal sanitation in "the Territories" and campaigned for temperance, social purity, and suffrage.[43]

After the closing of Ware High School, Haines Normal and Industrial School became the center of cultural life for the black community in Augusta. Laney organized a chorus and orchestra and persuaded an elderly German national to lead the two groups in public performances at the school and in the city. African Americans with national reputations, including Francis Grimke in 1904 and W. E. B. Du Bois in 1904 and 1917, spoke at Haines. The stage actor Richard Harrison taught drama classes part time at Haines from 1914 to 1922. On January 19, 1909, President-elect William Howard Taft visited Haines Normal and Industrial School after ignoring Atlanta University.

Taft later remarked in Carnegie Hall that he had "seen nothing in the way of efficiency and self sacrificing that could compare with the work of Lucy Laney."[44]

Some white males described Laney as unladylike in her fierce protection of her black students. When a white doctor arrived at Haines Normal and Industrial School to vaccinate schoolchildren for smallpox, he crowded all of the students into one room. The children became frightened and Laney demanded that the doctor vaccinate them in small groups or leave. Angered by her intervention, the physician sued Laney and won a ten-dollar judgment against her. During the trial the judge reprimanded Laney's white attorney for referring to her as "Miss Laney."[45]

Laney lived on the edge of poverty, spending little on clothes or other comforts. She considered no work beneath her dignity, from cooking for summer boarders to nursing an old furnace through cold winters. "She went hungry and she slept cold," Mary White Ovington recalled, describing Laney as a woman of "masterful ability and temper." Ovington, the wealthy white cofounder of the NAACP noted that "Lucy Laney never toadies. She may hold her tongue, but she does not pretend an acquiescence in what she believes to be wrong. During the war when the exodus from the South was under way, and Southern employees urged the Negro to stay home, she would not acquiesce in this doctrine."[46]

Some African American males criticized Laney as unqualified to head such a large educational institution because of her gender and nonelite background. As enrollments at Haines grew, these men questioned her right to be the principal, to stand on the platform in the morning, or to admonish students. They claimed that she had an "undignified way of sweeping up leaves in the yard or making biscuits in the kitchen, when she should have been sitting at her desk receiving visitors in her office."[47]

In 1897 Professor W. E. B. Du Bois of Atlanta University invited Laney to convene the second conference of the Women's Department. In her address Laney exhorted the audience: "To woman has been committed the responsibility of making the laws of society, [by] making environments for children. She has the privilege and authority, God-given, to help develop into a noble man or woman the young life committed to her care. There is no nobler work entrusted to the hands of mortals." Getting straight to the heart of the matter, Laney remarked, "Will not the intelligent mother gather to her heart her sons and daughters and teach them to be pure in life and chaste in conversation, and to see to it that there be no double standard set up in her home, and none in her community, if she is able to tear it down. . . . Women of today, awake to your responsibilities and privileges."[48]

At the third Hampton Negro Conference held in July 1899, Laney presented a paper entitled "The Burden of the Educated Colored Woman." She called on colored women to lift from the shoulders of the black masses "ignorance—with its inseparable companions, shame and crime and prejudice." Laney placed the blame for these troubles squarely on the institution of slavery, for there "true home life had been utterly disregarded." She argued that the "untidy and filthy" housing conditions of slavery, with no attention to the "gentle woman's molding" or a "father's responsibility" had resulted in intellectual and moral death. She believed that a lack of respect for marriage had resulted in a "shameful race inheritance." Laney lamented, "What other result could come from such training or want of training than a conditioned race such as we now have?" But she offered hope. "The crushing burden of immorality which has its roots in the disregard of the marriage vow, can be lightened. It must be, and the educated colored women can and will do their part in lifting this burden. . . . The burden of giving knowledge and bringing about the practice of the laws of hygiene among a people ignorant of the laws of nature and common decency, is not a light one. But this, too, the intelligent woman can help to carry." Finally, Laney turned to the burden of prejudice, "heavier in that it is imposed by the strong, those from whom help, not hindrance should come."[49]

To lift these burdens Laney recommended "homes—better homes, clean homes, pure homes; schools—better schools; more culture; more thrift; and work in large doses. . . . Can woman do this work? She can; and she must do her part, and her part is by no means small." For "nothing in the present century is more noticeable than the tendency of women to enter every hopeful field of wage-earning and philanthropy, and attempt to reach a place in every intellectual arena." Women must care for the young, teach, and become public lecturers who "will change a whole community and start its people on the upward way." Laney believed that "[t]he less fortunate women, already assembled in the churches, are ready for work. Work they do and work they will; that it may be effective work, they need the help and leadership of their more favored sisters," the educated colored women.[50]

Laney concluded her presentation by describing a telegram "elite white southern women of culture" had sent to Governor William J. Northen asking him about the early moral training of the Negro race. Reporting on the telegram, the southern press asked, "Who will teach the black babies?" When interviewed, several "elite white southern women of culture" responded that "Negro women fitted for the work could not be found, and no self-respecting white woman would teach a colored kindergarten." Laney retorted, "There is plenty of work for all who have the proper conception of a teacher's office, who know that all men are brothers, God being their common father. But the educated Negro woman *must* teach the 'Black Babies;' she must come forward and inspire our men and boys to make a successful onslaught upon sin, shame, and crime."[51]

By promoting separatism and working within the Jim Crow system, Lucy Laney and Haines Normal and Industrial School thrived. The school received financial assistance from the northern Presbyterian church, donations collected during lecture tours, gifts from alumni, and tuition payments. Laney joined in the effort to support the Allies during World War I. As a black suffragette, she celebrated when women won the franchise in 1920 and worked to register black women voters in Augusta.

By the early 1930s Laney showed the wear of a lifetime of service. She died on October 23, 1933. Dressmakers who had learned to sew at Haines made her burial clothes, and former students who now worked as undertakers offered the "best caskets that they could find as a final gift to their teacher." Haines students buried Lucy Laney on the grounds of her school.[52]

Whites too recognized Laney's dedication to the black community. The *Augusta Chronicle* ran her obituary on its editorial page. "By a life of sacrifice and devotion and the toil of half a century, by her work of faith and labor of love, Lucy Craft Laney has built a great school which is her monument, an institution which has sent out into the world a multitude of young men and women inspired by her example and equipped by the advantages this school has offered to serve their generation, their race and their nation." The editor recognized her contribution to social order. "Thoughtful men and women all over the country are beginning to realize that the stability of our institutions is dependent upon the kind of education which Lucy C. Laney endeavored to impart to the youth of the land and because of her influence, better homes have grown up in the community."[53] According to an article in the "Colored Section" of the same paper, thousands of people attended her funeral.

Thus through racial pride and self determination, Lucy Craft Laney responded to segregation. Unlike Amanda America Dickson Toomer, Laney did not attempt to define herself as a southern lady. Unlike Bishop Lucius Henry Holsey, Laney never relied on the aid and friendship of southern white men. Unlike the Harper-Ladeveze family, Laney never emphasized class dif-

ferences within the public sphere. Rather, Lucy Craft Laney appealed to a
higher authority for her values, relying on a deep Christian faith. "I am as
good as anybody else. God had no different dirt to make me out of than used
in making the first lady of the land."[54]

As the nineteenth century drew to a close, Augusta instituted an all-white
primary that disenfranchised most black men. New city ordinances segregated
streetcars, though a boycott by black patrons reversed the prohibition for a
short time. The segregation of other public accommodations followed suit.
In accepting de jure segregation, Augusta's white population no longer made
exceptions for the colored elite on the basis of talent, wealth, education, intelligence, or family background. In response to being dumped into a mono-
lithic black mass, Amanda America Dickson retreated into a world of private
privilege. Bishop Lucius Henry Holsey advocated a separate state for the educated and propertied colored elite. Some members of the Ladeveze-Harper
family escaped into the white world. Yet Lucy Craft Laney promoted racial
pride and separation in order to fulfill the hopes and dreams of her chosen
people.

Notes

1. Cable, *The Negro Question*; Gilmore, *Gender and Jim Crow*, xxii. For an analysis
of this racial transformation and the crisis faced by the aristocracy of color, see Eskew,
"Black Elitism."

2. Duncan, *Freedom's Shore*, xii; Drago, *Black Politicians*, 47; Wingo, "Race Relations in Georgia," 2; Kousser, "Separate but *Not* Equal," 15; E. Cashin, *Old Springfield*, 68, 74.

3. German, "Queen City."

4. Whitson, *Sketches*, 8–52; German, "Queen City," 23; *Augusta City Directory*,
1886, 1890.

5. German, "Queen City," 85.

6. Ibid., 89–91.

7. *Augusta City Directory*, 1888; *Atlanta Constitution*, July 19, 1887, 6; *Cleveland
Gazette*, October 23, 1886, 1.

8. First Presbyterian Church of Augusta had twenty-five black members in 1883.

9. Georgia Women's Temperance Union Records, Box 20, 1890–93, 1891, Georgia
Department of Archives and History, Atlanta.

10. John C. Ladeveze was descended from Raymond Ladeveze, a white refugee
from the Haitian revolution; *Augusta Chronicle*, February 24, 1990, 9A, 12A. Robert
A. Harper also was descended from Raymond Ladeveze as a free person of color in
antebellum Augusta. His white father sent him to Boston for an education as a musi-

cian and composer. Harper returned to Augusta and accumulated a fortune that placed him in the top 1 percent of wealthy free people of color in the state; see Kousser, "Separate but *Not* Equal." Judson W. Lyons served as register of the United States Treasury from 1898 to 1906. *Augusta City Directory*, 1886.

11. Hornsby, "Shifts in Wealth."

12. Frazier, *Black Bourgeoisie*; Gatewood, "Aristocrats of Color"; P. Murray, *Proud Shoes*.

13. The 1890 U.S. Census listed the total black population in Georgia as 858,996, with 773,682 black individuals, 72,072 mulattos, and 8,795 quadroons. Julian and Charles Dickson would theoretically be octoroons. See 1890 Federal Census, *Population*, 470.

14. Two-thirds of the black people of Georgia were illiterate in 1900; see Hornsby, "Shifts in Wealth," 105, 118–20.

15. *Augusta City Directory*, 1886–88.

16. *Nathan Toomer v. Pullman Palace Car Company*, Court of Common Pleas, City of Baltimore, Maryland, January 10, 1894, and Deposition of John M. Crowley, January 4, 1894, both in Maryland State Archives, Annapolis; McFeely, *Frederick Douglass*.

17. *Atlanta Constitution*, June 19, 1887, 6.

18. Wingo, "Race Relations in Georgia," 9; Matthews, "Studies in Race Relations."

19. *Atlanta Constitution*, July 19, 1887, 2; Bacote, "Negro Proscriptions"; Fredrickson, *Black Image*, 273; Hall, *Revolt Against Chivalry*, 135.

20. *Houston Home Journal*, July 21, 1892, 2. Houston County Court House, Deed Book L, 124–25. The family included the mother, Kit, a mulatto; Nathan, age twenty, mulatto; Walter, eighteen, mulatto; Patsy, sixteen, mulatto; Fanny, fourteen, mulatto; Trevor, eight, mulatto; Tom, six, mulatto; and Claudette, four, mulatto. The state valued the slave family at seven thousand dollars. Houston County Courthouse, Deed Book S, 532.

21. *Toomer v. Pullman*, Deposition of L. D. Stant; Darwin T. Turner, quoting Jean Toomer, in the introduction to *Cane*, xi; Leslie and Gatewood, "This Father of Mine."

22. *Toomer v. Pullman*, Deposition of Dr. Thomas D. Coleman.

23. Death certificate, "Amanda D. Toomer: 43 years old; color—colored; nativity—Georgia; occupation—housewife; married," Richmond County Department of Public Health, Augusta, Ga.

24. Embalming cost, twenty-five dollars, evidence used in *Toomer v. Pullman*; *Milledgeville (Ga.) Union Recorder*, June 20, 1893, 1; Bill from the Haggie Brothers Funeral Home, evidence in *Toomer v. Pullman*.

25. *Atlanta Constitution*, June 12, 1893, 2. Tribute paid by "A Friend," *Augusta Chronicle*, June 13, 1893, 2. I am grateful to Gordon B. Smith for this reference. The entrance to the Cedar Grove Cemetery is located on Watkins Street in Augusta. One paper reported "Amanda Toomer (or Dickson), the wealthy colored woman who was buried in the colored cemetery of Augusta last week was buried with some valuable

jewelry on her person. A policeman is guarding the grave to prevent robbery"; *Savannah Morning News*, June 19, 1893, 6.

26. Welter, *Dimity Convictions*; Leslie, "Myth of the Southern Lady"; Scott, *Southern Lady*; Amanda America Dickson Toomer's gravestone, Cedar Grove Cemetery, Augusta.

27. Guy-Sheftall, "Daughters of Sorrow," 155–56. Elizabeth Fox-Genovese observed that in the Old South "condescension was inseparable from charity"; see Fox-Genovese, *Within the Plantation Household*, 235.

28. On Holsey see Eskew, "Black Elitism"; Coleman and Gurr, *Dictionary of Georgia Biography*, s.v. "Holsey, Lucius Henry." Quotations from Caldwell, *American Negro*, 2:435; Holsey, *Autobiography*, 1; "Amalgamation and Miscegenation," in Holsey, *Autobiography*, 233.

29. Caldwell, *American Negro*, 436; Eskew, "Black Elitism," 110; Caldwell, *American Negro*, 436.

30. Kousser, "Separate but *Not* Equal," 5.

31. Eskew, "Black Elitism," 114; Caldwell, *American Negro*, 437.

32. Caldwell, *American Negro*, 433–38; Eskew, "Black Elitism," 107, 122.

33. E. Cashin, *Old Springfield*, 36; Sweat, "Free Negro," 157, 160; E. Cashin, *Old Springfield*, 32.

34. E. Cashin, *Old Springfield*, 47, 54, 59; Kousser, "Separate but *Not* Equal," 4, 17.

35. Kousser, "Separate but *Not* Equal," 19, 6; E. Cashin, *Old Springfield*, 65.

36. Kousser, "Separate but *Not* Equal," 20, 32, 40, 41.

37. Ibid., 46.

38. Cowan, "Haines Normal School," 138; Mordecai Johnson, president of Howard University, designated Laney as the "mother of the children of the people."

39. Griggs, "Lucy Craft Laney," 97; Cowan, "Haines Normal School," 138; Overton, *Portraits in Color*, 56–57.

40. McCrorey, "Lucy Laney," 161.

41. Coleman and Gurr, *Dictionary of Georgia Biography*, s.v. "Craft, Lucy Laney"; Kendall, "Lucy Craft Laney"; Griggs, "Lucy Craft Laney," 97–102, quotation on p. 98; Overton, *Portraits in Color*, 55; B. Brawley, *Negro Builders and Heroes*, 279–282.

42. Griggs, "Lucy Craft Laney," 98; Kendall, "Lucy Craft Laney," 8; Overton, *Portraits in Color*, 54; Cowan, "Haines Normal and Industrial School," 138.

43. Griggs, "Lucy Craft Laney," 99–100; Kendall, "Lucy Craft Laney," 11; Overton, *Portraits in Color*, 58; Cottingham, "Burden," 4, 90, 93–94, 104; see also E. Cashin, *Old Springfield*, 82.

44. Ovington, *Portraits in Color*, 57; Cottingham, "Burden," 102–104; Kendall, "Lucy Craft Laney," 13.

45. Kendall, "Lucy Craft Laney," 10.

46. Ovington, *Portraits in Color*, 59; Kendall, "Lucy Craft Laney," 12; Overton, *Portraits in Color*, 56, 60.

47. Ovington, *Portraits in Color*, 59.

48. Lucy Laney, "Address Before the Women's Meeting," 56–57.

49. Laney, "Burden."

50. Ibid., 341–42.

51. Ibid., 344.

52. Kendall, "Lucy Craft Laney," 13.

53. "Lucy C. Laney," *Augusta Chronicle*, October 25, 1933, 6; Griggs, "Lucy Craft Laney," 101.

54. Cottingham, "Burden," 82.

Standing on a Volcano:
The Leadership of William Jefferson White

BOBBY J. DONALDSON

I N AUGUSTA'S OLD HARMONY BAPTIST CHURCH on Hopkins Street, a large wood-framed portrait of the church's founder hung above the senior choir stand. The figure's solemn and dignified pose dominated the sanctuary. The curious gentleman had sharp, intense eyes, which were set off by bushy brows. A well-trimmed white goatee complemented his thin lips, small nose, high forehead, and penetrating blue eyes. A silver chain dangled from the vest of his immaculate black suit. In the eyes of any uninformed stranger, he was a white man—and the founder of a black Baptist church. But the congregation took great pride in knowing that their first pastor was a proud, self-professed "race man."[1]

Throughout his long life, Harmony's founder, William Jefferson White, steadfastly identified with the African American community and chided those who questioned his racial allegiance. The minister *chose* the life of a black man and courageously confronted the inescapable indignities of being black in the American South. As a minister and newspaper editor, he dedicated himself to the uplift of African Americans in Augusta and throughout Georgia. White's pioneering contributions to journalism, black education, and race relations, however, have received slight attention compared to the achievements of many of his contemporaries. The Augusta historian J. Philip Waring once remarked that there appeared to be a "quiet conspiracy to erase the old man from the historical record." This essay, probing largely untapped sources, begins by sketching out the contours of William White's remarkable life and concludes by examining how White and his community challenged the ascent of white supremacy and Jim Crow practices in an era Rayford W. Logan described as the "nadir of the Negro's status in American Society."[2]

Jim Crow's rising tide deeply affected the mind and mood of African Americans in Augusta and sparked social and intellectual debates within the black community over the most reasonable solution to the region's perplexing racial problems. Black leaders in Augusta largely avoided overt campaigns for civil rights and instead struggled to advance the cause of their constituencies through optimistic appeals for racial conciliation and moderation. In their private conversations and writings, however, many of these same leaders expressed a profound sense of anguish and despair about the social and political conditions that circumscribed their respective communities. A careful consideration of White's career illustrates the complexities and subtleties of black leadership in Augusta while underscoring the steps African Americans took to formulate and execute an alternative vision of the New South.[3]

Early Life

What little that is known about White's early life makes his later accomplishments seem the more extraordinary. It is a tale of considerable irony that a man equipped with an eloquent voice and learned mind exercised extraordinary reticence about his own past. Indeed, an investigation of White's life before his arrival in Augusta generates far more questions than answers. Surviving records indicate that White was born on December 25, 1832, in Ruckersville, a small town in Elbert County, Georgia. His father, William, was a white planter, and his mother was a mulatto named Chaney. Caroline Bond Day, a pioneering black anthropologist, described White's mother as nominally a Native American who "probably had Negro admixture." Even White's children seemed somewhat uncertain about their father's early years. Claudia Harreld, one of his youngest daughters, assisted Day with her research and recalled that "Mama did not know Papa's mother, for he himself did not see her after he was six. She must have been mostly Indian because she was not a slave, though married to one, a man named Tate."[4]

Some years later, another daughter, Mary White Blocker, recollected that her father was born in Ohio, where Chaney had been taken by a white man who strongly objected to her marriage to Tate. According to Blocker, William's father placed the ten-year-old boy in the care of a storeowner known only as "Uncle Dennis." A clerk in the store took White to stay with a farming family residing on the outskirts of Augusta. When the family later moved to South Carolina, young William joined them. During the early 1850s White returned to Augusta—then a thriving cotton trade center—in search of work as a skilled craftsman. In short order, he distinguished himself as an expert carpenter and cabinetmaker at both the W. H. Goodrich Company on Reynolds Street and the Platt Brothers undertaking establishment on Broad Street.[5]

During his apprenticeship as a carpenter at the Goodrich company, William White was sent out to repair a set of stairs at the home of an Augusta cotton merchant named Stephen Heard. The assignment was rather fortunate, for White made the acquaintance of an attractive mulatto seamstress named Josephine Elizabeth Thomas. Josephine, already wooed by White's friend George Dwelle (later pastor of Springfield Baptist Church), eventually agreed to a courtship with the talented carpenter. Claudia Harreld recalled that the relationship immediately posed a thorny problem for her parents. Up to that point young William "really was identified as white." If there remained any doubt about White's racial allegiance, Harreld remarked, "the question of his identity was solved then and there." Entranced by the young woman, White decided to attend her church, Springfield Baptist, where he was later baptized by the venerable pastor, Kelly Lowe, on October 7, 1855. Less than a year later, William, a free man, and Josephine, an enslaved seamstress, married and resided as husband and wife in what one daughter called the mistress's "big house." By the time their daughter Mary was born in 1875, White had "moved out to a two-story house, which he had built on the corner of Campbell and Gwinnett Streets."[6]

White devoted considerable time to perfecting his trade and raising a large family, yet he grew increasingly concerned about the paucity of educational opportunities for his children and other school-aged students in Augusta. Throughout the 1850s White, in defiance of state laws restricting the education of slaves and free people of color, organized clandestine schools in the homes of Augusta families. He conducted his first underground school "at night seven years before the civil war" in the home of Mr. and Mrs. Samuel Ketch on lower Greene Street. A minister, writing of White's accomplishment, discovered that "some of the best men and women of Augusta obtained their education in the secret schools of Mr. White during the days of slavery."[7] Four years after his baptism at Springfield, White secured Lowe's permission to establish a Sunday school in the church. The school, the first of its kind in Augusta, began on January 8, 1859, and quickly mushroomed to over 250 pupils.

White's tireless work on behalf of Springfield's Sunday school fortified his missionary zeal and piqued his interest in the ministry. Buoyed by his success before the war, White continued to assist African Americans as they adjusted to the anxiety and confusion that marked the sudden arrival of freedom. Alert to the growing need for churches in the outlying areas of Augusta, White worked with other members of Springfield to establish a church near South Boundary at Campbell Street on property donated by Mary Bouyer McKinley. On May 10, 1868, with the permission of Springfield leaders, White led a small band of parishioners and established a little church, which they eventually named Harmony Baptist. Harmony and other black congregations founded in the postwar period established schools, financed political campaigns, mobilized voters, promoted cultural activities, and trained and nurtured a generation of African American leaders. With his polished speech, congenial disposition, and courtly manner, White earned a reputation as an able and respected master of the pulpit, who deeply valued the marriage of religion, education, and political activity.[8]

An infectious excitement surrounded the gathering of the first meeting of the Georgia Equal Rights and Education Association at Springfield Baptist Church on January 10, 1866. Among the forty delegates in attendance, White emerged as an active and vocal member. The association, composed largely of black ministers and white Republicans, worked to educate freedmen and "to secure for every citizen, without regard to race or color, equal rights." White's ardent participation in the Georgia Equal Rights Association and the Republican Party came to the attention of General Oliver O. Howard, head of the newly established Freedmen's Bureau. In the spring of 1867, Howard, impressed by White's passion for education and his adept organizing ability, persuaded the minister to leave his profitable position at Platt Brothers and to travel around the state aiding Georgia's freed people in the building of schools.[9]

Father of Negro Education

William White's work with clandestine antebellum schools and his later involvement in public education after the Civil War earned him the honored title "Father of Negro Education" in Augusta.[10] Throughout the latter half of the nineteenth century, White's imprint and influence extended to nearly every development concerning the education of Augusta's African American community. His close friend Bishop Lucius H. Holsey, founder of Paine College, recalled:

> Perhaps no man in the state has done more to advance the educational interests of the people of color than he. For years, he traveled, lectured, planned, and labored for the establishment of a generous system of education for the state of Georgia, not for the people of color only, but for all

the people, and the Negro race today owes him a debt of gratitude and respect that duly belongs to him. All along, from pulpit and platform, with tongue and pen, he has battled for the rights of men, the freedom of the people and the redemption of the race from ignorance, from wrong, and from those oppressive and repressive measures that have been against their advancement in Christian civilization.[11]

By the fall of 1866, Augusta's growing black community increased the need for a trained cadre of ministers and teachers. Consequently, when Richard C. Coulter, an Augusta native, returned from Washington, D.C., to establish a branch of the National Theological Institute, he sought out William Jefferson White. Hoping to impose upon White's remarkable talents, Coulter visited the "coffin room" of Platt Brothers on Broad Street and presented the minister with a letter of introduction from the institute's head, Edward Turney. Coulter informed White of the proposed institute's mission and remarked, "You are the only man I know that can do anything with it, and so I have come to turn it over to you; if anybody can do anything with it, you can." White accepted the challenge and introduced the idea of the school to Springfield's pastor, Henry Watts, and the board of deacons. They enthusiastically accepted the proposal, and in February 1867 Augusta Baptist Institute began with a small enrollment of "deacons, preachers, and young men aspiring to the ministry."[12]

Despite the excitement surrounding Augusta Baptist's founding, the school's expressed commitment to black education placed its survival in jeopardy. Many of the white instructors who arrived in Augusta to work at the institute under the auspices of the American Baptist Home Mission Society were met with hostility and contempt. Augusta's white community, like that of most postwar southern towns, felt apprehensive about the relationships formed between northern white missionaries and black students. "Times were critical," remembered White, "and in some respects, dangerous, for whites engaged in teaching colored people." Charles H. Corey, who took over the leadership of the Institute in November 1867, grew increasingly frustrated by Augusta's tense racial climate and remained only nine months. "Times politically were unsettled," Corey recalled; "prejudices were strong, and with but few facilities, not very much was accomplished. I had some warnings from the Ku-Klux-Klan, and on a few occasions the city authorities, unsolicited by me, sent some policemen to protect our evening school." Faced with violence and strapped financially, Augusta Baptist lingered on the verge of collapse.[13]

Strapped financially, the institute encountered more problems in 1869, when the American Missionary Association announced the discontinuance of its educational programs in the Augusta area. White appealed to the association to reconsider and proposed a plan to acquire additional funding from the city. In a letter to Edward P. Smith, the AMA field agent, White, then serving as the assistant assessor of the Internal Revenue, wrote: "I am inaugurating a movement to secure if possible a portion of the State or county funds for the benefit of colored schools and desire to know if we should succeed in so doing if you will supply a number of teachers. . . . We are preparing to make a big fight with the County school board." Increased racial tensions surrounding Augusta Baptist, however, persuaded White to postpone his "big fight." In the fall of 1869, the institute, under the leadership of W. D. Siegfried, moved from Harmony Baptist Church to a larger space on Telfair Street. But the school's close alliance with northern missionary groups continued to spark community dissension. When Siegfried penned a letter to a northern journal describing the "maltreatment of colored people in [the] city," white Augustans grew indignant about the apparent blemish on their public reputation. Concerned about his own safety and the security of his family, Siegfried abandoned his duties at Augusta Baptist and hastily left the city.[14] Indeed, the treatment accorded Siegfried foreshadowed the aggressive efforts white Augustans would later undertake to defend the character and good name of their city.

By 1871 Augusta Baptist struggled desperately to remain afloat. William White worked to assuage community animosity by cultivating close associations with leading white citizens. One of his major benefactors was James Dixon, the influential pastor of Augusta's First Baptist Church. Dixon joined White in persuading Joseph T. Robert to assume leadership of the fledgling school. The talented and resourceful Robert worked to win community support and to secure financial help from local congregations and northern missionary societies. Harmony Baptist and the Shiloh Missionary Association, both led by White, actively contributed money. Robert described William White as his "constant friend and counselor," and together they increased Augusta Baptist's reputation throughout the state, expanded its curriculum, and attracted a talented core of students, including, William E. Holmes, Emmanuel K. Love, and Charles T. Walker. But by 1879 the school's location and meager endowment, as well as the lingering bad blood with white community members, persuaded Baptist leaders to support the relocation of Augusta Baptist Institute to Atlanta.[15]

Long before the institute closed, White acknowledged the limitations of Augusta Baptist's small budget and enrollment, and he began trying to procure public funding for staff and facilities for African American students throughout the city. In January 1873 White arranged for the newly established

Richmond County school board to take over schools once operated by the Freedmen's Bureau and the American Missionary Association. The following July he skillfully executed a campaign to convince the board that the city's growing population of black students merited expanded facilities and financial support. In a congenial letter to the board, White described the dearth of resources among black schools and concluded that conditions would only worsen without better buildings and additional teachers. White's appeal won the important backing of the editor of the *Augusta Chronicle*. "Colored children, under the law," the paper concluded, "are entitled to just the same privileges and the same advantages as the white children." In an endorsement that would ring with stinging irony twenty-five years later, the *Chronicle* argued that "if the whites have high schools, grammar, intermediate and primary schools, let the colored children have them also. Give both races exactly the same opportunities and equal advantages." A year later at the annual Emancipation Day celebration in Augusta, White, preaching before a crowd of two thousand, emphasized the inseparable link between public education and black progress and encouraged the audience to "educate themselves as rapidly as possible, and to conduct themselves with propriety."[16]

In October 1878, after successfully leading a campaign to increase the primary and grammar schools for Augusta's black children, White directed his attention toward advanced educational opportunities for the community. Along with twenty-four other citizens, the minister petitioned the board for an African American high school. Referring to an 1872 state law stipulating equal educational facilities for black and white citizens, the delegation requested that "as a matter of right under the law, that you provide a school commencing with the next school term to which these children of ours and others of like advancement may be sent." With determined resolve, White and other delegates, including Lucius Henry Holsey, James S. Harper, Alonzo McClennan, and Elbert Rogers, again went before the board in July 1880 bearing a list of potential students and a pledge from parents "to pay ten dollars for the scholastic year" for each pupil. Much to the chagrin of one school board member, Major Joseph Ganahl, who had argued in July 1879 that a black high school was impractical, departing superintendent William Henry Fleming supported the claims of the black leaders and contended that "to grant today the petition of the colored people would be only an act of tardy justice."[17]

The board voted in favor of the petitioners, and White, in hurried desperation, went in search of a talented person to head Georgia's first publicly funded black high school. As a member of the board of trustees of Atlanta University, White was well acquainted with the college's first valedictorian, Richard R.

Wright, who served as principal of Howard Academy in Cuthbert. White traveled to southwest Georgia and persuaded the dynamic young teacher to lead the Augusta high school. In October 1880 an enthusiastic Richard Wright and thirty-six students marched into a small building at 1109 Reynolds Street, marking the opening of "The Colored High School," later named in honor of Atlanta University's president, Edmund Asa Ware. The school faced many adversities, but Wright, a rising star in the Republican Party and an accomplished journalist, elicited strong praise from white leaders in Augusta.[18]

With Augusta Baptist off to a fresh start in Atlanta and Ware High School securely established, White could have easily retired to the comforts of his pastorate at Harmony, but he wisely gauged the political forecast for black southerners and realized that more ominous challenges lay on the horizon. As Reconstruction's fruitful promises withered away and the federal government grew increasingly indifferent to racial matters in the South, White remained a staunch supporter of the Republican Party. The establishment of Georgia's interracial Republican Party after the Civil War signaled an experimental turn in race relations in the South, and William White actively participated in nearly every significant development in the party. At the October 1875 Colored Convention, White, Henry McNeal Turner of the African Methodist Episcopal Church, and other black Republicans assembled in Augusta to deplore racial violence and to appeal for improved educational resources and land reform. The leaders, representing diverse ideological backgrounds, established the Georgia Agricultural, Educational, Emigration and Statistical Society.[19]

The Georgia Baptist

By the close of Reconstruction, William White wore many professional hats. He continued as pastor of Harmony Baptist Church; worked as a leading figure in the Georgia Missionary Baptist Convention; maintained positions on the boards of trustees of Atlanta Baptist Institute, Spelman Seminary, and Atlanta University; and traveled across the state championing black education and Republican Party causes. Though drained of time and energy, White seemed nearly indefatigable as he launched yet another project—the publication of a weekly newspaper. On October 28, 1880, White began publishing the *Georgia Baptist* in a small office on Ellis Street in downtown Augusta. As the primary organ of the Missionary Baptist Convention, White's newspaper included sermons of noted Baptist clergy and the minutes of church conferences, all of which illuminate the internal developments of black community life during the Jim Crow era. White's many travels, encounters, and contacts throughout the South informed much of the paper's commentary. As the paper's circulation grew, White's opinions carried significant weight in both political and religious circles. Throughout the state people hailed him as—what he called himself—the "Georgia Baptist man."

Disturbed by the treatment and depictions of African Americans in southern newspapers, White viewed the *Georgia Baptist* as a voice of social change. Early issues of the newspaper carried a masthead that read, "Great Elevator, Educator, and Defender of the People." W. E. B. Du Bois, a professor at Atlanta University from 1897 through 1910 and an avid reader of the paper, described it as "probably the most universally read Negro paper in the South." Although the *Georgia Baptist* filled an important need among black Augustans, the newspaper saddled White with enormous financial responsibilities and placed unlimited demands on his time. "My father's thoughts were absorbed by the Georgia Baptist," remembered Claudia Harreld. "Everywhere he went he carried it with him, literally, as well as figuratively. . . . No matter what the lack at home, the paper came out."[20]

Indeed, African Americans throughout the state viewed the *Georgia Baptist* as a proud symbol of black ingenuity and enterprise. John Hope, the first black president of Atlanta Baptist (later Morehouse) College, watched the *Georgia Baptist* unfold during his youth in Augusta. "How thrilling it all was to me as a boy," Hope recalled, "to look for the first time into that printing office of the *Georgia Baptist* in the little brick building on Ellis Street. William J. White showed me for the first time that Negroes could operate and own a newspaper; that amid fire and flood and earthquake a Negro newspaper could send itself forth every week for years and years."[21]

The Age of Redemption

When the Sumner Literary and Historical Society, a black lyceum and lending library in Augusta, invited White to deliver a paper at one of its meetings in 1885, he read an essay entitled "The Negro Problem, as Agitated in This Country," in which he drew attention to the failed promises of Reconstruction and the disturbing consequences of the South's recent turn toward racial demagoguery. White began by contending that a persistent and bitter memory of slavery constrained race relations and hampered the South's progress. African Americans, he reminded his audience, occupied a precarious position in the body politic of the nation. "Of all who came to this new found World," he intoned, "none but the black man came by compulsion.... As the country expanded territorially," he continued, "labor became more valuable, the accumulations of wealth were greater, the ruling class became less humane, and the cords of slavery were tightened.... The war is not, however, yet ended," White thundered. "The stronghold of caste and prejudice now confront us. This fortress is to be stormed and her walls leveled to the earth. I do not know that I can give any better name to this fortress than NEGRO PREJUDICE. . . . Negro prejudice lifts its head in every nook and corner of our land."[22]

White argued that "manhood recognition" between black and white southerners constituted the first step toward improved race relations. That mutual understanding, he insisted, "destroys forever the power of negro prejudice to injure him. This will solve the problem, and relegate the negro question from our civilization." White's appeal for a color-blind society seemed quite extraordinary during an era one historian described as "the vale of tears" for African Americans and when advocates of social Darwinism concurrently predicted the impending demise of black people.[23] At heart an optimist, White believed that solutions to the nation's race problem required innovative thinking and an unfailing faith in the working of Providence. Yet when the benevolent promises of white paternalists proved hollow and when laws failed to protect blacks against terror and humiliation, White suspended his customary protocol of deference and moral suasion.

Only three years after sharing his confident analysis of the race problem, White sensed the shortsightedness of his approach. The protracted subjugation and circumscription of black Americans incensed White and moved him to call upon other black leaders to meet and devise a concerted agenda to advance African American social and political causes. Therefore White invited "ministers of the gospel, school teachers, professional men, the farmer, the merchant, the mechanic, the artisan, and the wage worker" to Macon for a meeting of what he called the Georgia Consultation Convention. Three hundred delegates accepted White's invitation, and in the course of their deliberations, they agreed that there was "a predominating sentiment among their white fellow-citizens" designed "to keep them in a condition largely assimilating to their condition when held in bondage." The withdrawal of state money from the operating budget of Atlanta University, the "barbarous" chain gang and penitentiary system, and the "unlawful and inhuman practice" of lynching were only a few examples that confirmed their suspicions. Underscoring the value of self-determination, White encouraged his brethren to reject apathy and maintained that "a people who will not try to help themselves cannot expect others to help them."[24]

Not surprisingly, the impressions of the South depicted by William White and delegates of the Consultation Convention contrasted sharply with the images proffered by New South promoters such as the *Atlanta Constitution* editor Henry W. Grady. Although Grady trumpeted the commercial rebirth of the South, his New South philosophy carried with it a basic belief in the irrevocable inferiority of blacks. Black Augustans undoubtedly bristled as Grady traveled across the country informing audiences that African Americans were content with their subordinate social and economic positions. A. W. Wimberly, black editor of the *Augusta Methodist Union,* voiced clear disaffection for the paternalist promises of Grady and other New South spokesmen: "In the future the intelligent Negro will not accept gushing platitudes for friendship. He'll know his friends by their deeds; he has had enough of hypocritical professions, he now demands something substantial."[25] Both Wimberly and White championed racial cooperation in the South, yet they carefully insisted that congenial relations and civil discourse among citizens could be attained without passive acquiescence to white supremacy.

The Golden Blocks and the Terri

As racial divisions hardened and white supremacist campaigns reached higher decibels toward the close of the nineteenth century, Augusta's black community emphasized a message of self-help and increasingly relied on its own resources. Behind the racial veil, a generation of prosperous professionals emerged. A refined cadre of "New Negroes"—black intellectuals, preachers, attorneys, editors, educators, and artists—assumed positions of leadership and influence. Morehouse College President John Hope, a product of one of several interracial relationships in Augusta, marveled at the remarkable personalities that emerged from his hometown: "Then there was the group of people who independent of particular merit on their part, but because of circumstances, their relationships to their masters, received additional money or additional education and they were to that extent ahead of the people who had no money, no education, nothing. As a result there was at the close of the War a rather well organized Negro society, with its social metes and bounds, with its ideals and a great deal of culture."[26]

Hope's friend Channing Tobias, a graduate of Paine College and later a leading figure in the YMCA and NAACP, recalled that "there was something in that atmosphere" that enabled "a Negro in Augusta of the day of John Hope's boyhood to aspire to the heights and to receive encouragement from white people in doing so." Tobias surmised that the success of Augusta's black elite stemmed quite possibly from "the close relationship of men like W. J. White with the leading spirits of the white race [which] made it possible for men to see above the low level of things and not have it counted a crime that they should do so." The generous encouragement Hope and Tobias received from white citizens during their youth in Augusta highlight the significant contributions of "neopaternalists" like Joseph Robert and President George William Walker of Paine Institute, who displayed a consistent devotion to the moral and educational improvement of African Americans.[27]

A walk up the broad length of Campbell Street—from the Savannah River to the edge of the shanty quarters dubbed the "Territory"—revealed the impressive growth of black-owned institutions during the "nadir" period. From the doorway of William White's *Georgia Baptist* office, one had a clear view of Dugas Funeral Home and Dr. N. A. Mixson's Fountain City Drug Store. A few blocks over on Broad Street, the city's main commercial thoroughfare, James Harper, Robert Battey, and J. C. Ladeveze operated the Workingmen's Loan and Building Association. On the far end of Campbell at the intersection with Gwinnett, Dr. G. S. Burruss, a graduate of Atlanta Baptist and Meharry Medical School, operated a fully functional sanatorium, with twenty-seven rooms and twelve attendants. In 1886 the remarkable teacher Lucy Craft Laney, working in the basement of a Presbyterian church on Telfair Street, envisioned a school that would later become the highly successful Haines Institute. Nine years later, a dynamic young instructor from Mayesville, South Carolina, named Mary McLeod (later Bethune), assisted Laney and organized the Mission Sabbath School for the city's poorest children. In the Druid Park area near Paine Institute, members of the Shiloh Missionary Baptist Association financed the operation of the Gad S. Johnson Orphanage. In 1898 Thomas J. Hornsby, pastor of Antioch Baptist Church, joined his son Walter and cousin Solomon Walker to transform a small lot at 1348 Milledgeville Road into the enormously profitable Pilgrim Health and Life Insurance Company.[28]

Such astounding success stories gave black and white Augustans reason to view their city as a place of moderate race relations. As other southern urban and rural areas became hotbeds of racial violence and antagonism, Augusta, for a time, appeared little affected by growing dissension among black and white citizens. Henry L. Walker, who replaced Richard Wright as principal of Ware High School, informed delegates of the 1894 Negro State Teachers As-

Robert E. Williams, a prominent African American photographer in Augusta, portrayed informal scenes, as in this picture of two children on their way to church. (Courtesy Reese Library, Augusta State University)

sociation conference that "in Augusta you will find two races of people living together in such accord and sympathy as are nowhere else to be found in all this Southland." At the same conference, Silas X. Floyd, editor of the *Augusta Sentinel* and valedictorian of his class at Atlanta University, confidently declared that "Augusta has long been regarded as the garden spot of the country so far as the relations of the races go."[29] These accolades certainly seemed worlds apart from William White's stirring cry of "NEGRO PREJUDICE" in 1885.

Indeed, the boosterism displayed by Walker and Floyd conveyed a degree of truth. Both leaders spoke from the comfortable vantage point of successful black professionals. But beneath their expressions of civic pride, Walker and Floyd undoubtedly understood that black Augustans experienced the best of times and the worst of times. On one hand, a prosperous black professional class reflected the economic strides of a small group of African Americans. On the other hand, a languishing underclass magnified the expanding political, economic, and spatial gulfs that separated black and white Augusta. Even as Augusta entertained a vibrant black middle and professional class, working and living conditions for the vast lot of African Americans remained quite dismal.[30] That striking disparity, clear to anyone walking the city streets, troubled White. His regular interactions on Campbell Street, along with his work with the schools and the Gad Johnson Orphanage, placed him in daily contact with the city's black working poor. Moreover, his home, near the intersection of Campbell and Gwinnett, stood only a slight jaunt from the largely working class enclave known as the Terri.

Many residents of the Terri, described by John Hope as "human wrecks of swift emancipation," came to Augusta in search of the economic promises of Emancipation and Reconstruction. But like many African American migrants to southern cities, their inflated expectations differed sharply from their social realities. Even as Augusta's black leaders looked toward the new century with optimism, conditions in black working-class neighborhoods deteriorated. Wage earnings barely met basic subsistence needs; trash and debris piled up along the alleys and dirt streets of the community; stagnant water spawned mosquitoes and spread diseases; and drug use and crime became epidemic. Although conditions proved to be a "menace to the health of the whole community," city officials adopted few constructive measures of improvement. Material deprivations coupled with social and political subordination severely circumscribed black life in Augusta, and the constant attention given to successful African Americans, by both black and white citizens, only camouflaged severe inequities that haunted the community for many generations to come.[31]

With the turn of the twentieth century, Augusta's boosters grimly watched as the city's moderate reputation underwent critical challenges. Long regarded as a center of progressive politics, Augusta, once a bastion of Reconstruction Republicans, gradually dropped its paternalist mask and slowly marched in lockstep with the rest of the South. As racial divisions in Augusta and across the South hardened, black citizens watched nervously while advances in education and politics fell victim to a proliferation of racially discriminatory practices.[32] Certainly alarmed by the rising scale of segregation and racial violence, many black leaders tempered their distress with public entreaties toward moderation and the white paternalist ethos of the past. William White distinguished himself among black leaders in the South by his open and persistent critique of white supremacist ideology.

The city's failure to address eroding conditions in black neighborhoods disturbed White, and he used the pages of the *Georgia Baptist* to prod the consciousness of black leaders. White feared that the pool halls, bars, and crap houses that made up the city's red light district near his church on Hopkins Street contributed to a prevailing sense of political apathy and moral corruption. "Gambling on the streets of Augusta," he wrote, "has become disgustingly prevalent. . . . Our police force has been appealed to time and again but to no effect. . . . These gamblers are not only destroying themselves, but they are also dragging the race down to deeper and deeper degradation." White therefore appealed to leaders including Lucy Laney, Charles T. Walker, and A. R. Johnson to devise "some plan of systematic work" to repair and rehabilitate their community.[33]

The Problem of the Color Line

The intense debates within black communities over the best method to improve living conditions and race relations reflected the desperation and anxiety that attended the work of black leaders at the turn of the twentieth century. For most African Americans approaching the twentieth century, the path toward race progress seemed dimly lit. No class appeared immune to Jim Crow's indignities. In fact, the very autonomy and independence exercised by the growing black middle and professional classes posed a fundamental challenge to the color line and threatened to undermine Augusta's white paternalist tradition. W. E. B. Du Bois once observed that whites southerners feared "Negro ambition and success" more than they feared "Negro crime": "They can deal with crime by chain-gang and lynch law, but the South can conceive neither machinery nor place for the educated, self-reliant, self-assertive black man." When the prominent black barber Felix Holmes died in 1899, the *Augusta*

Chronicle offered an eloquent tribute to his service to white Augustans but used the occasion to sketch out the fine racial equations operating in the community. "Nowhere in the country," the paper claimed, "is the negro who deports himself properly so sure of kind treatment and friendly attention as right here in the south by the whites among whom he lives, who know his good traits and his foibles, his possibilities and his limitations, and are ever ready to make allowances for his shortcomings and accord praise for his commendable achievements."[34]

Events surrounding the appointment of a prominent black attorney, Judson W. Lyons, to the Augusta postmastership exposed the inherent inconsistencies of white paternalism in the city and underscored the glaring veracity of Du Bois's indictment. News of Lyons's potential appointment wrapped Augusta's attention for several months. Lyons, a member of William White's Harmony Baptist and a successful lawyer educated at Howard University, was an active figure in the national Republican Party. When newly elected President William McKinley nominated Lyons to the postmastership in 1897, white Augustans ignored his training and accomplishments and argued that the selection of a black man to such an important position was nothing less than an appalling affront to southern propriety. The *Augusta Chronicle*, which came out strongly against Lyons's appointment, cloaked its criticisms in paternalist gauze. "There is no community in this country," the paper reported, "where the negro is given fairer treatment than in Augusta." The paper listed a few examples of interracial cooperation in the city and concluded that "the two races live in harmony and contentment. . . . Now is it not the supremest folly for the negroes of Augusta to jeopardize this peace and good will to gratify the ambition of one of their number to fill an office in which he will not be acceptable to the community?"[35]

Postmaster General James A. Gary, sensing the rank political winds emerging from the controversy over Lyons, counseled McKinley to withdraw his offer. "I believe Lyons [is] a good-negro," Gary conceded, "but I also know well enough the temper and feeling [of] the southern people not to inflict upon them unnecessarily. I will oppose his appointment with the idea of giving him something better." Likewise, the *Augusta Chronicle* argued that "negroes cannot force themselves upon white people under circumstances where they are not acceptable." In a veiled threat, the paper called upon black leaders to encourage Lyons to back down and warned that "white men would, in many ways, show their resentment. In the schools, in the trades, in every avenue of life, the race would bear the penalty of the presumption of one of their number." Later in the year, McKinley pressed on to award Lyons for his loyalty to the Republican Party and appointed him register of the United States Treasury upon the death of the former Mississippi senator Blanche K. Bruce.[36]

Not long after the Lyons controversy, William Jefferson White and black Augustans again marshaled forces to protect black mobility and progress as the Richmond County Board of Education considered closing Ware High School.[37] The opposition to Lyons's appointment prompted subdued protest from Augusta's black leaders, but African American citizens viewed the closing of the only publicly funded black high school as a collective assault on the community. Undoubtedly, William Jefferson White viewed the decision to close Ware as a rebuff to his lifelong efforts to expand educational opportunities for black Augustans, and, not surprisingly, he stepped forward to lend his weight and wisdom to an organized attack against the decision.

At the board's monthly meeting in August 1897, members finally agreed to close Ware with the intent of directing more money toward primary education. With tremendous anxiety, several black leaders formed the Educational Union of Richmond County and rallied together in defense of the high school. Fifty citizens joined White and businessman John C. Ladeveze as they highlighted Ware's contributions to the Augusta community and submitted a petition of 150 names supporting its continuation. The appeal, however, did little to dissuade members, for they voted to close the school indefinitely by a vote of twenty-three to three.[38] Like other high schools in the county, Ware suffered from underenrollment; nevertheless, the school's very success in creating a small educated professional class accounted for its eventual demise. Closing Ware, board members argued, would make more money available for primary education. But the subtext of the argument was that Ware's emphasis on liberal arts training—not trade and industry—encouraged students to pursue professional careers, which threatened the security and longevity of white supremacy.

When Lawton B. Evans became the Richmond County school superintendent, he championed Ware and stressed the need for producing "teachers and leaders of their race." During the 1890s, however, Evans drastically changed his opinion about the merits of Ware's classical curriculum. Indeed, Evans's increasing lack of interest in the school's well-being mirrored public opinions among white Augustans. White citizens who supported African American education generally endorsed the industrial training pedagogy of Booker T. Washington's Tuskegee Institute. Throughout the 1890s Washington's program achieved wider support among champions of the New South. Washington's philosophy of political and social accommodation, eloquently articulated at the Atlanta Cotton States Exposition in September 1895, served as an agreeable counterpoint to the impatient, politically inclined leadership gradually taking root in African American communities. Augusta was no exception.[39]

Two months after Washington's electrifying performance in Atlanta, Lawton B. Evans expressed his position on the liberal arts/industrial education debate. Echoing Washington's speech, Evans observed that black children were "born to work . . . to work with their hands . . . they find their best service and happiness in manual labor." Ware's curriculum, Evans told the board, provided the "wrong kind of education." It was an education, Evans insisted, that made students "anxious to pursue some profession and obtain financial, social, and political, equality with the white race." Instead of admitting that black students suffered from an overall imbalance of financial and physical resources, Evans and the board inconspicuously used the need for elementary education as a foil to cover their clear dislike of liberal arts instruction. In the end, Ware's closing demonstrated how a putative benevolent concern for black education successfully masked discriminatory intentions that invariably undermined African American educational opportunities.[40]

As the new school term approached in the summer of 1897, William White and other black leaders found themselves against the wall, for there was little sign that Superintendent Evans and members of the board might rescind their opinion. With little other recourse, prominent black businessmen—Joseph W. Cumming, James S. Harper, and John C. Ladeveze—filed a lawsuit against the Richmond County Board of Education. The plaintiffs contended that the board disregarded an 1872 state law that called for a separate high school for the colored students. When Judge Enoch Callaway ruled against the closing of the high school, black leaders certainly felt a sense of relief and pride. But the board, with financial coffers exceeding those of black leaders, vowed to appeal the decision. A troubled William White watched the lawsuit unfold from the sidelines and penned several editorials in the *Georgia Baptist* decrying the unfairness of Ware's closing. White understood that the Ware case held national implications, for it tested the "separate but equal" doctrine upheld in the *Plessy v. Ferguson* decision. Even Booker T. Washington, the artful champion of industrial education, sensed the lasting impact of Ware's closing and sent John Ladeveze a small contribution to aid with legal costs.[41]

When the Georgia Supreme Court overturned Judge Callaway's decision in 1898, White responded with the headline "The Supreme Court of Georgia Decides in Favor of Wrong and Injustice." "We put it mildly," White wrote, "when we say that our leading colored citizens regard the supreme court decision as cruelly unjust." White argued that the court's ruling "gives the Board of Education the right to do as it pleases, in the matter of furnishing schools for colored children and colored parents have no recourse but to God and the United States Courts; which may be no better than State Courts when it comes to adjudicating the colored man's rights. . . . This is a hard blow at the colored man and tax payers of the county," he concluded, "who are to be compelled to pay taxes to furnish education to white children. God is not dead though he some time seems to sleep."[42]

In December 1899, three years after the landmark *Plessy v. Ferguson* decision, the arduous fight of Joseph W. Cumming, James S. Harper, and John C. Ladeveze came to a disappointing end before the United States Supreme Court. The court, unconvinced that the board had acted in a prejudiced manner when closing Ware, ruled against the plaintiffs. In a poignant way the *Cumming* case reminded Augusta's prominent black leaders of the liberalism of Jim Crow. Editor White described the decision as a perpetuation of "wrong and injustice upon the colored citizens of Richmond county. . . . The colored citizens of Augusta have vindicated their manhood in a manly way," White boasted, and "they have made a record which they may justly feel proud."[43] The travesty of the *Cumming* decision dealt a heavy blow to community leaders who sacrificed time and money to halt Jim Crow's creeping advances. Moreover, the extraordinary measures black Augustans employed to correct an egregious wrong exposed the growing fissures within a community that carefully presented itself as a paragon of racial harmony.

While black Augusta struggled to defend Ware, greater challenges appeared on the horizon as local and state governments took measures to dilute African American voting strength. Under the guise of progressive reform, Augusta's officials proposed the adoption of an exclusive white primary to thwart political corruption in city elections. In September 1897 a petition circulated around the city stating that "a white primary will be the greatest reform that can, at this time, be accomplished. It will rid us of practices that in the past have been many times disgraceful." Reformers charged that the principal culprits of election fraud were black voters who, after being seduced by promises of money and whiskey, succumbed to the demands of party bosses. H. L. Embry, the pastor of Saint Luke's Methodist Church, took to the pages of the *Augusta Chronicle* and chastised local Christians for tolerating "a miserable gang of men with white skins hugging Africans and rushing them on" to the ballot box.[44]

Disturbed by such public outcries, political leaders in the city concluded

Mayor Joseph B. Cumming attempted to uphold the standards of the Old South in his writing and oratory. (Courtesy Reese Library, Augusta State University)

The descendants of the plaintiffs in the Ware High School case (*Cumming et al. v. County Board of Education of Richmond County*) gathered in Augusta for the unveiling of a marker on the occasion of the one hundredth anniversary of the 1899 decision. Back row, left to right: Nathaniel Ingram, Ramona Ingram Jones, Cecilia Osborne Johnson McGhee (niece of John Ladeveze), Mary Bruce Harper Ingram (niece of James Harper), Gwendolyn Marjorie Johnson Connally (niece of John Ladeveze), Edith Dean, Mildred Ingram Singleton, David Singleton (in front of his mother, Mildred), Judge Cecilia Ellen Connally (partly obscured); the other three girls are children of Ramona Ingram Jones. (Courtesy Peggy Hargis)

that the best way to achieve honest elections was to make voting a "white man's business." Although blatant ballot frauds occurred in wards throughout the city, white leaders directed their ire toward the corruption of the black vote and made African Americans the scapegoats for the larger problem of machine politics in Augusta. The white primary, the *Augusta Chronicle* pointedly confessed, "is the safeguard of our people; it not only guarantees white supremacy, but it is our greatest protection against political fraud."[45]

Fearing the loss of political influence, Augusta's black leaders opposed the introduction of a white primary and adamantly resisted the effacement of African Americans from public political life. William Jefferson White, Charles T. Walker, and other members of the Baptist Pastoral Union denounced political corruption in the city and appealed for "honest elections." White similarly criticized disfranchisement campaigns on the state level. When the Georgia legislature, led by the combative Thomas Hardwick, crafted a disfranchisement platform similar to the ingenious plan adopted by Mississippi, which crippled black suffrage through the implementation of grandfather clauses, poll taxes, and literacy tests, White turned to the *Georgia Baptist* and argued that "what is needed today in the South is real Americanism, and this Americanism to be real must be colorless. The thought of white supremacy and negro domination should be eliminated from the public mind."[46]

Representative Hardwick ignored petitions for racial reconciliation and shamelessly appealed to white Georgians' latent fears of black domination. Hardwick argued that African Americans must be removed from the voting pool "not because they are black, but because they lack virtue and intelligence." The legislator then attempted to spur racial divisions with disturbing evocations of Reconstruction and the 1898 Wilmington, North Carolina race riot: "Will you wait until your streets are filled by Negro officeholders . . . until some unprincipled minority which arise in this state will place the negroes in county and city offices . . . until the outrages of North Carolina are repeated in Georgia, and the people rise to demand the enactment of this law."[47]

William White, who labored incessantly for the education of the city's African American youth, resented aspersions on black respectability and strongly denounced public discussions about the shortcomings of blacks' intellectual abilities. "Six prosperous Negro physicians, three successful drugstores, hundreds of grocers, shoemakers, carpenters and other business establishments in a population of fifteen thousand Negroes," he insisted, "make talk about inferiority cheap."[48]

"Such Incendiary Negroes"

The precipitous rise in lynching and heightened cries of white supremacy signaled the white South's increasing intolerance of black appeals for social justice and economic mobility. Segregation and disfranchisement served their purposes, but violence betrayed the desperation of those with vested interests in maintaining and expanding racial hierarchy. Black Augustans gathering in shops and stores along Campbell Street certainly discussed the unfolding horror of violence that gripped the nation at the turn of the century. Amid sensational stories about the Spanish-American War, readers of the *Georgia Baptist* learned of the racial atrocity that visited Lake City, South Carolina, on February 22, 1898, when an enraged mob set fire to the black postmaster's house and then killed the defenseless man and his infant son. Augustans knew full well that the divisive elements that contributed to the explosion in Lake City were all too prevalent in their own city and surrounding region. Nine months later, they heard tale of the brutal deaths of seven black men shot by a raging mob of over six hundred people in the Phoenix riot in Greenwood, South Carolina. A short while later, from across the river in nearby Edgefield County, South Carolina, came word that a white mob had strung three black men to a tree and lynched them under suspicious charges.[49]

Although bewildered and grieved by these tragic turn of events, William Jefferson White boldly denounced apologists of racial violence. After the Edgefield episode White charged that "a halt in lynching in the South must come, and come it will." But violence against black people persisted and continued to receive greater social legitimacy and official sanction. Many black leaders, understandably threatened by the convulsive racial climate, carefully censored their public commentary about violence and appealed to white southern moderates. White stood out among his peers for his courageous—some said foolish—stand against racial violence and disfranchisement. Enraged by the Wilmington riot in November 1898, White avowed that many white southerners "like a nigger as a nigger in a nigger's place, with his hat in his hand calling them master and cringing as a slave. . . . When it comes to recognizing the Negro as a man and a full fledged citizen of these United States," he concluded, "the great bulk of white people in the south 'ain't in it'."[50]

A few weeks later, in the final edition of the *Georgia Baptist* for 1898, White again conveyed a level of resignation and contempt that mirrored the frightened attitudes among black Augustans:

The dark clouds of internal discord have gathered in some localities and the murderous lyncher, though walking around with the blood of his brother almost dripping from his fingers, goes unpunished. The deadly fire-arm, the deadly hemp, and well-lit torch have all been called into service by irresponsible and irrepressible mobs; many lives have paid the penalty and the appetite of blood thirsty lynchers is unsatisfied. 1898 has witnessed the most atrocious crimes of many years, but in this respect the tide turns with the closing of the year and the Tillmanish brutality has seen its best days.[51]

Five months later, however, Reverend White's prayerful words fell on deaf ears. The following April, "Tillmanish brutality" exploded in Georgia with the odious murder of Sam Hose, a black itinerant laborer, in Coweta County, south of Atlanta. Hose, accused of murdering his white employer, Alfred Cranford, and raping his wife, embodied all the worst fears that white southerners entertained about a roving band of black rapists. Myths and rumors of Hose's villainous deeds swept through newspapers, creating a heated climate of rage and anticipation. His eluding of the police only added tension to an already tragic drama. Upon Hose's capture by police, news of his impending lynching swiftly reached Atlanta. In short order, trains of onlookers came to Newnan to witness the festivities. Amid a cheering white throng, Hose's black body was hoisted, mutilated, and burned.[52]

Dismayed by the ghastly events in Newnan, black leaders in the state responded with a mix of restrained anger and conservative appeals for racial cooperation. Charles T. Walker, regarded by black and white Augustans alike as the spokesman for African Americans in the community, approached the Hose affair with a cautious tone. He warned his congregation against adopting "incendiary measures" to avenge Hose's murder. Instead, he appealed to Augusta's white paternalist tradition and reminded his church that the most important thing to do was "to make a sympathetic appeal to the ruling class; that is to the white people." Echoing the sentiments of his friend Booker T. Washington, Walker shied away from cries of outrage and exercised characteristic prudence: "There should be none of politics and a great deal more of business. Thrift and industry in the pursuits of life was sure to open the gateway to a more perfect American citizenship." William White, mindful of the recent closing of Ware High School and the adoption of a white primary, disagreed, arguing that Walker's optimistic prescription blurred the clear reality that African Americans—regardless of their accomplishments—would always be regarded as second-class citizens. William Jefferson White Jr., displaying the activist zeal of his father, scathingly denounced the Newnan lynching and charged that Hose's death "is not the vaporing of a blinded prejudice nor the hasty alusion of a novice. . . . It is anarchy pure and simple."[53]

By the spring of 1900, the rash of violence circulating through the state grew to a fever pitch in Augusta and severely tested William White's resolve. During the third week of May, the *Georgia Baptist* carried extensive coverage of the lynching of William Wilson, a black painter accused of murdering Aleck Whitney, the son of a prominent white cotton merchant, aboard a streetcar on Sunday evening, May 13. When Wilson and Whitney argued over a seat, a fight ensued and Wilson fatally shot Whitney through the eye. After police tackled Wilson and spirited him away to jail, a crowd of over seventy-five persons gathered near the murder scene and amid "yells of vengeance and cries of defiance" called for Wilson's immediate lynching. J. T. Plunket, pastor of First Presbyterian Church, arrived on the scene and attempted to quiet the clamor by reminding the crowd that their actions held profound implications for the city. "You have a reputation to sustain," he said, "the fair name of Augusta is at stake. Let's be reasonable now. The law shall be vindicated." For a few hours tensions subsided, but calls for Wilson's death increased again when protestors came across Whitney's youngest brother wailing with grief on a city street.[54]

Unable to guarantee Wilson's security and with a potential riot brewing, George Hood, the chief of police, decided to send the prisoner to Atlanta for protection. On that evening Wilson and two deputies boarded the Georgia Railroad bound for Atlanta. When they reached the county limits—near Belair, a mob ambushed the train and pulled Wilson from the locomotive. Before officials from Augusta could arrive, the crowd, numbering around thirty-five, hanged the terrified painter from a tree and riddled his body with over one hundred bullets. The *Savannah Tribune* reported that the "ears, nose, and fingers were in time hacked from the helpless victim." Satisfied that justice had been rendered, the angry mob placed in Wilson's shirt pocket a card that read, "Warning to all Georgia Negroes."[55]

The death of Aleck Whitney and the brutal lynching of William Wilson threw the city "into a wild state of excitement." Whatever distinction Augusta enjoyed as a place of tranquil race relations rapidly eroded as tensions on both sides of the color line flared. White, sensing the ominous consequences of Wilson's lynching observed in the *Georgia Baptist* that Augusta "is fearfully wrought up, and feeling everywhere is tense and bitter." Likewise, the *Savannah Tribune* reported that the murder and lynching "disgraced a city, and caused a bitter feeling of antagonism between the races in a community that has boasted of its goodness, culture, and civilization." Silas Xavier Floyd, the accomplished poet and preacher who years before celebrated Augusta's peaceful race relations, lamented that the "passions of men seem to burst forth like the pent-up fires of a burning volcano" and despairingly announced that "many say that the relations between the two races, hitherto so pleasant in Augusta, are now strained forever and that the breach can never be healed." Floyd understood, as did Augusta's black elite, that violence weakened the threads of paternalism and paved the way for more perverse forms of racial control.[56]

Before Whitney's death, city officials discussed the need for greater spatial distance among blacks and whites, especially on modes of transportation, and White and other black leaders feared that the murder would galvanize public support for stricter legalized forms of segregation. At Wilson's funeral, held in Thankful Baptist Church, the Methodist minister H. Seb Doyle, who had gained notoriety as a supporter of Tom Watson, called for calm and cautioned local officials against using Whitney's death as a excuse to institute segregation on city streetcars. "We don't think this is necessary," charged Doyle before the mourning crowd, "only one black and white man in every thousand ever clash." Doyle informed the congregation that if city officials insist "on humiliating the whole race for the deed of one, I move that we stay off the cars and walk." M. H. Daughtry, echoing the ideas of Henry McNeal Turner and Lucius Henry Holsey, encouraged listeners to join the African emigration movement and abandon the South.[57]

Although White disagreed with Daughtry's plan for migration, he too viewed plans for racial segregation as a concerted effort "to humiliate the colored people." "They speak of the Negro in this day of freedom," he wrote, "just as they spoke of them in the days of slavery. They propose to make this law and that law for the Negroes just as they would for horse and cows. . . . The colored people of Augusta," he reminded readers, "are keeping off the street cars because of the revival of Jim Crowism on them, and some of the white papers of the city are howling about it. They howl if colored people ride on the cars and howl if they stay off of them. What in the name of high heaven do the white people want the colored people to do?" he asked.[58]

White's candid and critical examination of Augusta's changing racial climate cost him dearly. The weekly sneers he directed toward the city's Jim

Crow policies and their proponents infuriated many local Augustans. In Augusta there remained an unspoken understanding that the safekeeping of the city's reputation was first and foremost. White apparently pushed matters to an inexcusable limit by reprinting an editorial from the *Washington Bee* that condemned Wilson's lynching. Calvin B. Chase, the paper's editor, repudiated the lynch mob, called Whitney a "white wretch," and hailed Wilson as a "martyr in defense of female virtue." Few white Augustans were aware of Chase's charges until the article reappeared in the *Georgia Baptist.* White citizens viewed the reprint as an endorsement of Chase's sentiments. The *Augusta Chronicle* went so far as to describe the article as "too contemptible a production; too vile to be reproduced in these columns." As emotions flared, William Jefferson White became the object of obsessive white hostility.[59]

On Saturday afternoon, June 2, about three weeks after Wilson's lynching, a group of white men consisting of business leaders and working-class laborers gathered on Reynolds Street to discuss a response to the *Georgia Baptist* article. The debate went on for some time before someone "suggested that the crowd should march in a body to the office of the *Georgia Baptist,* demolish the office, tar and feather the editor, and give him a few hours to leave town." The group, seeking a public rebuke of White, left the meeting and marched two miles from the river up Campbell Street to White's house and office. By the time they passed through the Irish enclave of Dublin and crossed Calhoun Street, the crowd numbered between three and five hundred people. They encircled the house and office, and a frightened Josephine White and her youngest daughter nervously informed the crowd that the editor was away.[60]

Several prominent white business leaders in the audience cautioned the crowd to refrain from violence, but many seemed eager to harm the editor and his property. Meanwhile, the Whites' neighbors interceded as the rabble threatened to ransack the *Georgia Baptist* office and destroy its printing presses. Dr. George Burruss, a respected black physician, stood guard in front of the office and appeared to jot down names of the rioters. One of White's neighbors, a member of the Harper family, accosted the crowd and was badly beaten. While the legion of white men gathered around his home, White caught wind of the episode and hastily made his way to the city jail, where he successfully secured the protection of Police Chief George Hood. Throughout the evening and for the next week, White's office and home remained under police surveillance. On the following Sunday morning, however, White returned to his neighborhood, made his way to the pulpit of Harmony Baptist, and rendered a sermon fittingly entitled "Walk in Love."[61]

In the days following his public humiliation, White made several efforts to heal the breach caused by the inflammatory clipping. In a lengthy public apology in the *Augusta Chronicle* the day after the riot, White expressed regret and puzzlement over the inclusion of the editorial in his newspaper. "Among my most valuable friends and counselors for years have been leading white citizens of Augusta and common sense would teach me not to willingly or intentionally do anything to alienate the friendship. . . . I do not even know how the article got into the *Georgia Baptist* and believe it was entirely accidental." On the same day, White informed his son Lucien of events and confided that "fortunately for us white friends persuaded the mob not to destroy the *Georgia Baptist* office." White was particularly proud of the black neighbors who came to his defense. "Our friends are true as steel. I was surprised at the staunch friendship shown by colored men & women. It was surprising and alarming because they were ready to make any sacrifice."[62]

In the June 7 issue of the *Georgia Baptist*, White sharpened his apology by expressing strong disapproval of the contents of the *Bee* editorial. On the front page of the paper, White wrote: "I deprecate, repudiate and denounce the article and all the sentiments it contains, and further guarantee to the white people of Augusta that it is not the intention of the Georgia Bapt. to offend by upholding any such dastardly acts as that referred to in the article in question." "The GEORGIA BAPTIST MAN," he said, "would a thousand times rather die himself and go to heaven than to do anything that would cause riot and bloodshed in this community." White's private anguish remained hidden as he displayed a public face of contrition and expressed optimism about the eventual resolution of the South's racial problems; nevertheless, his correspondence to his son Lucien revealed a man deeply pained by the seemingly hopeless state of affairs. "The mob did me no injury," he wrote, "except in the outrageous injustice and meanness of their procedure. I am not decided as to whether or not I will continue my residence here." In a later letter, he assured Lucien that things were relatively calm, but cautioned that "the police force continue to strongly guard our place at night and they would hardly do so unless they saw the need of it." The potential danger faced by his family and his community pushed the editor to a position that he resisted for some time. "I shall say in the GaBapt only what appears necessary in the GaBapt.," he sadly avowed; "we seem to be standing on a volcano."[63]

William White's harrowing ordeal magnified the widening social and spatial gulf among black and white Augustans. As long as White kept to the domain of his ecclesiastical duties, white citizens regarded him as an acceptable

Negro. Yet when the minister stepped beyond those boundaries and offered critical political or social commentary about the city, he invited rancor and consternation. Major Joseph Cumming, one of the leading white citizens of Augusta, admitted as much when he was invited to address the Peabody Colored Institute at Union Baptist Church. Cumming, clearly influenced by recent events in the city, encouraged the black congregation to "be prudent, careful and wise" and to remember that they were always at the "mercy of the white people of this land." "Down with your editors of the *Bee!*" he exclaimed. And then, without mentioning William Jefferson White or the *Georgia Baptist*, Cumming concluded: "If in your newspapers you wish to discuss the issues of politics of the day, do it in a conservative manner. In your pulpits preach the Gospel and let politics alone as the Gospel is enough for any man to preach. Be sober, be honest and industrious and strengthen the arms of your friends and confound your enemies."[64]

The shameful rebuke of his honor by both the white mob and local newspapers and his declining favor among white leaders such as Major Cumming grieved White deeply. Nonetheless, he remained in the city, and despite his earlier reservations, he seemed ever more determined to speak openly and truthfully about conditions that saddled African American progress and mobility. On the occasion of the twentieth-fifth anniversary of the *Georgia Baptist* in 1905, White wrote at length about the perplexing tensions between accommodation and confrontation. "Quiet submission to injustice, to wrong treatment, is often times the wise thing to do," White observed, "but this will not be the thing to do forever. There is a time to speak, a time to act. There is a time to prove your own inherent manhood if you possess it." Buoyed by W. E. B. Du Bois's establishment of the Niagara Movement in 1905 and its advocacy for political rights, White observed, "The time has fully come when the colored men of Georgia should come together and give a statement to the white people of Georgia and the balance of mankind as to what their position is upon questions now before this state and especially those which have reference to the colored man as a citizen and his relation to other men and the commonwealth as a whole."[65]

White invited African American leaders from across the state to assemble in Macon on February 13 and 14, 1906, to establish the Georgia Equal Rights Convention. The editor hoped that the delegates would fashion a creative defense against the menacing advances of white supremacist ideology. In the "Call to the Colored Men & Women of Georgia," White observed that "the

Left: An enlargement of this photograph of William J. White is preserved in the church he founded, Harmony Baptist Church in Augusta. (Courtesy Josephine Harreld Love, granddaughter of William J. White)

Below: William J. White posed for this portrait at the Broad Street, Augusta, studio of black photographer Robert Williams. (Courtesy Josephine Harreld Love)

time has fully come when the colored men of Georgia should meet in solemn conclave and confer with each other fully and freely upon questions that involve their own well being and the well being of their posterity." Moreover, White argued that segregation and racial violence robbed black men of their manhood and weakened their ability to defend their homes and families. "If they [black men] are content with present conditions let them say so; and if they are not content let them as men, in a manly way, say so."[66]

Many prominent black Georgians accepted White's invitation, but a vocal minority, largely supporters of Booker T. Washington, rejected calls for political agitation and ridiculed public demands for social equality. Benjamin J. Davis, the editor of the *Atlanta Independent*, a black weekly newspaper, emerged as White's harshest critic and halfheartedly predicted that the meeting opened the door for a race riot. "The Blood will be on Dr. White's Head," read a headline in the *Atlanta Independent*.[67]

Clearly conscious of the potential dangers surrounding the gathering, more than two hundred leaders traveled to Macon and assembled at the Cotton Avenue Baptist Church on February 13, 1906. J. Max Barber, editor of *The Voice of the Negro*, observed that the "men who shaped all the policies of the body were fearless men . . . who find no pleasure in forever kissing the chastening rod of oppression; who believe that only drastic and precautionary correctives will suffice to save the race of utter spoliation."[68] The impressive list of attendees included Barber; Bishop Henry M. Turner, of the AME Church, who served as vice-chairman along with Augusta CME Bishop R. S. Williams; Hugh Proctor, pastor of Atlanta's First Congregational Church; E. R. Carter, Atlanta pastor and president of the Educational Society of the Missionary Baptist Convention; Atlanta University professor W. E. B. Du Bois; Peter James Bryant, pastor of Wheat Street Baptist Church; Adam Daniel Williams, pastor of Ebenezer Baptist Church (and grandfather of Martin Luther King Jr.); and John Hope, professor at Atlanta Baptist College.

Standing before the convention, White appealed for cooperation among black and white Georgians but expressed disaffection with Booker T. Washington's patience and moderation. He acknowledged that "a large percentage of Georgia's white people are fair-minded and Christians" and not "disposed to do the colored people any injustice." White expressed willingness to "cooperate with them for the highest good and best development of this grand old commonwealth that is as dear to us as Georgians as it is to them. . . . The signs of the times," White continued, "tell in language unmistakable that the ruling element of the white people of Georgia have determined to eliminate the colored man from the high prerogatives of manhood citizenship." Careful not to draw undue public criticism of his remarks, White again underscored the need for interracial cooperation. "Brethren of the white race, living together as we do, let us be friends, and not enemies. Let us not stir up the darker, fiercer passions. Let us strive together, not as master and slave, but as man and man, equal in the sight of God and in the eyes of the law, eager to make this historic state a land of peace, a place of plenty and an abode of Jesus Christ."[69]

White's platitudes about cooperation, however, did not weaken the forceful tenor of the convention's final resolutions. The delegates called for the cessation of lynching and governmental indifference to racial violence and demanded the right to enter the Georgia militia, black representation on juries, equal and adequate educational opportunities, and the franchise qualified by equitable property and literacy rules. "Voteless workingmen are slaves," the leaders declared, "without the defense of the ballot we stand naked to our enemies, helpless victims of jealously and hate, subjected to, and humiliated by an unreasoning caste spirit, which grows by what it feeds upon." The convention's platform concluded with a poignant appeal. African Americans, the leaders observed, "must agitate, complain, protest, and keep protesting against the invasion of our manhood rights; we must besiege the legislature, carry our cases to the courts and above all organize these million brothers of ours into one great fist which shall never cease to pound at the gates of Opportunity until they fly open."[70]

Seven months after the celebrated gathering in Macon, White and his associates watched as their political dreams and social hopes collapsed in a caldron of racial violence during the Atlanta race riot. Throughout the summer of 1906, a tense climate—provoked largely by incendiary political rhetoric and sensationalist news stories describing the assault of white women by "black beast rapists"—draped across the city and extended throughout the state. On the evening of September 22, the perplexing "Negro Problem" exploded. A ring of white mobs engulfed Atlanta and thrashed through neighborhoods firing guns and pummeling blacks with batons and stones. The mob, working under the mute consent of law enforcement, left bruised and slaughtered black bodies along streets and allies. An estimated twenty-five African Americans lost their lives in the Atlanta riot.[71]

As news wires transmitted the violent episodes in Atlanta, ripples of unrest and fear surged from the epicenter throughout the state and region. White Augustans immediately turned their attention to William Jefferson White. On

the very day that events in Atlanta reached a boiling point, an editorial criticizing White appeared in the *Augusta Chronicle*. The newspaper condemned
the *Georgia Baptist*'s endorsement of a streetcar boycott in Savannah and
went on to describe White's recent editorials as downright traitorous:

> The Chronicle is no advocate of harsh measures in dealing with our
> very acute negro problem—for we have faith in the intelligence and
> conservatism of the best men of both races to cope with this problem
> rationally and successfully—but negroes like White ought to be made to
> leave the South, the place for them is, either where there are no Jim
> Crow laws or where it is too hot for street cars. Augusta has no room for
> such incendiary negroes, and we should waste no time in letting them
> know it.[72]

Meanwhile the *Atlanta Constitution* reported that the Augusta police came
upon an outfit of men, purporting to be members of the Ku Klux Klan, who
were preparing to embark on a terror mission to White's home and office.
Despite years of warning, White continued to take chances and published
strongly worded editorials in the *Georgia Baptist*. Now aware of the sensitive
nerves among whites and blacks and the direct threats placed against his life,
White abided by the wisdom of his family and friends and informed Mayor
Richard Allen that he was leaving the city. The *Augusta Chronicle* noted that
White's departure signaled that "the only possible fear of friction between the
races is thereby removed." Although rumors of riots continued to circulate
around the city, the paper concluded that "there is absolutely no cause for
alarm in Augusta. The better element of negroes—and they are unusually
numerous here—are working with the white people to prevent anything that
might cause any resentment and consequent outbreak and the cessation of
hostilities in Atlanta, all fear is dissipated."[73]

The Atlanta race riot damaged the illusion that Atlanta and Augusta were
New South paragons of racial harmony. For the larger South, however, these
events suggested the inevitable collapse of Booker T. Washington's 1895 cov-
enant, described then as the "augury of the future of the races." The severe
language directed against White reflected a perilously unstable society, exposed the delicate racial boundaries in Augusta, and suggested that paternalism succeeded to the extent that blacks acquiesced to subordinate roles. For
White, the forced expulsion from his home and family was a moment of utter
humiliation. Nevertheless, an unfailing religious faith that had inspired his
social activism seemed to sustain him through adversity. "God knows how to

comfort his children," he wrote. "I think it not strange that I must suffer persecution." Writing to a distraught daughter, White assured her that he would persevere: "I have stood as a good soldier of Jesus Christ battling against sin and wickedness in high places and it is not strange that the wicked seek my life.... God works in mysterious ways his wonders to perform and though his way be mysterious, he never forgets to care for his children."[74]

White spent time among friends in Denmark and Charleston, South Carolina, before returning to the city later in the fall. Despite the threats against his life, he continued to express his impatience with the festering state of race relations in Georgia. In early 1907 he managed to organize and convene a second meeting of the Georgia Equal Rights Convention. But the pugnacity and enthusiasm of the first convention were noticeably absent in the subsequent meeting. White assumed a much more conciliatory demeanor, which undoubtedly reflected the painful personal challenges of the previous year. The delegates made conspicuous alterations to the program to reduce any cause for alarm. Not only did they change the name from the Equal Rights Convention to the less threatening Georgia Colored Association, but they also solicited the participation of white leaders known for their racial moderation. Judge Emory Speer, the Augusta lawyer William Fleming, and the former governor and Southern Baptist Convention president William Northen were among the guests who spoke at the 1907 Macon conference.

Although the delegates refrained from making direct demands, White succeeded in raising the issue of elective franchise. "No man can be said to be a citizen in the full meaning of the term," he argued, "who is without the ballot; it is the badge, the sign, the shield of a citizen of this republic." The *Atlanta Constitution* congratulated the delegates for a sober dialogue and reported that "the speakers were conservative, and no references were made to social equality." Benjamin Davis of the *Atlanta Independent* was far less complimentary and noted that "the same set of men elected or appointed by nobody, representing nobody . . . elect themselves to empty offices, issue an address and adjourn."[75] Indeed, White's efforts proved futile. The harsh racial calculus of the region remained unchanged.

Into the Sunset

As crusades of white supremacy threatened black life and property, weakened African American voting power, depleted public schools of necessary funding, and relegated blacks—regardless of class or status—to Jim Crow quarters, African American leaders continued to preach a message of self-determination and race consciousness. William Jefferson White's life offers one vantage point from which to view black leadership and race relations in Augusta. His long life reflected both the rise and the collapse of the paternalist sensibilities that governed race relations after the Civil War as well as the multifarious efforts of African Americans to reconfigure the color line. Although William White had every incentive to leave his home, he remained in Augusta until his death and continued to render an honest and critical assessment of African American struggles for social and political equality.

Travelers along Campbell Street found the old editor busy at work in the *Georgia Baptist* office, holding court on his front porch, or tending to his prized vegetable garden. On Sundays they could still find his stooped frame preaching to the congregation at Harmony. Periodically, students at Spelman and Atlanta Baptist would find the venerable sage visiting his family or attending board meetings. But toward the end of his life, White, with failing eyesight and rheumatoid arthritis, recognized his own physical shortcomings and attempted to find others to assume financial control of the *Georgia Baptist*. He generously lent his support to the work of younger leaders, like John Hope. In a poignant letter to Hope, White confessed, "For a time, I may remain around and then I may take [the] train for another and perhaps better land any day."[76]

When he died, at sunset on April 17, 1913, William Jefferson White's fame and influence extended well beyond the limits of Georgia. When hearing of White's death, Booker T. Washington telegraphed a letter of sympathy to the family and informed them that he honored the minister for his "great unselfishness; for his pride in his race and for his unflinching devotion to its best interests." The Augusta writer Silas X. Floyd overlooked his own political differences with the belated editor and reported that White "was not selfish with what he had been taught, but imparted as best he could what he had learned to the less fortunate." Floyd surmised that "in more respects than one, Dr. White was our most remarkable colored citizen. The story of his life, when told, sounds like romance." The celebrated evangelist Charles T. Walker postponed an out-of-town revival and returned to Augusta in time to eulogize his former adversary. Walker too shied away from their celebrated public spats and instead predicted that "the future historian cannot write a complete history of our race in general and of the Baptist denomination in particular without giving conspicuous and honorable space to the life, character and deeds of Dr. Wm. J. White." After Walker finished his stirring eulogy before a teeming crowd at Springfield Baptist Church, "not a dry face was to be seen in the audience."[77]

Yet when Claudia Harreld reflected on her father's career, the irony of Walker's remarks were not lost. She noted that "he might have spun off a list of hardships to resemble those of Paul if he had chosen to dwell on that aspect of his experiences. For he was mobbed, he was threatened with death, he was forced to be a wanderer from his own city, he was falsely accused by his own brethren, he was prosecuted by them, he was left sometimes to stand apparently alone; however, he lived thru it all, accomplished his work, and died triumphant." White undoubtedly understood his place in history, for there were many monuments to his credit throughout the state. His close confidante W. E. B. Du Bois noted that "as editor, educator and leader, he held a hundred thousand people in the hollow of his hand." Nevertheless, White remained remarkably humble and modest about his accomplishments "My comfort," he reminded his daughter, "is that whatever I have done during my long life has been done conscientiously without a thought of my fellow men's applause. . . . My highest ambition," he concluded, "is that my children may be proud of me when I am gone."[78] In perhaps the most fitting tribute to William Jefferson White's life, his "other children"—nearly a thousand black students from the public and private schools in the city—escorted his coffin along Augusta streets to a crypt in Cedar Grove Cemetery and then one by one showered the minister's grave with a stream of roses.

Notes

1. As a young child attending Harmony Baptist, I too looked at White's portrait with puzzlement and intrigue. Over the years, many people assisted me in uncovering the mysteries of William Jefferson White. I gleaned a great deal from my friend Phil Waring (1912–97), and I deeply miss his wise counsel and guidance. I owe a tremendous debt to White's granddaughter Josephine Harreld Love for sharing her family's history and for providing me with invaluable source material and generous words of encouragement. I also wish to thank Randall Burkett, Dan T. Carter, Lawrence Carter, Leroy Davis, Elizabeth Fox-Genovese, Eugene Genovese, David Godshalk, Philip Lapsansky, Kent Leslie, Christine Miller-Betts, Gregory Mixon, Leslie Pollard, Jane Robinson, Virginia Shadron, the late Isaiah Washington, and the members of the Mellon Southern Studies Seminar at Emory University. Many thanks to the kind audiences at Harmony Baptist Church, the Lucy Laney Museum, Paine College, and Dartmouth College.

2. William White's skin color and ambiguous parentage raise many interesting

questions about the constructions and perceptions of racial identity in the American South. For an insightful analysis of the social construction of race, see Fields, "Ideology and Race." For a discussion of miscegenation and interracial relationships, see Williamson, *New People*. Interview with J. Philip Waring, Augusta, January 14, 1995; Logan, *Betrayal of the Negro*, 52.

3. For a discussion of black leadership at the turn of the century, see Meier, *Negro Thought in America*; Wilson Moses, *Golden Age*; Franklin, *Black Self-Determination*; K. Gaines, *Uplifting the Race*; Gilmore, *Gender and Jim Crow*. As the historian Wilson Moses notes, black leaders during this period struggled to maintain a "new spirit of confidence and assertiveness" and engaged in impressive efforts to curb white hostility, achieve social and political equality, and surmount prescribed social roles. Wilson Moses, *Wings of Ethiopia*, 201. For discussions of African American life during the age of Jim Crow, see Ayers, *Promise of the New South*; N. McMillen, *Dark Journey*; also see Lamon, *Black Tennesseans*; Newby, *Black Carolinians*.

4. Pegues, *Our Baptist Ministers*, 526–27. On the occasion of his seventy-ninth birthday, White penned a short autobiographical sketch for the *Georgia Baptist* and noted that he was born in 1832, which contradicts Pegues's 1831 date; *Georgia Baptist*, April 24, 1913. Day, *Negro-White Families*, 30. Claudia Harreld to Caroline Bond Day, May 1, 1930, Caroline Bond Day, Box 1, Folder 13, Peabody Museum of Archaeology and Ethnology, Harvard University, Cambridge, Mass.

5. White worked in the office of Platt Brothers as a cabinetmaker and coffin designer and earned an estimated twelve hundred dollars a year. E. Jones, *Candle in the Dark*, 20–21; Simmons, *Men of Mark*, 1095–96; Pegues, *Our Baptist Ministers*, 526–39. For an extensive discussion of Augusta's role in the cotton trade, see J. Harris, *Plainfolk and Gentry*.

6. William White later described Josephine as "one of the handsomest girls ever given to the world by Augusta," *Georgia Baptist*, October 19, 1905; Claudia White Harreld, "Memoirs," winter 1952, 15–16, typescript, Schlesinger Library, Radcliffe College, Cambridge, Mass.; Interviews with William Jefferson White's children, Ridgely Torrence Papers, Firestone Library, Princeton University, Princeton, N.J.; E. Jones, *Candle in the Dark*, 21. The 1872 Augusta directory notes that White lived near the corner of Campbell and South Boundary; *Haddock's Augusta, Georgia Directory*, 184.

7. For a discussion of education and slavery, see Cornelius, *"When I Can Read"*; Woodson, *Education of the Negro*. White instructed Ketch, his wife, and their four children. He established other schools in the homes of Deacon Anderson Hartwell (who later moved to Liberia) and the Reverend Peter Johnson, and on the property of Judge W. T. Gould. Pegues, *Our Baptist Ministers*, 529–30; *Georgia Baptist*, March 16, 1899; Pegues, *Our Baptist Ministers*, 529–30.

8. White answered the call to the ministry and received his license to exhort in September 1858 and his license to preach on February 16, 1862. Pegues, *Our Baptist Ministers*, 531–33, notes that he was ordained on April 1, 1866. Later White received

one of the coveted honorary doctorates from the State University of Kentucky in Louisville, where the prominent Baptist leader W. J. Simmons presided. He received the degree in 1890 along with the Augusta minister Charles T. Walker. Two years after establishing Harmony, White joined other ministers in the founding of the Missionary Baptist Convention of Georgia and the Shiloh Baptist Association; Cathcart, *Baptist Encyclopaedia*, 1238. For an extended discussion of the role of ministers and religion in Reconstruction politics, see Drago, *Black Politicians*, 21; Hildebrand, *Times Were Strange*; Montgomery, *Under Their Own Vine*. White's friend W. E. B. Du Bois noted that the black preacher "is the most unique personality developed by the Negro on American soil. A leader, a politician, an orator, a 'boss,' an intriguer, an idealist"; Du Bois, *Souls of Black Folk*, 141.

9. Drago, *Black Politicians*, 27. After two years with the bureau, Edwin Belcher, the first black assessor of Internal Revenue appointed by President Ulysses Grant, named White assistant assessor; Pegues, *Our Baptist Ministers*, 533–35.

10. E. Cashin, *The Quest*, 9.

11. Cade, *Holsey*, 178.

12. William Jefferson White, "The Founding of Atlanta Baptist College," speech to the Alumni Association of Morehouse College, May 13, 1904, Alumni Office, Morehouse College, Atlanta; Davis, *A Clashing of the Soul*, 103–4.

13. Swint, *Northern Teacher*, 98; W. J. White, "Founding of Atlanta Baptist College"; Range, *Rise and Progress*, 24; E. Cashin, *Old Springfield*, 53–56; E. Jones, *Candle in the Dark*, 30–34. For a discussion of the experiences of northern teachers, see J. Jones, *Soldiers of Light and Love*. B. Brawley, *History of Morehouse College*, 17; E. Jones, *Candle in the Dark*, 31–32.

14. In April 1870 White and Siegfried joined others at the Augusta City Hall to celebrate the ratification of the Fifteenth Amendment; *Augusta Chronicle*, April 28, 1870. White, "Founding of Atlanta Baptist College."

15. After Augusta Baptist relocated to Atlanta in 1879, White remained a member of the board of trustees of the school (later Morehouse College). He also served on the board of trustees of Atlanta University and was one of the original incorporators and vice president of the board of Spelman Seminary in Atlanta; Bacote, *Story of Atlanta University*, 97. Range, *Rise and Progress*, 108; Reed, *The Story of Spelman*, 93.

16. Wm. J. White to Rev. Edw. P. Smith, August 12, 1869, no. 22739, microfilm, AMA Archive, Amistad Research Center, Tulane University, New Orleans; see also White to Smith, July 27, 1869, no. 22712, and September 8, 1869, no. 22760, AMA Archives. June Patton, "Black Community of Augusta," 49; Richmond County Board of Education, Minutes, January 11, 1873, 17, and April 12, 1873, 59, Richmond County Board of Education, Augusta; see also *Augusta Chronicle*, April 13, 1873. Editorial in *Augusta Chronicle*, July 20, 1873, July 22, 1873. Emancipation Day speech report in *Augusta Chronicle*, January 3, 1874.

17. Patton, "Black Community of Augusta," 50; Richmond County Board of Education, Minutes, October 1878, 36; Patton, " Black Community of Augusta," 50; Rich-

mond County Board of Education, Minutes, July 10, 1880, 137; E. Cashin, *The Quest*, 19, *Old Springfield*, 65.

18. Haynes, *Black Boy of Atlanta*, 67–68; E. Cashin, *The Quest*, 20. White also invited Wright's classmate Lucy Craft Laney to come to Augusta and assume charge of the Fourth Ward Grammar School; see Torrence, *Story of John Hope*, 55. E. Cashin, *Old Springfield*, 65.

19. E. Cashin, *Old Springfield*, 64, and *Story of Augusta*, 158. Turner was a frequent visitor and highly regarded speaker in Augusta. For information on Turner, see Angell, *Bishop Henry McNeal Turner*.

20. *Georgia Baptist*, October 13, 1881; Torrence, *Story of John Hope*, 55. Harreld noted that the office was initially outfitted by white workmen; Mrs. Kemper Harreld, "The Founder," *Georgia Baptist*, n.d., courtesy of Josephine Harreld Love.

21. Torrence, *Story of John Hope*, 63; *Georgia Baptist*, December 10, 1930.

22. White, "The Negro Problem," 6–7, 13.

23. B. Brawley, *Social History*, 297–340; for a discussion of social Darwinism, see George Fredrickson, *Black Image*, 228–55.

24. The delegates, including the Augusta attorney Judson Lyons and the Savannah minister Emmanuel K. Love, agreed to name their new organization the Union Brotherhood of Georgia; "Minutes of Consultation Convention, Macon, Ga., January 25, 1888," in Aptheker, *Documentary History*, 2:697–703.

25. Quoted in Davis, *Henry Grady's New South*, 136–37.

26. Torrence, *Story of John Hope*, 54. For a discussion of Augusta's black aristocracy, see Gatewood, *Aristocrats of Color*, 90–91; Kousser, "Separate but Not Equal: The Supreme Court's First Decision on Racial Discrimination in Schools," *Journal of Southern History* 46, no. 1 (1980): 17–44; Davis, *Clashing of the Soul*.

27. "Dr. Tobias Speaking at the Memorial Service of the Interracial Commission for Dr. John Hope, April 15, 1936," Ridgley Torrence Papers, Firestone Library, Princeton University, Princeton, N.J. For a clearer assessment of the neopaternalist school of southern thought, see Fredrickson, *Black Image*, 198–227.

28. For a discussion of Georgia's wealthy black elite, see Hornsby, "Shifts in Wealth." Phil Waring, whose father operated a grocery and restaurant on Campbell Street, recalled meeting many of the luminaries of the "Golden Blocks" during his boyhood; interview with J. Philip Waring, Augusta, January 14, 1995.

29. Kousser, "Separate but *Not* Equal," 15; *Augusta Chronicle*, June 21, 1894, June 24, 1894.

30. Harvey, "The Terri"; German, "Queen City," 37; *Augusta Chronicle*, May 1, 1899.

31. Torrence, *Story of John Hope*, 42; German, "Queen City," 384–85; *Augusta Chronicle*, December 31, 1900.

32. C. Vann Woodward's *Strange Career of Jim Crow* outlines the steps the South took toward a capitulation to racism. For a discussion of postbellum paternalism, see Fredrickson, *Black Image*, 198–227.

33. *Georgia Baptist*, February 9, 1899.

34. Litwack, *Trouble in Mind*, 101; Du Bois, "Religion in the South," 180; *Augusta Chronicle*, April 4, 1899.

35. Interview with Waring; *Atlanta Constitution*, April 22, 1897, May 10, 1897, July 24, 1897; *Augusta Chronicle*, May 18, 1897.

36. *Atlanta Journal*, May 10, 1897; *Augusta Chronicle*, July 2, 1897, May 18, 1897, March 23, 1898.

37. Edward Cashin notes that an announcement of Ware's closing appeared to be an annual event after the departure of Richard R. Wright in 1891. E. Cashin, *Story of Augusta*, 181; *Augusta Chronicle*, June 9, 1897; Kousser, "Separate but Not Equal."

38. Richmond County Board of Education, Minutes, June 12, 1897, 370–72, July 15, 1897, 379–80; *Augusta Chronicle*, August 29, 1897.

39. Kousser, "Separate but *Not* Equal," 8. For a glowing endorsement of Booker T. Washington's leadership and a speech he delivered at Thankful Baptist Church, see *Augusta Chronicle*, April 28, 1899.

40. Commissioner of Education Report, 1895, in Richmond County Board Minutes, November 9, 1895, 309; Patton, "Black Community of Augusta," 53. For a statistical study of the sharp disparities between black and white education in Richmond County, see Kousser, "Separate but *Not* Equal," 24–27. In his analysis of New South paternalism, George Fredrickson offers some conclusions that seem quite consistent with the motivations behind Ware's closing: "Their [neopaternalists'] program for Negro uplift amounted, in the last analysis, to moral guidance and a willingness to provide certain educational facilities, especially industrial education. At best, it was an effort to prepare blacks more adequately for scratching out a living at the lower levels of a capitalist society; at its worst it openly capitulated to racial discrimination to such an extent that even this modest goal was endangered"; Fredrickson, *Black Image*, 210–21.

41. E. Cashin, *The Quest*, 39; *Augusta Chronicle*, September 22, 1897. When Judge Enoch Callaway supported the petition of the plaintiffs on December 22 1897, the board appealed to the Supreme Court of Georgia. The case was argued on January 24 and 25, and a decision was handed down on March 23, 1898. The U.S. Supreme Court decision was handed down on December 18, 1899. E. Cashin, *The Quest*, 39–40, *Old Springfield*, 77–80; Kousser, "Separate but Not Equal," 32.

42. *Georgia Baptist*, March 31, 1898.

43. *Georgia Baptist*, December 21, 1899.

44. *Augusta Chronicle*, September 15, 1897. The effort to weaken African Americans' voting power came after they proved to be the decisive swing vote in the 1897 election of Patrick Walsh as mayor; see E. Cashin, *Story of Augusta*, 185. German, "Queen City," 46.

45. *Augusta Chronicle*, January 17, 28, May 12, 14, 1897; German, "Queen City," 380, 389.

46. *Augusta Chronicle*, October 12, 1897; *Georgia Baptist*, June 15, 1899.

47. *Atlanta Journal*, November 28, 1899.

48. *Georgia Baptist*, September 6, 1900; E. Cashin, *Old Springfield*, 81. Local jurisdictions successfully adopted disfranchisement measures, yet the Hardwick bill momentarily failed. See Dittmer, *Black Georgia*, 101–4.

49. For a discussion of the rise in lynching and racial violence in the South, see Brundage, *Lynching in the New South*, and *Under the Sentence of Death*; Hall, *Revolt Against Chivalry*; MacLean, *Behind the Mask*; Wright, *Racial Violence in Kentucky*. Gatewood, *Black Americans*, 32. Mays, *Born to Rebel*, 330–35; *Georgia Baptist*, November 24, 1898; Butterfield, *All God's Children*, 56–57.

50. *Georgia Baptist*, November 3, 1898, December 1, 1898.

51. *Georgia Baptist*, December 29, 1898.

52. *Atlanta Constitution*, April 16, 1899. For a discussion of the Sam Hose lynching see Capeci and Knight, "Reckoning with Violence"; Eskew, "Black Elitism," 658–59; Litwack, *Trouble in Mind*, 280–83; Hale, *Making Whiteness*, 209–16.

53. *Augusta Chronicle*, May 1, 1899; Charles T. Walker and William J. White lived only a few blocks from each other, but their social philosophies were often worlds apart. Interview with Waring; Meier, *Negro Thought in America*, 156, 221–22. *Georgia Baptist*, April 27, 1899.

54. *Augusta Chronicle*, May 15, 1900; *Georgia Baptist*, May 17, 1900.

55. *Savannah Tribune*, May 19, 1900.

56. *Augusta Chronicle*, May 16, 1900; *Macon Telegraph*, May 15, 1900; *Georgia Baptist*, May 17, 1900; *Savannah Tribune*, May 19, 1900; *Savannah Tribune*, May 26, 1900; *Augusta Chronicle*, May 21, 1900.

57. *Georgia Baptist*, May 31, 1900; E. Cashin, *Old Springfield*, 75. For a discussion of the streetcar boycott, see *Augusta Chronicle*, May 21, 1900. For a discussion of Seb Doyle, see Woodward, *Tom Watson*, 239–40.

58. *Georgia Baptist*, May 31, 1900. Despite black protest, the city council passed an ordinance permitting racial segregation on the streetcars.

59. Quoted in E. Cashin, *Old Springfield*, 84; *Augusta Chronicle*, June 3, 1900.

60. *Augusta Chronicle*, June 3, 1900; E. Cashin, *Story of Augusta*, 187–88; Harreld, *Remembered Encounters*, 8. Josephine Elizabeth White died in January 1902.

61. *Augusta Chronicle*, June 3, 1900; E. Cashin, *Old Springfield*, 84; *Georgia Baptist*, June 7, 1900.

62. *Augusta Chronicle*, June 3, 1900; William Jefferson White to Lucien Hayden White, June 3 and 7, 1900, courtesy of Josephine Harreld Love. In addition to Burruss and Harper, the *Augusta Chronicle* reported that "one woman stood with half a brick in her hand, as if ready to throw it, but did not do so"; *Augusta Chronicle*, June 3, 1900.

63. *Georgia Baptist*, June 7, 1900; William Jefferson White to Lucien Hayden White, June 3, 1900, June 7, 1900. While White publicly extended the olive branch and contemplated his future in Augusta, his longtime friend Bishop Henry McNeal Turner

denounced the public humiliation of the editor. "For four hundred men to band together to go and lynch a man seventy odd years of age," he wrote, "is proof positive
that they were four hundred cowards. . . . Nobody but a set of worthless cowards
would dream of such a thing"; *Voice of Missions*, June 1, 1900.

64. *Augusta Chronicle*, July 6, 1900.

65. *Georgia Baptist*, October 19, 1905. Lewis, *W. E. B. Du Bois*, 326–27. When Du
Bois and other members of the Niagara Movement marked the centenary of William
Lloyd Garrison's birth at Atlanta's Wheat Street Baptist Church, White was one of
the featured speakers; *Atlanta Independent*, December 2, 1905.

66. Several prominent Augustans were among those who signed the call: W. J.
White, Bishop R. S. Williams, Isaiah Blocker, Dr. E. T. Robinson, the Reverend C. S.
Wilkins, A. R. Johnson, G. W. Dwelle, Dr. George N. Stoney, and Dr. G. S. Burruss.
Lucy Craft Laney, founder of the Haines Institute, appeared to be the only woman
from Augusta who endorsed the convention. Surprisingly, White succeeded in securing the signature of C. T. Walker. Many who supported the call did not attend the
actual convention in Macon. "Call to the Colored Men & Women of Georgia," microfilm reel 1, W. E. B. Du Bois Papers, University of Massachusetts, Amherst.

67. *Atlanta Independent*, January 20, 1906.

68. *Voice of the Negro*, March 1906, 177.

69. "Georgia Equal Rights Convention," February 13 and 14, 1906, and "The
President's Address," W. E. B. Du Bois Papers, microfilm, reel 1.

70. "Address of the First Meeting of the Georgia Equal Rights Convention," W. E.
B. Du Bois Papers, microfilm, reel 1; Dittmer, *Black Georgia*, 173.

71. Grant, *The Way It Was*, 204; Crowe, "Racial Violence" and "Racial Massacre in
Atlanta."

72. *Augusta Chronicle*, September 22, 1906.

73. *Atlanta Constitution*, September 26, 1906; *Augusta Chronicle*, September 26,
1906; Dittmer, *Black Georgia*, 165.

74. Grant, *The Way It Was*, 210; William Jefferson White to Mamie, October 1906,
courtesy of Josephine Harreld Love.

75. *Georgia Baptist*, March 14, 1907; *Atlanta Constitution*, February 15, 1907. The
Augusta lawyer William Henry Fleming was one of the strongest defenders of black
Augustans and a vocal critic of white supremacy. See Fleming, *Slavery and the Race
Problem* and *Treaty-making Power. Atlanta Independent*, February 23, 1907.

76. White served as pastor of Harmony until 1904. He resumed the pastorate in
1911 and served until his death. White to John Hope, January 7, 1913, March 12, 1912,
John Hope Papers, Moorland-Spingarn Research Center, Howard University, Washington, D.C.

77. Booker T. Washington letter, reprinted in *Georgia Baptist*, May 1, 1913; *Augusta
Herald*, April 20, 1913; *Georgia Baptist*, April 24, 1913; *Atlanta Independent*, April 26,
1913.

78. Mrs. Kemper Harreld, "The Founder," *Georgia Baptist*, n.d.; Torrence, *Story of John Hope*, 55; White to Claudia White, December 12, 1912, courtesy of Josephine Harreld Love. Seven months after White's burial, in a sign of things to come, the Augusta City Council passed an ordinance that legalized neighborhood segregation. Not surprisingly, one of the leading detractors of the ordinance was William Jefferson White Jr.

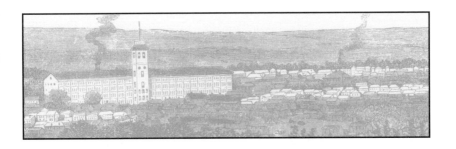

Rolling Religion down the Hill:
Millworkers and Churches in Augusta

JULIA WALSH

I N MAY 1882 THE REVEREND EDWIN WEED of the Episcopal Church
of the Good Shepherd decided to build a new church. His parish of predominantly middle- and upper-class worshipers in the increasingly fashionable Summerville or "Hill" district of Augusta needed a larger building
than the simple wooden structure that had stood on Walton Way since 1869.
At the same time, Weed and concerned members of the Ladies Sewing Society of Good Shepherd decided to sponsor a mission church in the developing mill district of Harrisburg, down by the Augusta Canal. In the summer of
1882, after donations by wealthy parishioners made the new church a possibility, the old church structure was, according to oral histories, rolled on logs
down Battle Row and placed on the corner of Eve and Greene Streets in Harrisburg, facing the Sibley and King textile mills. Although the *Augusta
Chronicle* did not mention this extraordinary sight, the paper noted on July
11, 1882, that Christ Church (Episcopal) had just been completed in Harrisburg and was "a very pretty structure."[1] The image of Christ Church rolling
down the hill to become a mission to the millworkers of Augusta is interesting
in both its physical and its symbolic dimensions. What motivated those who
sent the church to Harrisburg, and how was it received by the workers for
whom it was intended? Were city elites and upper-class congregations genu-
inely interested in millworkers' religious lives, or did they see churches helping to create a docile and passive working class? Which denominations were
concerned with the working class? What about workers themselves and their
notions of faith and church?

As the historian Edward Ayers has noted, religion was one of the constants of New South society, permeating all aspects of life. Religious belief was shared by almost all southerners—rich and poor, black and white, churchgoers and the unchurched. I. A. Newby suggests, in his study of rural millworkers in the New South, that textile workers were no exception. "Religion," he explains, "was the well-spring of their understanding of things."[2]

Yet historians of the working class have been slow to look at the religious lives of workers in a serious way. Some of this hesitation is no doubt due to the difficulty of finding sources; religious records and histories often consist of the voices of only middle- and upper-class worshipers. More fundamentally, however, historians have ignored religion because they do not take it seriously. Many scholars of the working class consider race, class, and gender as more tangible and influential determinants of choices and values.

This essay explores working-class religion in Augusta after the Civil War, focusing on white millworkers.[3] Augusta is an excellent site for this type of study. Besides being an important industrial center in the New South era with a swelling working-class population, Augusta was, and still is, a city of churches. The very visibility of religion on the landscape symbolizes its importance to the dynamics of city life. By analyzing the roles of various denominations in the lives of the city's millworkers, this essay investigates the more difficult question of what religion and churches may have meant to ordinary people and how that connected to their political lives. The contemporary political climate demonstrates that, even in a society where church and state are "separate," religious values and symbols are at the forefront of politics. This essay is also about the ways different groups in the city came to terms with industrialization, particularly mill development, and with one another in a context of evangelical Christianity. As leading citizens became industrialists and capitalists, and rural farm folk moved to the city to become "workers," shifting class and cultural relationships were negotiated within a Christian milieu.

The strong role played by city elites, particularly mill owners and investors, in the religious lives of millworkers indicates that religion and churches could provide a form of social control. This issue of social control has continually interested scholars in the field of working-class religion. The classic work in this field is Liston Pope's *Millhands and Preachers*, a pioneering sociological analysis of the bitter textile strike in Gastonia, North Carolina, in 1928. Pope studied millworkers' churches in detail and concluded that they were usually an instrument of control, as ministers expressed public approval of mill owners, inculcated labor discipline through moral supervision, and preached acceptance of one's lot on earth.[4]

Christ Church (photo ca. 1950) was the first Church of the Good Shepherd (Episcopal), until it was "rolled down the hill" to its new location at Greene and Eve Streets to make way for a new Church of the Good Shepherd. (Courtesy Reese Library, Augusta State University)

The Sibley Mill (ca. 1940) before its windows were bricked up for air-conditioning. The tall chimney in front is the only extant structure of the Confederate Powerworks. (Courtesy Reese Library, Augusta State University)

Edgerton Garvin's photograph (ca. 1915) shows the Sibley Mill across the Harris-burg mill village. (Courtesy Augusta Museum of History)

Recently, historians have modified this rather one-dimensional view of mill religion. Books by I. A. Newby, Jacquelyn Dowd Hall et al., Allen Tullos, and Douglas Flamming on nineteenth- and twentieth-century millworkers, all of which pay attention to religion, acknowledge the role of mill owners in establishing and funding churches as well as the conservatism of most preachers.[5] But these studies also emphasize the agency of millworkers in constructing their own religious lives. Even if there was only one church in town, and pressure put on workers to attend, what people actually took away from services was harder to control. These works show, furthermore, that "church" was not synonymous with "faith." Even workers who were not church members or regular churchgoers saw their world in religious terms and showed familiarity with the Bible. Many who did not formally join a church participated in religious events such as revivals and went to hear famous speakers like Dwight Moody and Sam Jones.

This study, then, analyzes the interplay between rich and poor whites in churches and Sunday schools, looking at how class and culture interact with faith. Rather than labeling action by rich whites as purely social control, it looks at the motivations of these wealthy benefactors and the efforts of Augusta's elite to "teach" Christianity to millworkers. The study investigates the actions of Augusta's industrialists and how they fit into a national context of reform. The essay considers the reception of millworkers to the industry-supported churches and presents evidence of how workers created and interpreted their own religious worldview. While acknowledging that religion is not the same as church, one finds that much of the evidence of religious activity comes from denominational records. Yet by considering burial association records and working-class newspapers, one can catch glimpses of workers' attitudes. While the diverse people who called themselves Christians in Augusta often spoke the same language of faith, its meaning was filtered through experience, just as faith gave meaning to experience.

The first stage of textile mill development in Augusta actually came before the Civil War. The Augusta Factory was built in 1847, after the completion of the first part of the Augusta Canal, and soon became one of the biggest textile factories in the South. The first employees were white Protestants from Augusta's rural hinterlands. Some of the early workers were widows and their children, who found it difficult to maintain farms without a male head of household. More often, entire families came to the city, although it was usually only the children and sometimes the wife who actually worked in the mill. In the antebellum South, as in the northern mills of New England, textile work was considered female or child labor. The male heads of household took other jobs in the town or attended to garden plots at home.[6]

With a primarily female and child workforce, it is not surprising that an atmosphere and rhetoric of paternalism characterized these early mills. William Gregg, who developed the Graniteville Mill, from where many of the city's millworkers later came, epitomized this early paternalism. After building houses and stores for his workers, he banned alcohol from the town he had created. He established an elementary school and demanded that all children attend till the age of twelve, when they entered the mill. He also built a Methodist and a Baptist church in the town and demanded that workers attend one or the other. Workers not adhering to Gregg's strict rules were dismissed.[7]

The mainline Protestant denominations in Augusta also worried about the religious lives of the mill families in their community. The Augusta Factory was in a developing area of town not served by the existing churches. The denominations responded by building mission churches and, especially, Sunday schools. In 1852 the Episcopal Church of the Atonement was consecrated "in the upper part of the city in a new manufacturing area." The church was unusual because it was the first Episcopal church in the city where churchgoers did not have to pay rent for the pews that they sat in, suggesting the church was intended for working-class worshipers. In 1856 Saint John Methodist Church established a Sunday school, which soon became known as Asbury Mission. Not to be outdone, the Baptists formed a mission church known as Kollock Street Baptist Church, later called Second Baptist Church.[8]

From the start, mill development emphasized white racial identity. In Augusta, as in most of the South, textile mills were regarded as white spaces. Efforts throughout the antebellum South to use slave or free black labor in cotton mills failed. In a somewhat tacit pact, millwork became viewed by elites and workers alike as a special type of privilege for poor whites. In this formulation rural whites, though destitute, did not have to drop to the level of African Americans; instead, they could move to the mill. Such a rationale divided the South's poorest workers along racial lines and engendered racial pride, the psychological "wage" of whiteness, among the white working class.[9]

White native-born workers, then, received jobs and churches as their numbers increased in the city, while African Americans and immigrants fought for steady employment and worked to establish their own places of worship. In return, millworkers were expected to behave in ways that did not challenge the political, economic, or even religious status quo. These connections among economic, political, and religious power indicate that paternalism and the use of religion as a controlling force would be a constant factor in the development of the city's mill churches.

The Civil War dealt a fierce blow to the confidence of the South's white Protestant denominations. Secular and religious leaders alike felt that military defeat showed that "God was against us." Most denominations remained separated from their fellow northern counterparts. At the same time, an increasing number of African Americans left southern white churches, unwilling, now that they were free, to remain second-class citizens in the churches of their former masters. As the southern white Protestant denominations began to recover financially and structurally in the 1870s and 1880s, they needed a new focus to invigorate their organizations. Missions became a crucial rallying point for most of the southern churches, becoming as important as they were to many northern denominations. The southern Baptist, Methodist, and Presbyterian churches, in particular, slowly began to send missions overseas and out West to the Indians. But through the nineteenth century the most important field for evangelization remained in the South itself, particularly in industrializing towns such as Augusta.

Though less affected by the ravages of war than most Georgia cities, Augusta was transformed in the late nineteenth century. The most visible change in the city was probably the rise of manufacturing establishments, especially the nine textile mills that dominated the city's geography by the 1890s and earned the city the title of "Lowell of the South." As in most of the South, the textile workforce in Augusta continued to be mainly white, native-born Protestants who had recently moved to Augusta after generations of working farms in Georgia and South Carolina. The workers in the antebellum mills had been predominantly women and children, but disastrous economic conditions for southern farmers in the late 1880s increased the number of male textile workers. For example, in Augusta in 1880, men over sixteen constituted only 23 percent of the cotton mill workforce. By 1890 they made up 39 percent of the total. As before the war, mill work remained a predominantly white and native-born job. Some African Americans worked in the city's mills, but they usually were given the least desirable jobs at the "edges" of the mill, loading cotton into the mill or cleaning up outside. None appear to have worked on the mill floor alongside white employees. Efforts by Augusta's African Americans to establish their own mill failed because they could not raise the necessary capital for the expensive machinery, although Riverside Mill, a cotton-waste factory owned by a white man, had an exclusively African American workforce.[10]

Harrisburg was a new center for white working-class settlement, developing after the canal expansion in 1875. As work began on the Sibley and J. P. King Mills in June and October 1880, mill owners began to build houses for future employees. In 1882, as the mills neared completion, Harrisburg, along with the smaller adjacent neighborhoods, Rollersville and Hicksville, was formally incorporated into the city limits. The *Augusta Chronicle* noted that "the great improvement in this section shows what manufacturing enterprise accomplished for a place."[11] But despite the optimistic report from Augusta's leading newspaper, the area had few amenities or churches. It was to this neighborhood that Weed sent Christ Episcopal Church on its logs in May 1882.

The interest of the Episcopal church in millworkers is particularly intriguing. The Protestant Episcopal Church was known generally as an elite church, not given to evangelization among working people. Yet Weed, who would later become the bishop of Florida and an influential church leader, was very concerned with home missions. As pastor of the Church of the Good Shepherd, he oversaw a black Sunday school. Already Augusta Episcopalians had established a white mission church—Atonement—in the Augusta Factory area. The Harrisburg mission may also have been an attempt to bring Episcopalianism to workers who had grown up Baptist and Methodist. Many Episcopalians thought that these evangelical denominations were too emotional and prone to "fire and brimstone" preaching.[12]

But the Episcopalians were not the only Christians concerned with the influx of millworkers. The Methodists began Saint Luke's as a mission church of Saint John Church in 1875, and the First Christian Church of Augusta developed Second Christian (later known as Central Christian) in 1882. Both these churches were on Crawford Street in the heart of Harrisburg, as was Berean Baptist Church, begun in 1881, later known as Crawford Avenue Baptist Church. In fact, the street was so full of houses of worship it became known as Church Street.[13] The Presbyterians, like the Episcopalians, had a mission church and Sunday school nearby.

A blend of evangelism and competitiveness motivated the churches of Augusta to provide mission churches and Sunday schools for Harrisburg's workers. Denominations were concerned that the millworkers lacked churches and Sunday schools in Harrisburg and that if their particular denomination did not establish a mission, workers might commit to a different church. Edwin Weed of Good Shepherd explained that there was a lack of churches near the workers and that it was too far for them to walk to the "First Churches," which were predominantly in the center of town, or to the new churches up in Summerville, where his church stood. Yet there are hints that this preference for building new, separate "mission" churches for millworkers "was not entirely in the spirit of evangelism." Central Christian Church records indicate that "affluent church members" of First Christian Church felt that " 'lint heads' would be better served by churches closer to their own mill villages," implying that the mill hands would not be welcome in the city's respectable First Churches.[14]

One reason church elites were so keen to support missions was that churches had a stabilizing influence in a community and would thus create a more steady and dependable workforce. Certainly, mill owners in Augusta gave generously to church missions in the mill neighborhoods. The Methodist church, for example, received financial help from the Augusta Factory to establish Asbury Mission in the 1850s, and the mill eventually sold a plot of land to the Methodists to build Asbury Chapel. William Sibley, owner of the Sibley Mill, was a prominent member of the First Presbyterian Church of Augusta. "Seeing the needs of the factory operatives for the gospel," he determined to bring Presbyterianism to the millworkers of Harrisburg.[15] In 1880 he established and financed the building of a Presbyterian Sunday school and mission church on Broad Street opposite the mill, deeding the land to the Presbyterian church. While the church was being completed, services were held in the Sibley Mill office. One can imagine that the sermons preached in there would have emphasized the godliness of hard work, discipline, and obedience. The church, which was fully established in 1891, was appropriately named Sibley Presbyterian. The congregation, presumably, were left with few doubts about the connections between their everyday and religious lives.

William Sibley was only the most obvious example of the connections between influence in Augusta's churches and influence at the city's mills. Mill owners, managers, and investors were typically prominent members of city churches. H. H. Hickman was an elder at First Baptist Church and the treasurer of the local Hephzibah Baptist Association, as well as president of the Graniteville Mill in South Carolina. Emily Tubman, the richest woman in Augusta, was a leading philanthropist and a major investor in local industry, holding two hundred shares in the Sibley Mill. Julia Weed, wife of Edwin Weed, held fifty shares in the Sibley Mill, even after the Weeds moved away to Florida.[16]

Such connections certainly suggest that many of the civic leaders providing churches and ministers for the millworkers of Augusta had vested interests in maintaining social order and stability. Yet this does not mean that mill owners were without genuine religious motives. The Sibley family in Augusta, especially, donated money for schools and chapels throughout the city. William Sibley was a reformed alcoholic whose wife, Jane, the president of the state Women's Christian Temperance Union and one of Augusta's earliest Progressives, had aided him in "taking the matter to Christ" to cure his condition.[17] Jane Sibley involved herself in many of the city's charitable causes. She was especially devoted to Prohibition and was criticized in the 1890s for her outspokenness on political matters.

The wealthiest and probably most powerful woman in Augusta after the Civil War was Emily Tubman. When Tubman's husband died, in 1836, he freed the family's slaves in his will. But Georgia law prohibited such action, so Emily Tubman became an active member of the American Colonization Society, and her former slaves went on to settle the town of Mount Tubman in Liberia. Tubman used her wealth to fund the public high school for white girls in Augusta, which was named in her honor, and to establish a widows' home in the city. Her financial generosity and religious devotion greatly aided the church-building efforts of her own denomination, the Christian church.[18] She founded Central Christian in the Harrisburg mill neighborhood in 1883 with Charles Estes, the former mayor of the city, who had joined the denomination late in life, in 1880. Estes was the president of the J. P. King Mill, the city's second largest factory. Even after her death in 1885, Tubman's endowments paid for a minister at Central Christian.

Emily Tubman's donations gave her a measure of control of the institutions she funded that was unusual for a woman at this time. In 1883, while she was in Kentucky, where she spent most summers, she wrote to First Christian telling the church which sort of music to play while she was gone; after all, she funded the organist.[19] Such an example indicates the level of control she had even in a church attended by the city's elite. Tubman gave large amounts of her wealth away and used her investments in mills and other Augusta industries to aid churches, schools, and hospitals. But her actions, like her mission to send her slaves to Liberia, were within the limits of benign paternalism. In a context of industrial capitalism rather than racial slavery, her actions reinforced her power and influence as well as her class position.

It is significant that women played a significant role in religious philanthropy in Augusta. Indeed, LeeAnn Whites argues that the lead taken by women in so-called paternalistic activities in the city suggests that *maternalism* might be a better term to describe the relationship between millworkers and the social elite.[20] Whites adds that the focus by historians on men—both as mill employers and as workers—has obscured the roles played by women, both as upper-class philanthropists and as workers.

Certainly women like Emily Tubman and Jane Sibley were active in mission efforts, for they were the women who actually headed aid committees, raised funds, and went into the mill communities and churches. They established women's organizations in their own churches to coordinate these efforts and networked to pool resources. In Emily Tubman's and Julia Weed's cases, the money donated actually belonged to them. Yet Tubman's control within her church, particularly of charity and mission efforts, was unique. No women sat on the board of her, or any other, church. Most of the women leading charitable efforts were the wives, sisters, or daughters of mill owners or prominent churchmen. There is little evidence that their activities went against the dictates of their husbands and fathers. They too existed within the bounds of a religious and social paternalism that affected all classes of society.

Hamilton Hickman illustrates many of the connections between religious and worldly power. Hickman, the president of Graniteville Mills, was a prominent member of First Baptist Church of Augusta and the Hephzibah Baptist Association. The *Christian Index*, Georgia's white Southern Baptist newspaper, reported in 1892 that he had subscribed to the paper for a record forty-eight years. A profile of him in *Helping Words*, a newsletter produced by First Baptist's minister, described Hickman as a "sweet" old man and said that the women of the church, in particular, turned to him for advice. His apparently gentle manner was considered both a manly and a Christian quality. In a glowing eulogy in the Hephzibah Association's minutes for 1904, the association recognized his forty-two years as treasurer of their group. Hickman, who apparently grew up in poverty, had become a business success, managing several mills in Georgia and South Carolina. The minutes continued: "If every corporate President in the United States would follow [his] example in the manner of treating employees there would be no great strikes and capital and labor would dwell together in the greatest harmony. . . . His employees' welfare" was apparently a top concern, and the people who worked for him never "asked him for aid but what he administered to [their] wants," for his "purse was always open to worthy subjects. . . . He was economical but not miserly, liberal yet not extravagant," reported the minutes. As evidence of his popularity, a large number of millworkers—who saw him as a "faithful friend"—had attended his funeral.[21]

Although it would be wrong to doubt Hickman's generosity on a personal level and his popularity among some millworkers, statements he made about mill employees belie his "liberal" spirit. In 1877, when questioned about the low wages received by southern millworkers, Hickman announced that they could live "for half the expense of those at the North" although the cost of living in southern cities like Augusta was little cheaper. His generosity to common folk also did not spread to funding education. During a debate about whether to levy a tax for public high school education, Hickman conceded that he would pay "to teach any child, white or black, the rudiments of education." But he felt that teaching beyond that level was sometimes counterproductive, announcing that "there [were] some people that the more you educate them the less they amount to."[22] At his Graniteville Mill he ended the compulsory education that William Gregg had demanded for mill children before the Civil War.

Hickman's comments show the nature and limits of his paternalism. He advocated personal giving to those in what he considered "genuine" need; indeed, his eulogy indicates he saw this as his Christian duty. But as a group, he saw millworkers, indeed all workers, as occupying a particular place in Augusta's class system. Extra compensation for work, just like extra education, was unnecessary for those in this stratum. While he would hear petitions of needy workers as individuals, as man, woman, or child, he discouraged any dealings with workers as a united group. Hickman was the most vociferous opponent of the Knights of Labor during the 1886 strike and urged other mill owners to refuse to even meet with the union.

Hickman was certainly not a progressive in his Christian viewpoint and took a very different approach from Emily Tubman, for example. Yet there are similarities in their worldview. Both used charity in religious and individual ways to resolve being both Christians and industrialists. These actions assuaged any hint of guilty feelings about inequalities in society. The *Augusta Chronicle* in an 1878 editorial declared that "the charitable institutions of Augusta bespeak the philanthropy of her people. Humane and charitable institutions evidence the civilization, culture and practical religion of a people."[23] Charity was seen as proof of genuine religious feeling.

The focus of most churches in the South (and the North) in the late nineteenth century was on the personal behavior and salvation of church members. Sin was considered a personal depravity rather than a result of social conditions. *Helping Words*, the newsletter published by Lansing Burrows, the minister of First Baptist in Augusta, announced that humans "sin as individuals," and that "the idea and fact of personal accountability are impressed at every step in the Bible." In another article he urged those who felt they were too poorly dressed to attend church to come anyway, for finding religious "salvation" could lead to earthly wealth. In language of which H. H. Hickman, elder of the church and industrialist, would have heartily approved, he suggested that "the poor man who gets a new heart will not be long before he gets a new coat." Leading evangelists, particularly Dwight Moody, who preached a similar message, were very popular in the city. Although increasingly rarely in urban settings like Augusta, churches—particularly Baptists—still expelled members for personal sins such as dancing, drinking, and swearing.[24]

The Social Gospel movement challenged this purely individualistic form of religion. Advocating social reform as a goal of churches and, in more radical manifestations, suggesting that the evils of society could be solved on a collective as well as an individual level, the Social Gospel was slow to influence southern churches. As C. Vann Woodward notes, the South was as distinct and "solid" in its religion as in its politics. J. Wayne Flynt has shown, however, that the churches did make efforts to alleviate the sufferings and improve the quality of life of their congregations, even if they more rarely critiqued the political and social environment that led to such sufferings. As Keith Harper's book on white southern Baptists and the Social Gospel explains, even conservative churches contemplated social aid beyond simple charity for the destitute. Social control and the Social Gospel were not necessarily mutually exclusive. Many white religious leaders figured that workers who were well fed, well clothed, and educated in basic reading and domestic skills would be likely to make good workers and good Christians. In this respect Augusta's missionizing leaders were very similar to northern progressives, especially those connected with Social Gospel work. Just as social control and Social Gospel blended together in action, so too did progressivism give multivalent meaning to actions. In the 1860s Asbury Mission reported that two hundred "factory children" attended the mission's Sunday school, "which had a larger number of poor than any other . . . in the city." Part of the reason may have been that Asbury also provided free clothing during the winter. Between 1867 and 1872 Anne McKinnie Winter of First Presbyterian Church ran a sewing school for the children of the Augusta Factory workers at the Greene Street Presbyterian mission. Though a 1904 historian discusses the sewing school in rather condescending tones, suggesting the children "took their first uncertain stitches, while they learned lessons of gentleness and courage and noble behavior," the skills taught would have been useful to mill families.[25]

Some ministers seem to have been particularly energetic in providing for the poor. In November 1902 John Chipman of Christ Episcopal Church reported in his new parish newsletter that in October "one hundred poor were helped with either food, fuel, clothes, or medicine, about 250 visits made, about fifty dollars cash spent, about eighty garments given." Chipman's newsletter provides an illuminating insight into at least one minister's notions of his mission's duty. Christ Church's mission, he wrote, was to "to feed the hungry, clothe the naked, warm the cold, visit and relieve the sick."[26]

Reverend Chipman proved especially eager to fulfill his mission statement. In 1901 Christ Church opened a library that provided Harrisburg residents with one of their few opportunities to read and borrow books. In 1902 the library was followed by a pool and gym, which were open to all millworkers, as well as an evening school for working girls. The turn of the century saw an increasing interest on the part of the churches in the social welfare of the city's millworkers. In 1897 the Methodists established a industrial school in Augusta under the control of the Women's Home Missionary Society of the North Georgia Conference. After the 1916 floods the First Baptist Church found the Sibley Mill Settlement House, which taught skills to 747 children as well as delivering relief.[27]

It is significant that this type of activity increased in the early 1900s. Churches in Augusta and the South appear to have stepped up their social programs at the turn of the century, tapping into the developing movement of progressivism. At the end of the century, Ted Ownby argues, the South became increasingly open to national popular culture, rather than trying to stay out of the world.[28] Though the Civil War and the Lost Cause were not forgotten, southern lifestyles became increasingly similar to those in the North. Rather than shutting out the world as before, southern churches tried to make the world respect them. As Gregory Wills explains, the numbers of expulsions in Southern Baptist churches declined as the denomination moved its focus from the personal actions of church members and focused instead on establishing moral order in society in general. The struggle to pass Prohibition at local and eventually national levels was only the most obvious manifestation of these efforts.

The increase in settlement houses in southern cities like Augusta shows a similar preoccupation with reformist goals as well as reflecting the rise of industrialization, which affected the South later than the North. It is significant that the southern Methodist Women's Missionary Union split into domestic and foreign missions in 1897, as textile mills and other factories went up in Atlanta, Macon, Athens, and Columbus as well as Augusta.[29]

Certainly, by the end of the century, the city's First Churches, especially their women's organizations, stepped up their efforts in Harrisburg. Rather than using the mission churches in the neighborhood as a conduit for support and influence, the First Churches became directly involved in settlement houses, Sunday schools, and charitable relief. One reason for this was that some mission churches were relatively independent and started their own missionary and charitable projects. Even a church as small as Christ Church had its own mission Sunday school in the late 1890s, as did Central Christian.

In other cases, the reason First Churches took new initiatives in social work was just the opposite. Some mission churches had such difficulty surviving that they had little time for new missionary efforts. For example, the white Baptist efforts after the 1916 flood came from First Baptist rather than the local Berean Baptist. Berean had experienced problems at the turn of the century regarding finances and personnel and had just reestablished itself in 1908 as Crawford Avenue Baptist Church. Finances, in fact, were one of the many problems besetting the churches in mill neighborhoods. Most working-class churches were established initially as missions of wealthy First Churches. Funds for the new mission churches—including all or part of the ministers' salary—came from the sponsoring church. Mission churches, however, were expected to become self-supporting and gain full church status eventually. Some churches changed status a number of times. In 1890 Asbury Church was an independent church with its own mission, known as Wesley Chapel, but by 1900 the minister was wondering if the church would have to return to mission status. The Church of the Atonement, for example, had become a full church by 1908 but returned to mission status by the 1950s.[30]

The financial difficulties of the churches in the old mill area around the Augusta Factory were partly the result of the shift of industrial concentration to the Harrisburg area, but even churches in Harrisburg found it difficult to survive. Many churches could not afford a permanent minister and often shared pastors with another church, sometimes even a different denomination. Christ Episcopal Church, for example, relied on ministers from Good Shepherd and Saint Paul's to lead services between 1883 and 1893, as the church could not afford its own minister in residence. Sibley Presbyterian was without a minister at the turn of the century, and services were conducted by pastors from Greene Street Baptist Church. This fluid interdenominationalism between different Protestant groups suggests that in hard economic times it was more important for churches to get their message to the people than worry about who exactly was preaching.[31] Church maintenance was also a constant problem. The parish accounts of 1896 for Christ Episcopal show that the church still owed the outgoing pastor, Rector Kimball, for the previous year's electric light bill.

The economic situation of the mills could drastically affect church finances.

A historian of Saint Luke's stressed that the church was "largely composed of persons . . . whose business is dependent on the mills." In 1889, in a report to the Baptist City Mission Board, Berean Baptist Church announced a vacant pulpit. The church could not afford to pay a minister, because flooding had temporarily closed mills. The heart of the problem was the poverty of the missions' congregations. Ministers despaired about the problems of maintaining a church in an area where few people were financially secure. In 1894 W. L. Kilpatrick noted that Berean Baptist "had labored under the difficulties of its membership being largely drawn from a population not permanently located in homes of their own."[32]

But sometimes the problem was not that millworkers did not give enough money when they came to church, but rather that they did not come to church at all. Workers may have been embarrassed by their poverty and lack of suitable clothing to wear to church. In March 1870 Asbury Mission reported a decline in Sunday school attendance. The minister suggested that one reason was "want of suitable outfits . . . to make a decent appearance in school." The church was "too poor" at the time to remedy the lack of clothing. When facing empty churches during the winter, ministers blamed the weather and resulting illnesses. In the first quarter of 1879 Pastor J. B. Bryan of Asbury Methodist suggested that "only a small proportion of the large membership has attended church because of the "cold and disagreeable weather." In the early record books of Christ Church, the minister would carefully calculate the Sunday attendance, putting low numbers down to the "bad weather" or "rain."[33]

Not surprisingly, empty churches and emptier collection plates frustrated many ministers. The mission churches had a high turnover of leadership in the late nineteenth century. Berean Church, for example, had five ministers in its first decade of existence. Another problem may have been the class differences between ministers and their congregations. Episcopalian and Methodist ministers, in particular, were often college-educated and may have felt a social and cultural distance between themselves and their often barely literate flock. The quarterly reports of one Asbury Methodist Church minister hint at this cultural gulf. R. B. England, a new minister, reported in 1899 that he had done "no special work as yet, down among the children. I recognize them and try to get close to them." In the supplement to the year's record, he was still having problems: "It seems a difficult matter to get our young people interested in this work." He worried "that the matter of family worship [was] much neglected" but thought that "most of [the] people are reasonably moral."[34]

Ministers worried about communicating with their flocks, especially if the congregation was younger and from a different social class.

If poor attendance and shaky finances were often discouraging, ministers also saw much evidence of religious enthusiasm among the millworkers, showing that religion and church were an important part of some workers' lives. W. L. Kilpatrick wrote in 1894 that although millworkers did "not represent the monied wealth of the city," they did "very largely represent the piety and the devotion to the Master's cause." Revivals proved particularly important in working-class religious life. Revivals were usually a series of nightly prayer meetings and services spread over a week or so. Their goal was to increase religious enthusiasm and prompt conversion. "A genuine and wide sweeping awakening" affected the workers at Augusta Factory in 1856, encouraging the Methodists to develop Asbury mission. The Reverend J. S. Meynardie wrote in 1886 that after a "gracious revival" the "spiritual condition of the church was good" and baptisms had increased.[35]

Some revivals seemed to happen spontaneously and take on their own momentum. A new minister might engender new enthusiasm and inspire conversions. But most revivals were planned events. Churches would set aside a week in the year as revival time. A traveling evangelist or a minister from another church—sometimes from a different denomination—might lead the revival services. In fact, revivals were a time when millworkers would attend a church regardless of their own denomination. People with no church affiliation were more likely to attend services during a revival. Revivals were exciting events, and the preaching was particularly good. With large crowds from different churches all over the mill neighborhood, people could feel more anonymous as they attended the services. Other revivals took place on the streets of Harrisburg. One Sunday in April 1895, the Reverend Beckman of the Christian church held an "open-air meeting near the King mill." The subject, illustrated with Bible charts, was "the Kingdom of Heaven." The *Daily Tribune*, a working-class newspaper that carried a notice of the event, announced that "everybody was cordially invited."[36] These open-air meetings emphasized how revivals transcended the bounds of church and denomination. Though ministers led the proceedings, services in the street were a working-class community experience.

Another common type of revival, especially among Methodists, was the camp meeting. Usually in a rural location, camps were sites where visitors could set up tents or sleep in cabins. These meetings could last for several weeks or even longer and were an important event on many southerners' social and religious calendars. Fitting in with the cycle of rural life, the meetings usually took place between planting seasons and provided both a vacation and a spiritual experience. Richmond County's main campground was just outside the city. Some millworkers probably attended and met rural relatives there, but it was harder for city workers to take protracted breaks from work if the mills were running. But millworkers often moved to the country during planting and harvest. These country revivals were a special time for them to share their faith with their rural kinfolk.

Pastor Bryan's report on Asbury Mission in 1879 indicates, however, that revival enthusiasm could be short-lived. In the first quarter of the year it was his "decided conviction that a revival of religion [was] greatly needed," and he saw "manifest tokens" of revivalism by the spring. By the third quarter a revival had affected the church, attracting new members, encouraging old members, and swelling church membership. Yet by the end of the year many of these new members had ceased to attend services.[37]

Millworkers were particularly receptive to revivalists and ministers who appeared to identify with working-class people. W. L. Kilpatrick of Hephzibah Baptist Association was impressed with the missionizing efforts of Thomas Walker of Second Baptist (Kollock Street) whose "sphere of work [was] so greatly directed to the citizens of Augusta residing under the shadows of the Augusta mill." Part of Walker's success in this "difficult field" was attributed to his previous experience at Graniteville and Vaucluse Mills in South Carolina and also because he was a self-educated man who presumably came from the same social class as most millworkers. Reverend Chipman at Christ Church, who was responsible for much of the improvements and programs there, had also worked in the mills before becoming a minister, although as a trained engineer his income was relatively high.[38]

Church historians suggest that millworkers also preferred a more informal atmosphere. In a 1920s history Isabella Jordan discussed the mission work of Fred Lockhart at Berean. Lockhart was described as the Baptists' "first vital contact with the industrial population of the city." Among his "innovations" were "a Floating Sunday school on a canal barge . . . and his 'Whistling Choir.'" The choir and school boat may not have been equally appealing to the respectable congregation of First Baptist.[39]

Sunday school appears to have been particularly important to millworkers. Even when few attended church services, Sunday schools thrived. In 1900 Christ Church had 57 communicants but 190 Sunday school pupils. Even

Christ Church had its own mission Sunday school, Saint Andrew's, with an additional 22 pupils. In 1891 Saint Luke's Methodist Church had a Sunday school enrollment of 531, of whom over 220 attended on average.[40] Of course, Sunday schools enrolled many children who were as yet ineligible for full church membership. Yet many adults attended Sunday school rather than church services. Church membership alone cannot be a gauge of religious interest. Millworkers may have felt that they were not ready for full church membership but that they were interested in religious education for themselves and their children.

Many workers did not formally join milltown churches because they still retained membership in country churches.[41] While such evidence is difficult to find, there is some indication that Augusta millworkers, who had often recently moved from the countryside, remained connected to country churches. Many may have initially felt that they would return to their rural homes and hence did not need to formally join a city church.

The records of the Augusta Factory's burial union, a group into which members paid a small monthly fee that then paid one's burial expenses, are suggestive. Even at the turn of the century, a period when some millworkers would have considered themselves permanent Augusta residents, records show that many millworkers returned to family graveyards near country churches at their death. Some returned to the more rural Graniteville Mill area and others to the Richmond Factory area outside Augusta. Millworker Georgia Weeks, who died at age twenty-eight of consumption, was "buried in the country near Richmond Factory."[42]

The burial unions are themselves an indicator of people's belief about the afterlife. By 1896 the Augusta, Enterprise, Sibley and J. P. King Mills all had burial unions. These appear to have been successful and filled an important role at a time when burials were expensive. Members well knew the burden burial expenses could place upon their families. Yet these associations also suggest that millworkers were concerned about their afterlife and wanted a respectable funeral and burial. Most of the members of the Augusta Factory burial union in the late 1890s—which had many members who worked outside the mill—appear to have been connected in some way to the mission churches around the factory. Most funerals documented in the union's records took place at Kollock Street Baptist, with a lesser number held at Asbury Methodist, the Church of the Atonement, and even the Catholic Sacred Heart. Some members appear to have been connected to a number of churches. Mrs.

S. P. Cooper, who died in September 1898, was a member of Berean Baptist Church in Harrisburg, and her funeral was at Kollock Street Baptist. But she also attended Saint Luke's Methodist.[43]

Interestingly, some members of the union had no funeral service listed or had services in their homes. These members may have belonged to no church, and yet their membership suggests that they wanted a proper burial. Religion was important to many millworkers who never attended churches or went to Sunday school. Millworkers, therefore, did have a choice in their religious lives. They could decide which church to attend, which ministers to listen to, or whether to go to church at all. Dissatisfied churchgoers could change congregations or just decide to stay at home. Workers might go to church as release from their ordinary lives, to learn about the Bible in Sunday school, through a sense of duty, or out of genuine piety. They may have been attracted by food parcels, gymnasiums, and an opportunity to learn to read, as well as sermons and prayers. Just as many upper-class worshipers did not want "lintheads" at their services, many millworkers felt more comfortable in a mill community church than in the First Churches downtown. Mill churches engendered a sense of community.

Prayer meetings were another place where millworkers could feel comfortable expressing their Christianity with fellow workers. In 1895 the *Daily Tribune* reported a "cottage prayer meeting" at the home of Henry Neese for the following Saturday night. The meeting would be led by a B. Durham. Neese lived on Poor Row, near the Sibley Mill, and Durham was listed as a mill operative in the city directory. The "invitation" to pray "was extended to all Christians and sinners." The meeting was clearly interdenominational. The prayers were led by a lay millworker rather than a minister. Another prayer gathering a few days later was described as "devoid of a formality likely to crush the spirit of brotherly love."[44] This description perhaps juxtaposed these meetings with formal church services. In small meetings in their homes, led by friends from their own class, religious millworkers could express "brotherly love" with more openness. These groups focused around prayer but may have become involved in other religious activities. In March the "mission Band of little Christian workers" met at the home of M. B. Arthur, a millworker, although there was no description of what they did. These meetings in the homes of ordinary working people provided an alternative network to formal church sessions. Although many of those participating probably belonged to churches in Harrisburg, others may have had no affiliation.

The notices for these meetings were printed in the *Daily Tribune*, a strongly

political newspaper that worked to connect working-class religious independence with political activism. But the cottage meetings in small mill houses
throughout Harrisburg were not necessarily political. Instead, they expressed
a Christianity that existed apart from the mission churches and settlement
houses that connected Augusta's millworkers to the congregations of the city's
First Churches. In a critique of Robert Ingersoll, the infamous atheist who
was speaking in Augusta, the *Tribune*'s editor "beg[ged] the boys of the West
End not to go." Instead, they were urged to take their Bibles and "read the
fifth chapter of James" to "hear something worthy of . . . attention."[45] After his
talk, which was apparently poorly attended, the newspaper refused to interview him, thinking "he could not say anything worth repeating to a Christian
community." The editor, then, saw Harrisburg (which he called the West End)
as a Christian "community." His comments suggest that it was a community
not necessarily in opposition to, but certainly distinct from, other Christians
in the city.

If churches in mill neighborhoods were not merely sources of social control for mill owners and city fathers, neither were they usually a source of
radical opposition to the status quo. Newby states that mill folk "did not understand religion to be an instrument of reform or revolution."[46] Nevertheless, there is evidence that both ministers and millworkers in Augusta were
frustrated by the contradictions between the messages preached in church
and working-class reality.

The Reverend Chipman of Christ Church, a particularly active minister
bringing a new energy to his mission church in Harrisburg, faced many of the
frustrations common to mission ministers. Parish records show that he was
constantly worried about low turnout at church and lack of money to pay bills
and expand church activism. The first edition of his parish newsletter hints
that his frustrations at times extended to a dissatisfaction with the system itself. He wrote, "Work that is done in the name of Jesus is holy. Why should
not the altruistic idea make further conquests? We have churches, on which
enormous sums are spent, that are beautiful manifestations of the spirit of love
towards God and towards one another. Why not have factories and workshops built under the same plan?"[47]

That Chipman connected work to holiness is clear from the name of his
newsletter, *Work*, and his parish community group, called the Willing Workers. But Chipman's experience in the mill community led him to a radical
critique of the mills. "If a cotton factory," he suggested, "were built as a testimony of love to God and man, and run as God's factory by trustees for Him,

would that not make holy all the work done in good heart, within the factory?"[48] Such a mill would be organized very differently from the mills running in Augusta at that time.

> If a mill were owned by wise trustees, for God's glory, the work would be run so as to make men holy, and women and children sacred. The profits, whatever are made after paying fair wages to all, and after providing pleasant surroundings and healthy work for those employed, would be used, to give God glory in an honest worship, and to obey Him in giving loving help to men, and to redeem the world, acre by acre, to obedience to Him.[49]

Chipman's call for safe working conditions was not unusual by the turn of the century. Many progressives, in and outside the churches, were concerned about working conditions. Others, too, argued, as Chipman did, that women and children should be sacred and not work long hours in factories from a young age. Chipman's suggestion that men should be paid fair wages so that their families did not have to work was also common, particularly in labor circles, where the notion of the family wage was a key platform. More unusual, however, was Chipman's suggestion that profits should be used "to give God glory," although he did not elaborate on what this entailed.

Chipman appears to have unusual attitudes compared to most ministers. There is little evidence to suggest how his newsletter and sermons were received. He remained at Christ Church for eight years (1897–1905), which was longer than most rectors stayed, and he worked hard to improve the material and spiritual lives of Harrisburg people. There is no evidence, however, linking him to political or radical activities.

J. S. Meynardie of Berean Baptist church, however, did become involved in working-class activism and created a furor in Baptist circles about the proper role of the clergy in society. Meynardie, the son of a Methodist minister from South Carolina, became pastor of Berean in 1885. The three years he served there saw renewed energy in the church and an increase in revivalism and membership. The summer of 1886 was a particularly intense period of revival energy. Church histories do not mention, however, that Meynardie had been hounded out of South Carolina because of his efforts there to organize millworkers. Meynardie soon began organizing in Augusta, and by the beginning of 1886 had established Local 5030 of the Knights of Labor, a national labor organization. Meynardie headed the union as master workman. The presence of the Knights of Labor in the textile mills ignited the already tense relations between labor and management, and in June 1886 the workers at Algernon Mill went on strike. Though the Algernon workers did not strike as a formal action of the Knights of Labor and soon returned to work, Augusta's textile mills became a hotbed of walkouts and disputes. In July workers struck at the Sibley Mill and the Augusta Factory, the biggest mills in the city. The action soon spread, in the form of a management lockout, to Augusta's seven other textile mills and left production at a standstill for more than three months in the summer of 1886.[50]

The workers wanted recent pay cuts rescinded, and some complained of bad working conditions and unpopular and unfair overseers. The strike was by the rank and file—the Knights of Labor leadership being wary of walkouts—and was supported by many Augusta storeowners, who extended credit to the striking families. Nevertheless, the power of the newly formed Southern Manufacturers Association, which organized nonunion labor, particularly from South Carolina, and the failure of the national Knights of Labor initially to assist the strikers either financially or emotionally broke the strike. Meynardie had what appears to have been a nervous breakdown and never fully recovered from the strike. He was replaced as master workman and left Berean two years later.[51]

There are excellent accounts of the Augusta strike by the historians Melton McLaurin and Merl E. Reed. Yet these accounts, though acknowledging that Meynardie was a minister, give little indication that this is significant. In particular, neither study attempts to link the strike with the revivals at Berean in that same year. One link between the strike and the church is the delegations that Berean sent to the local Hephzibah Baptist Association meetings. In October 1885 the Hephzibah Baptist Association met in Waynesboro, Georgia. The Berean Church sent a full contingent to the meeting, including Meynardie and his brother C. W. Meynardie, listed as the Berean Sunday school superintendent. The three other representatives, E. W. Collier, Green B. Lively and W. R. Cox, were all listed in the 1886 Augusta city directory as weavers at the Algernon Mill, where the early strike began. In 1886 Berean sent seven representatives to the Hephzibah Baptist Association meeting. They included three Algernon millworkers, two Sibley Mill hands, and a worker from the Augusta Factory. Meynardie was away in Richmond, Virginia, at the Knights' annual general assembly and could not attend the association meeting. The men sent by their church to the local meetings were generally leaders in the church. Although no church minutes from Berean have survived to tell how that church decided on sending these messengers, usually the church as a whole proposed and voted for representatives, normally with the approval of the minister. These Algernon weavers, then, probably were trusted leaders of their church community whose opinions were valued. These same men would probably have been involved in the weavers' strike and may have been leaders on the factory floor. Such a coincidence suggests that religious and political authority intertwined.[52]

Religion and politics also intertwined at the revival services held at Berean in July of 1886. In his report to the Baptist City Mission Board Meynardie mentioned that Berean church was in the midst of a revival. He reported that "after a gracious revival, the spiritual condition of the church is good. During the four weeks and a few days, nothing marred the dignity or solemnity of the meeting. Baptized 22, yet to baptize 6 or 8, by letter 5, under watch care 6, Sunday meetings, 2 prayer services a week, sometimes as many as 4 funerals a day." Although "the financial condition of the church [was] not good," Meynardie could not find "sitting room" for his evening congregations.[53]

Meynardie emphasized to the City Mission Board, which reported back to First Baptist Church, that the revival was solemn and dignified. He probably wanted to assure the city's Baptist leaders that his meetings were spiritual rather than political, as his position as master workman appears to have been commonly known. Yet revivals created a sense of spiritual excitement.[54] Worshipers would meet many times a week, as Meynardie's report indicates, and the Berean revival appears to have gone on for several weeks. While some would renew their faith, others would be converted for the first time. Many would go to a revival at a church they did not usually attend, and many without a church would come to these special events. Methodists, Christian church members, and Episcopalians would attend Baptist revivals, especially if the church was near their homes.

The Berean revival, then, was a time for millworkers throughout Harrisburg and other parts of town to come together on a social as well as a spiritual basis. As well as praying and singing together, the workers probably discussed the events at the mill, either in church or on the way home. The revival came early in the summer, when the Algernon walkout had already proven effective and workers were optimistic about their efforts to affect labor relations in the city. The many walkouts, strikes, and other actions that spun through the city's mills in July suggest a state of excitement akin to revival emotion. Indeed, the *Atlanta Constitution* reported that Augusta's millworkers were in a "state of feverish excitement" as walkouts spread from one factory to another.[55] Religious and political enthusiasm appear to have gone hand in hand.

Although evidence is scanty, there is enough to suggest that Meynardie's tenure as preacher at Berean is important to an understanding of the 1886 strike. Both the successes and the failures of the strike may be linked to the church. It may have been easier for Meynardie to organize a Knights of Labor local in such a short period because the church gave him a organizational base and an arena to disseminate his ideas. As a minister he was already in a leadership position, and people would find it more natural to look up to him. The church may also have helped the strikers psychologically and financially. Yet at the same time the connections with Berean may also have proved problematic. As minister, Meynardie had other responsibilities, and it certainly appears that he took too much upon himself. The strike may also have been identified with the members of just one church, making non-Baptists less likely to become involved. Meynardie reported to the *New York World* in the midst of the strike that he was "boycotted by the churches outside [his] own." There is certainly enough evidence to indicate that labor historians must pay attention to religion and churches when they discuss working-class activism.[56]

Although church histories say little about Meynardie's activities in the Knights of Labor, it appears that his behavior was discussed in Baptist circles in the city and the state. In 1894 an article appeared in the *Wool-Hat*—Richmond County's Populist newspaper—that reexamined the events of 1886. Silas Reed Jr. wrote a letter to the newspaper in response to an article in the *Christian Index*, Georgia's dominant and conservative Southern Baptist newspaper, arguing that Berean Church was ruined by politics.

Reed recalled how Meynardie was invited by Baptists in Augusta to the pastorate at the Berean Church. "Everything went well with the church for a while and Mr. Meynardie was loved by his own congregation and the denomination generally." Yet when Meynardie was "chosen" to lead the Knights of Labor "on account of his popularity with the working people," the minister who had invited him to Berean declared Meynardie "a bad man." In Reed's account the Baptist establishment's persecution of Meynardie after the defeat of the strike led him to an "untimely grave," "all because he had 'gone into politics.'"[57] Reed's argument was that it was rather the politics of the Baptist establishment that was so ruinous to Berean Church. Reed had personal reasons for making such statements. He and a fellow working-class politician had supposedly been dismissed from the church because of their political activities.

The *Wool-Hat* is important because it offers an unusual glimpse at more popular views of religion and, in particular, Augusta's churches and their relationships to the city's working class. The newspaper was begun by William Henning in 1892 as a local voice of the Populist Party. He saw his newspaper as providing an alternative to the prestigious *Augusta Chronicle*, a fiercely Democratic broadsheet.[58] The *Wool-Hat*, which was initially published in Gracewood, a rural Augusta suburb but moved to Augusta in 1895, certainly did not represent the views of most working people in Augusta or even all millworkers. The paper does, however, show some of the interweaving of political and religious debates in the city.

The language of the newspaper was deeply religious and evangelical. It reported the news of country churches and the city mission churches of which it approved. Occasionally even the Roman Catholic churches in town received a good word. Temperance, moral conduct, and prayer were commonplace issues in the newspaper. Prayer meetings and political meetings were mentioned side by side, as if attending a Baptist revival in a city mission church were much the same cultural activity as listening to a Populist lecture on the evils of the money system. For the working-class Populists in Augusta, politics and religion were intertwined.

Generally, however, the *Wool-Hat* was very critical of established churches in Augusta, accusing them of supporting elite values and Democratic politics. Saint Luke's, the Methodist mission in Harrisburg, came under particular attack. In an article in November 1892, the *Wool-Hat* responded to an article in the *Augusta Chronicle* entitled "To Starve Him Out" in which the Reverend Timmons of Saint Luke's complained the church did not receive enough income to support him. Referring to the strike of 1886 and subsequent layoffs, the *Wool-Hat* suggested that "the poor members of his flock . . . had very little to pay" because they, "true to their convictions, had dared to use their rights as honest christians and for that reason had been discharged by bosses more heartless than the taskmasters of Egypt."[59] The newspaper equated activist workers with Christians and mill owners became the Egyptian masters who had enslaved the Israelites.

Timmons came under personal attack in the piece. "By posing as a martyr in Shylock's cause," the Methodist minister was promised "strong probability of easy access to Shylock's coffer." Shylock obviously represented Augusta's money interests and the Democratic Party. That the attack on Timmons was of a political nature is evident too in the claim that the minister, while preaching abstinence from alcohol, "joins hands with those who put 'the bottle to the mouth.'" Populists enjoyed equating whiskey and the Democratic Party. Populists generally favored temperance and antiliquor laws, but the Democrats, including Patrick Walsh and his *Augusta Chronicle*, supported the rights of liquor dealers. Through his affiliation with the Democratic Party, Timmons was associated in the minds of the Populists with alcohol and all its un-Christian evils. The anti-Semitic references in this article—Timmons as a pawn of Shylock—emphasized that the *Wool-Hat* did not consider the minister a true Christian. The article ended with a warning to Timmons that perhaps "the christians are forced to the necessity of separating themselves from such a worldly organization."[60]

The *Wool-Hat* also emphasized that the Christians were those who suffered from the injustices of class oppression. The *Augusta Chronicle* printed an article entitled "Empty Pews" about a lack of church attendance and the tendency for poorer people to give more than they could afford. Rather than simply agreeing with this sentiment, the *Wool-Hat* used this as evidence that the whole economic system was flawed, because people could not afford to give freely at church. In a similar vein, the newspaper criticized the new emphasis by Augusta churches on foreign missions when there were so many in need at home. "Forty thousand" missionaries were needed "right here in the Tenth District of Georgia."[61]

But the *Wool-Hat* did have some good things to say about some of the Augusta churches. On March 11, 1893, the newspaper began a series entitled "Crawford Avenue News," which reported on the Harrisburg churches. Prominent in the news was a "protracted meeting" at the Berean Church led by the minister of Second Christian Church. The "spirit" at these "well attended" meetings where "much good is done" was contrasted with the ineffectiveness of churches that had "Democratic pastors." Again, the Populists emphasized that "whiskey and Christianity will not mix."[62]

Certainly, the political agenda of the *Wool-Hat* makes it difficult to use as a source for understanding the religious feelings of ordinary workers. The newspaper does demonstrate, though, that the language and centrality of religion and the churches was evident in working-class politics in the city. To the Populists who wrote for the newspaper and perhaps attended one of the Harrisburg mission churches, religion and politics were inextricably intertwined. A minister who preached a message that supported the unholy Democratic Party could not be truly Christian.

Although most Augusta workers were not so politically active and did not consider the churches as political in any way, religion and the church were part of their everyday experiences. It is too simple to say that churches were either an instrument of social control on the part of employers and city elites or an arena for working-class expression and consciousness. In the early twentieth century, the rise of grassroots Holiness and Pentecostal churches would frighten city elites. These churches appeared to challenge social norms and question worldly authority. But for most of the late nineteenth century, this was not the case. Returning to Christ Episcopal, the church that moved between two different worlds in Augusta, leafy Summerville, and industrial Harrisburg, one wonders to which world exactly the church did belong. The answer is that it belonged to both worlds. Religion provided both a bridge in which the sewing societies and mission boards of the city could interact with the working class, and a symbol and language through which workers could express their own separate identity.

Notes

1. See the file on Christ Episcopal Church in "Histories of Augusta's Churches," Richmond County Historical Society, Special Collections Room, Reese Library, Augusta State University, Augusta, Ga.; I am also grateful to Claude Hill, historian of Christ Church, for further information on the church. *Augusta Chronicle*, July 11, 1882, microfilm, Augusta State University, Augusta, Ga.

2. Ayers, *Promise of the New South*, 160; Newby, *Plain Folk*, 390.

3. This study forms part of my dissertation, which investigates the religious lives of all working-class Augustans. Forty percent of the city's population was African American. African Americans were predominantly working class, employed in service and manual labor jobs. Working-class immigrant and ethnic groups were also important in the city after the Civil War. Irish American Catholics, for example, worked in the city's railroad yards and building trades; Augusta's small but prominent Chinese population ran grocery stores and laundries. All these groups had important religious traditions in which class, ethnicity, and race interacted. See Julia M. Walsh, "Horny-Handed Sons of Toil."

4. Pope, *Millhands and Preachers*, esp. chap. 2. Other early studies that came to similar conclusions include Holland Thompson, *From the Cotton Field*; and Harriet Herring, *Welfare Work*.

5. Newby, *Plain Folk*; Hall et al., *Like a Family*; Tullos, *Habits of Industry*; and Flamming, *Creating the Modern South*. See also Carlton, *Mill and Town*.

6. The key for textile development in these early years was proximity to water for power and transport of cotton. Several mills in the rural hinterland around the city started even earlier than the Augusta factory. The Richmond textile factory began on Spirit Creek, ten miles from Augusta, in 1834, and about the same time the Belleville Factory started to produce a mixed wool and cotton cloth known as "Georgia plains," which was used by many planters to clothe slaves. See E. Cashin, *Story of Augusta*, 87.

Mills also developed early on across the Savannah River in South Carolina. William Gregg, usually considered the father of antebellum southern textiles, developed the Vaucluse Factory in Aiken, South Carolina, in 1837 and opened the Graniteville complex in 1848. From the very start the connection between these South Carolina mills and the Augusta factories was strong. Shareholders invested in both state's mills, and managers and workers moved between the two groups of factories. For an overview of early mill development, see DeTreville, "The Little New South." Whites, *Civil War as Crisis*, 237 n. 5. In the more rural Graniteville mill environment, William Gregg enticed families in the 1840s by offering plots of land for men to work while their families labored in the mill. For a study of antebellum New England textiles, see Dublin, *Women at Work*.

7. Burton, *In My Father's House*, 52–57. Many families balked under Gregg's strict rules. Burton estimates that the persistence rate for heads of households in Graniteville was lower than average for both blacks and whites from 1850 through 1880.

8. Malone, *Episcopal Church in Georgia*, 84; "A Chronicle of Christian Stewardship: Sesquicentennial of St. John's Methodist Church, 1798–1948," n.d., and Kilpatrick, *Hephzibah Baptist Association Centennial*, 227, Special Collections Room, Reese Library, Augusta State University.

9. For a telling introduction to the notion of whiteness, see Roediger, *Wages of Whiteness*. For studies that analyze millworkers in terms of their racial identity, see Flamming, *Creating the Modern South*, and Newby, *Plain Folk*, esp. chap. 16.

10. German, "Queen City," 1–34. For an explanation of the long-term economic factors affecting small southern farmers, see G. Wright, *Political Economy*, chap. 6. The figures for the mill workforce are from Whites, "Southern Ladies and Millhands," 191. Her estimates are based on the interviews of Augusta mill presidents carried out in 1883 by the U.S. Senate Committee on Education and Labor. See U.S. Senate, Committee on Education and Labor, *Report upon Relations*, 4:687, 699. Whites's figures parallel those given by Newby in *Plain Folk*, 122–23. Newby estimates that in 1880 in Georgia and the Carolinas, men over sixteen constituted only 28.6 percent of the mill workforce. By 1890 they made up 42.5 percent and by 1900, 53.3 percent of the workforce. Whites estimates that African Americans made up only about 4 percent of the mill workforce before 1900; "Southern Ladies and Millhands," 228. E. Cashin, *Story of Augusta*, 201.

11. *Augusta Chronicle*, July 11, 1882.

12. Weed was a minister of considerable personal wealth and married one of Augusta's richest young heiresses. Such personal fortune allowed him to be particularly generous in his missionary efforts. See interview with Allan Clarkson, Augusta, Ga., February 25, 1996, in possession of the author. Claude Hill of Christ Episcopal Church suggests that distrust of emotionalism may have been one of the reasons behind the Christ Church Mission.

13. The Methodists had started a mission church to the "suburban population" of

Harrisburg earlier in 1868, but the mission closed in 1870. In 1874 the conference appointed a new city mission minister, and Saint Luke's church was established a year later. See *Minutes of the North Georgia Conference, Methodist Episcopal Church, South, 1867–1875*, microfilm, Georgiana Project, Pitts Theological Library, Emory University, Atlanta. Tom Hunter, "The Harrisburg Story," *Augusta Magazine* 2, 3 (1984): 26. Most of these churches continue today, although Central Christian and Crawford Avenue Baptist have built larger meeting places next to the original churches. Only the Presbyterian church has moved; its old meeting place is now Free Will Baptist Church.

14. "Christ Episcopal Church"; John Whitaker, "Central Christian Church, 1882–1982: A Brief History," (Augusta, n.p., 1982), Special Collections Room, Reese Library, Augusta State University. Current parishioners suggest that a similar divide between First Christian and Central Christian members continued into the 1930s and 1940s. Interviews with Mary O'Tyson, Sonny Switzer, and Tony Switzer, February 29, 1996, and Wheldon Hair, March 7, 1996, in possession of the author.

15. "Through the Years at Asbury United Methodist Church," 3, pamphlet, Augusta Genealogical Society Library, Augusta, Ga.; Quotation from Federal Writers Project, Works Progress Administration, "Georgia Historical Records Survey, Church Records Inventory 1936–41: Inventory of Presbyterian Church Records in Georgia," microfilm, Georgia Department of Archives and History, Atlanta.

16. Information on shareholders from Sibley Mill Dividend Book, 1887–1900, Special Collections, Woodruff Library, Emory University. Richard German estimates that investment in the mill before it opened totaled about Seven hundred thousand dollars. Each share cost one hundred dollars, suggesting that Emily Tubman's investment, for example, totaled twenty thousand dollars, a small but significant amount of the total investment. See German, "Queen City," 25.

17. Quoted in Whites, "Southern Ladies and Millhands," 291.

18. Biographical information on Tubman from loose folder at Disciples of Christ Historical Society Archives, Nashville, Tenn. Tubman gave varying amounts to different causes, spending more on Christian church projects. For example, while she gave five hundred dollars for the widows' home, she spent over thirty thousand dollars on the foundation of Central Christian. See Whites, "Southern Ladies and Millhands," 127. First Christian Church, *Minutes*, February 4, 1884, microfilm, Disciples of Christ Historical Society Archives.

19. First Christian Church, *Minutes*, March 5, 1883, Disciples of Christ Historical Archives.

20. LeeAnn Whites, "Paternalism and Protest in Augusta's Cotton Mills: What's Gender Got to Do with It?" (paper presented at the "Race, Religion and Gender in Augusta" Conference, Augusta, Ga., March 1, 1996). Whites's title echoes that of Melton McLaurin's book on southern textile workers and employers, a study which Whites critiques for its concentration on males alone as both paternalists and protesters. See McLaurin, *Paternalism and Protest*.

21. *Christian Index*, March 24, 1892, 9, microfilm, Special Collections, Georgia Baptist Historical Depository, Mercer University, Macon, Ga.; *Helping Words*, December 15, 1889, microfilm, Georgia Department of Archives and History; Minutes, Hephzibah Baptist Association Annual Meeting, 1904, 27–28, microfilm, Reese Library, Augusta State University.

22. Quoted in Whites, "Southern Ladies and Millhands," 54, 99.

23. Ibid., 146.

24. Newby, *Plain Folk*, 394; *Helping Words*, September 15, 1888, 2, Georgia Department of Archives and History. The most detailed study of Baptist discipline is Wills, *Democratic Religion*. Wills's analysis of church discipline contends that this self-regulating aspect was one of the central defining features of southern Baptists, both black and white, till late in the century.

25. Woodward, *Origins of the New South*, 448; Flynt, "Southern Protestantism"; Harper, *Quality of Mercy*, 11–14; "Through the Years at Asbury," 3; Wadley, *One Hundred Years*, 44.

26. John Chipman, *Work*, November 1, 1902; Parish Register, Christ Church, Augusta, Ga., 1887–1904, in Episcopal Diocese of Georgia, Miscellaneous Records, microfilm, Georgia Department of Archives and History. This appears to be the only extant copy of *Work*.

27. Christ Episcopal Church, in "Histories of Augusta's Churches"; Jordan, *Century of Service*, 59.

28. Flynt, "Southern Protestantism," 136; Ownby, *Subduing Satan*, 207; Wills, *Democratic Religion*, 133.

29. Records of the Women's Home Missionary Society of the North Georgia Conference of the Methodist Episcopal Church, South, 1897–1910, Pitts Theological Library, Emory University.

30. "Through the Years at Asbury"; Supplement B, 3d Quarter, 1900–1901, Quarterly Conference Records Book, Asbury Methodist Episcopal Church, Augusta Genealogical Society Library, Augusta, Ga; Malone, *Episcopal Church in Georgia*, 84.

31. Christ Episcopal Church, in "Histories of Augusta's Churches"; Federal Writers Project, Works Progress Administration, "Inventory of Presbyterian Church Records in Georgia," Georgia Department of Archives and History, Atlanta. Churches in mill neighborhoods in this era appear to have had cordial relations with little evidence of antagonism, although a concerned Methodist minister claimed in a March 1870 report on Asbury mission that another church was taking "undue advantage" of his Sunday school children to "force" them to attend another Sunday school. He suggested this was "very unfair dealing." The minister may have been referring to either the Episcopal or the Baptist church, both of which had established mission churches near Asbury by the 1870s. See Second Quarterly Report, 1870, Quarterly Conference Records Books, Asbury Methodist Episcopal Church, Pitts Theological Library, Emory University, Atlanta.

32. G. Smith, *One Hundred Years*, 58; Mrs. J. L. (Iris Epps) Hewett Jr., "Crawford

Avenue Baptist Church, 1881–1981," 4, in "Histories of Augusta's Churches," Richmond County Historical Society, Special Collections Room, Reese Library, Augusta State University; Kilpatrick, *Hephzibah Baptist Association Centennial*, 205–6.

33. Newby, *Plain Folk*, 394; Second Quarterly Report, 1870, and First Quarterly Report, 1879, Quarterly Conference Records Books, Asbury Methodist Episcopal Church; Parish Register, Christ Church, Augusta, 1887–1904, Episcopal Diocese of Georgia, Miscellaneous Records.

34. Supplements, 1899 and 1900, Quarterly Conference Records Books, Asbury Methodist Episcopal Church.

35. Kilpatrick, *Hephzibah Baptist Association Centennial*, 227. For a good description of southern revival meetings, see Ownby, *Subduing Satan*, chap. 8. G. Smith, *One Hundred Years*, 45; Hewett, "Crawford Avenue Baptist Church," 4.

36. Older members of Central Christian remember how everyone in their community seemed to come to Central's annual revival week, regardless of denomination. Many would join the church that week but soon drop away again. Interviews with Sonny Switzer, Tony Switzer, and Mary O'Tyson. *Daily Tribune* (Augusta), April 6, 1895, 1, microfilm, Georgia Department of Archives and History.

37. Quarterly Reports, 1879, Quarterly Conference Records Books, Asbury Methodist Episcopal Church.

38. Kilpatrick, *Hephzibah Baptist Association Centennial*, 258; information from conversation with Claude Hill.

39. Jordan, *Century of Service*, 48.

40. History of St. Luke's United Methodist Church, filed in "Histories of Augusta's Churches."

41. Newby, *Plain Folk*, 401.

42. Augusta Factory Burial Union Records, 1897–1903, Historic Augusta, Augusta, Ga.

43. *Supplement to Augusta Directory*, 51–52; Augusta Factory Burial Union Records, September 1898.

44. *Daily Tribune*, January 29, 1895, 1, and February 2, 1895, 1.

45. *Daily Tribune*, February 6, 1895. The fifth chapter of the letter of James is a warning to those who have "piled up wealth" and a call for "brothers" to be "patient . . . until the Lord comes." The passage choice reflects the political radicalism of the *Tribune* as well as the editor's familiarity with Bible verses.

46. *Daily Tribune*, 403.

47. Chipman, *Work*, 2.

48. Ibid.

49. Ibid.

50. McLaurin, *Paternalism and Protest*, 94. The strike is described in detail in McLaurin, *Paternalism and Protest*, 92–112; and Reed, "Augusta Textile Mills."

51. Rumors at the time suggested that Meynardie also became addicted to alcohol or drugs. A letter from two of Berean's prominent members in the *Christian Index* in

February 1887 suggested that the labors of Meynardie in 1886 caused him to have "two attacks of paralysis" which led to such "nervous prostration" that people "might have supposed him to be under the influence of strong drink." Because of his strange behavior "many slanderous and malicious rumors [had] been put about to injure Bro. M." The church had investigated these accusations and resolved that the minister was "not intoxicated." Interestingly, the letter made no reference to Meynardie's role in the 1886 strike, although it did mention the "three glorious outbursts" of revivalism that had occurred that year. See *Christian Index*, February 10, 1887, 2–3.

Sexton's Book records show that a J. S. Menardie was buried at Magnolia Cemetery in Augusta on January 16, 1890. Menardie was listed as being born in South Carolina, having lived in Augusta for five years. He was listed as married, age forty, and a farmer by occupation, although his residence was listed as Broad Street in the Fifth Ward—the mill neighborhood—of Augusta. His cause of death was listed as heart disease. Although there are no indications in the record that this Menardie was a minister, this listing is probably J. S. Meynardie's death record. See Sexton's Book, Book C, C119, Magnolia Cemetery, Augusta, microfilm, Reese Library, Augusta State University.

52. McLaurin suggests that Meynardie's zeal for organizing workers demonstrates a "touch of a messianic complex," indicating that Meynardie could be a charismatic leader in a religious way; McLaurin, *Paternalism and Protest*, 96. Reed notes that "Meynardie's union activity did not interfere with his preaching"; "Augusta Textile Mills," 233 n. 11. Minutes of the Hephzibah Baptist Association, 1885, 11; *Augusta City Directory*, 1886; Minutes of the Hephzibah Baptist Association, 1886, 4; *Augusta City Directory*, 1886. Minutes of the Hephzibah Baptist Association, 1886, 4. The politics of these association meetings are intriguing. Millworkers and farmers appear to have attended these annual meetings alongside such elite figures as H. H. Hickman, who was treasurer of the association for forty-two years. Hickman, as indicated above, was a prominent member of First Baptist, was president of the Graniteville and Vaucluse mills in South Carolina, and one of the founders of the Southern Manufactures Association, which worked to crush the 1886 strike.

The church minutes for Springfield Baptist Church, an African American church in Augusta, suggest this was the usual pattern for selecting representatives among Baptists. The *Atlanta Constitution*, June 15, 1886, 2, lists the names of the five men who led the walkout at the Algernon weaving room. None of these names matched with those attending the Hephzibah Baptist Association meeting. Thus it cannot be told if the strike leaders were members of Berean Baptist.

53. Hewett, "Crawford Avenue Baptist Church," 4.

54. Ownby, *Subduing Satan*, chap. 8. Urban revivals were very similar, although those attending would return home each night rather than stay at a campsite. But many textile workers would have attended rural revivals as children before they moved to the city, or in the summer when they moved to the country to work on the harvest.

55. *Atlanta Constitution*, July 16, 1886.

56. Some of the evidence suggests that Meynardie's personality limited the success of the strike. Reed calls him "rash" and "boastful" with "deficiencies of leadership"; "Augusta Textile Mills," 233. But the Augusta Knights had more forces working against them than the character of their leader. Meynardie's remark quoted in Reed, "Augusta Textile Mills," 233. In his interview Meynardie, in a melodramatic depiction of Augusta millworkers which outraged most Augusta citizens, declared he "buried two children a day on average" as a result of poverty and disease brought on by mill life; ibid, 234. Another useful line of inquiry may be an analysis of religion and gender during the strike. As LeeAnn Whites suggests in her gendered study of Augusta millworkers, striking was usually considered a male action, yet for the 1886 strike to last as long as it did, women must have been involved; see Whites, "Southern Ladies," 233–35. At the same time, women were a proportionately high percentage of churchgoers. This connection between the church and the strike may have been particularly appealing to women. Evidence of such links is difficult to uncover.

57. *Wool-Hat*, May 19, 1894, microfilm, Georgia Department of Archives and History, Atlanta.

58. Murray, "William John Henning," 10.

59. *Wool-Hat*, November 19, 1892.

60. Ibid. There is some debate about the level of anti-Semitism in the Populist movement. Certainly, the Populists used a language of anti-Semitism, especially when discussing the money system.

61. *Wool-Hat*, January 28, 1893, April 29, 1893.

62. *Wool-Hat*, March 11, 1893.

Bibliography

MANUSCRIPT AND ARCHIVAL MATERIAL

Atlanta, Georgia

GEORGIA DEPARTMENT OF ARCHIVES AND HISTORY

Augusta Tax Digests, 1794–1797
Catherine Barnes Rowland Diary
Episcopal Diocese of Georgia Records
Federal Writers Project, Works Progress Administration, Georgia Historical Records
Survey, Church Records Inventory, 1936–1941—Inventory of Presbyterian Church
Records in Georgia
Federal Writers Project, Works Progress Administration, Church Survey, District 2,
Richmond County
Georgia Women's Temperance Union Records
Helping Words
Richmond County Census
Richmond County Estate Records
Richmond County Inferior Court Minutes
Richmond County Ordinary Estate Records
Richmond County Probate Records, Estate Appraisements
Richmond County Tax Digest

EMORY UNIVERSITY, PITTS THEOLOGICAL LIBRARY

Christian Advocate (General Conference daily), April 1866
Georgian Project Records
Journal of the General Conference of the Methodist Episcopal Church, 1848
Journal of the General Conference of the Methodist Episcopal Church, South, 1866,
1870, 1874
Women's Home Missionary Society of the North Georgia Conference of the Meth-
odist Episcopal Church, South, records
Yearbooks and Minutes of the North Georgia Conference, 1867–72, 1879–1910

EMORY UNIVERSITY, ROBERT W. WOODRUFF LIBRARY

Enterprise Manufacturing Company, Augusta, Records, 1877–1960
George Foster Pierce Papers
Methodist Leaders Papers
Sibley Mill Records

GEORGIA STATE UNIVERSITY, PULLEN LIBRARY, SPECIAL COLLECTIONS

Terence V. Powderly Papers, microfilm

Augusta, Georgia

AUGUSTA CITY HALL

Minutes, 1885–1901

AUGUSTA GENEALOGICAL SOCIETY LIBRARY

Asbury Methodist Episcopal Church Quarterly Conference Record Books
Jack Steinberg, "United for Worship and Charity: A History of Congregation Children of Israel"

AUGUSTA STATE UNIVERSITY, REESE LIBRARY

Hephzibah Baptist Association, Annual Meeting Minutes, 1904
T. S. P. Lewis, "Condensed Historical Sketch of Tabernacle Baptist Church, Augusta, 1885–1904"
Magnolia Cemetery Records, Sexton's Books
Craig Morrison, Enterprise NEU Company, Historic American Engineering Record, National Park Service, 1977, copies of drawings in vertical folder, Augusta Collection, accompanying text by Robert Spude
Alan J. Steiner and Robert Jorgensen, John P. King Manufacturing Company and Sibley Manufacturing Company, Historic American Engineering Record, National Park Service, 1977, copies of drawings in vertical folder, Augusta Collection

AUGUSTA–RICHMOND COUNTY PUBLIC LIBRARY

"Oral Histories of Augusta's Citizens," Augusta Oral History Project

HISTORIC AUGUSTA, INC.

Augusta Factory Burial Union, Record Book, 1897–1903
Session Minutes of First Presbyterian Church of Augusta, microfilm

Macon, Georgia

MERCER UNIVERSITY,
GEORGIA BAPTIST HISTORICAL DEPOSITORY

Christian Index
Helping Words, Augusta
Records of First Baptist Church, Augusta, microfilm
Records of Springfield Baptist Church, Augusta, microfilm
Minutes of the Hephzibah Baptist Association Annual Meetings, microfilm
Minutes of the Walker Baptist Association Annual Meetings, microfilm

Chapel Hill, North Carolina

UNIVERSITY OF NORTH CAROLINA,
SOUTHERN HISTORICAL COLLECTION

Thomas E. Watson Papers

Durham, North Carolina

DUKE UNIVERSITY, SPECIAL COLLECTIONS DEPARTMENT

Elizabeth [Johnson] Harris Memoir, 1867–1942

Winston-Salem, North Carolina

MUSEUM OF EARLY SOUTHERN DECORATIVE ARTS

Chatham and Richmond Counties Research Files

Aiken, South Carolina

UNIVERSITY OF SOUTH CAROLINA AT AIKEN, SPECIAL COLLECTIONS

Gregg-Graniteville Collection

Nashville, Tennessee

DISCIPLES OF CHRIST HISTORICAL SOCIETY ARCHIVES

Emily Tubman Folder

PUBLIC RECORDS

City Records

Augusta City Directory, 1886–90. Augusta: Chronicle Book and Job Rooms, 1886–90.

Augusta City Directory, 1888. Atlanta: R. L. Polk, 1888.

Augusta Directory and City Advertiser 1841. Augusta: Browne and McCaffery, 1841.

Haddock's Augusta, Ga. Directory and General Advertiser. Augusta: E. H. Pughe, 1872.

Hooper's Augusta City Directory and Business Register, 1874–75. Augusta: George W. Hooper, 1874.

Rowland, Arthur Ray. *Index to City Directories of Augusta, Georgia, 1841–1879.* Augusta: n.p., 1991.

Sholes' Directory of the City of Augusta of 1877. Augusta: Chronicle and Constitutionalist, 1877.

Sholes' Directory of the City of Augusta. Augusta: Chronicle and Constitutionalist, 1879.

Supplement to the Augusta City Directory, 1896–1897. Augusta: Maloney Directory Companies, 1897.

County Records

Houston County Realty Books. Superior Court Clerk's Office, Courthouse, Perry, Ga.

Richmond County Realty Books: 2-Y, 3-C, 3-H, 3-L, 3-T, 3-Y. Superior Court Clerk's Office, Courthouse, Augusta.

State Records

Candler, Allen D., ed., *The Colonial Records of the State of Georgia.* 30 vols. Atlanta: various printers, 1904–16.

Lamar, Lucius Q. C. *A Compilation of the Laws of the State of Georgia, 1810–1819.* Augusta: T. S. Hannon, 1821.

Marbury, H., and W. H. Crawford. *Compilation of the Laws of Georgia.* Savannah: Seymour, Woolhopter, and Stebbins, 1802.

Federal Records

Aggregate Amount of Persons within the United States in the Year 1810. Washington, D.C., n.p. 1811.

Contested Election Case of Thomas E. Watson v. James C. C. Black. House of Representatives Report, 1894.

Report upon Relations between Labor and Capital. Investigation of Senate Committee on Education and Labor, vol. 4. Washington, D.C.: Government Printing Office, 1885.

The State of the Population of the United States. Washington, D.C., n.p., 1872.

U.S. Census Office. *Second Census*. Washington, D.C.: n.p., 1801.

———. *Tenth Census*. Washington, D.C.: U.S. Government Printing Office, 1881.

———. *Eleventh Census*. Washington, D.C.: U.S. Government Printing Office, 1891.

———. *Twelfth Census*. Washington, D.C.: U.S. Government Printing Office, 1901.

U.S. Senate. Committee on Education and Labor. *Report upon Relations between Labor and Capital*. Washington, D.C.: U.S. Government Printing Office, 1885.

MEMOIRS AND OTHER PRIMARY SOURCES

Abbott, B. A. *Life of Chapman S. Lucas*. Baltimore: Christian Tribune, 1897.

Aptheker, Herbert, ed. *A Documentary History of the Negro People in the United States*. New York: Citadel Press, 1969.

Augusta Exchange. *The Industrial Advantages of Augusta, Georgia*. Augusta: Akehurst, 1893.

Cable, George Washington. *The Negro Question*. New York: Charles Scribner's Sons, 1890.

Caldwell, Erskine. *Tobacco Road*. 1932. Savannah, Ga.: Beehive Press, 1974.

Cathcart, William, ed. *Baptist Encyclopedia: A Dictionary of the Doctrines, Ordinances, Usages, Confessions of Faith*. Philadelphia: L. H. Evarts, 1881.

Chipman, John. *Work*. Parish Register, Christ Church, Augusta.

"A Chronicle of Christian Stewardship: Sesquicentennial of St. John's Methodist Church, 1798–1948." N.p., n.d.

Cowan, E. P. "Haines Normal and Industrial School, Augusta, Georgia." *Church at Home and Abroad*, August 1893, 138.

Cumming, Joseph B. *New Ideas, New Departures, New South*. Augusta: Chronicle, 1893.

Cumming, Mary G. Smith. *Two Centuries of Augusta: A Sketch*. Augusta: Ridgely-Tidwell-Ashe, 1926.

Day, Caroline Bond. *A Study of Some Negro-White Families in the United States*. Cambridge: Harvard University, Peabody Museum, 1933.

Dow, Lorenzo. *History of Cosmopolite; or, The Writings of Rev. Lorenzo Dow*. Cincinnati: Applegate, 1855.

Du Bois, W. E. B. *Souls of Black Folk*. Chicago: A. C. McClurg, 1903.

———. "Religion in the South." In *The Negro in the South: His Economic Progress in Relation to His Moral and Religious Development*, edited by Booker T. Washington and W. E. B. Du Bois. Philadelphia: G. W. Jacobs, 1907.

Dunlap, W. C. *The Life of S. Miller Willis, The Fire-Baptized Lay Evangelist*. Atlanta: Constitution, 1892.

"The Exposition Edition of the *Augusta Chronicle*, 1891." Richmond County Historical Collection, Special Collections, Reese Library, Augusta State University, Augusta.

Federal Writers Project of the Works Progress Administration, Augusta Unit. *Augusta American Guide Series*. Augusta: Tidwell, 1938.

Fleming, William Henry. *Slavery and the Race Problem in the South, with Special Reference to the State of Georgia Alumni Society of the State University, Athens, June 19, 1906*. Boston: D. Estes, 1906.

———. *Treaty-Making Power: Slavery and the Race Problem in the South*. Boston: Stratford, 1920.

Floyd, Silas X. *The Life of Charles T. Walker*. 1902. Reprint, New York: Negro Universities Press, 1969.

Force, Peter. *American Archives*. 5th ser. 3 vols. Washington, D.C.: Mt. St. Clair and Peter Force, 1848–53.

Gaines, Wesley J. *African Methodism in the South; or, Twenty Five Years of Freedom*. Atlanta: Franklin Publishing House, 1890.

Gibbes, Robert W. *Documentary History of the American Revolution*. 1853. Reprint (3 vols. in 1), New York: *New York Times* and Arno Press, 1971.

Gilmer, George Rockingham. *Sketches of Some of the First Settlers of Upper Georgia, of the Cherokees, and the Author*. 1855. Reprint, Americus, Ga.: Americus Book Company, 1926.

Harrald, Claudia White. *Remembered Encounters*. Atlanta: B. F. Logan Press, 1951.

Harrison, W. P. *The Gospel among the Slaves*. Nashville, Tenn.: Publishing House of the M.E. Church, South, 1893.

Haygood, Atticus G. *Our Brother in Black: His Freedom and His Future*. Nashville, Tenn.: Southern Methodist Publishing House, 1881.

Haynes, Elizabeth Ross. *The Black Boy of Atlanta*. Boston: House of Edinboro, 1952.

"Histories of Augusta's Churches." Richmond County Historical Society, Special Collections Room, Reese Library, Augusta State University, Augusta.

"History of Catholicity in Augusta, Georgia, from the earliest period to the present date, with Ceremony of Consecration of St. Patrick's Church, cost, and time of completion, Augusta, Georgia, March 17, 1897." Augusta: Chronicle Job Printers, 1897.

Holsey, Lucius Henry. *Autobiography, Sermons, Addresses, and Essays*. 2d ed. Atlanta: Franklin, 1899.

Hood, James Walker. *One Hundred Years of the African Methodist Episcopal Zion Church; or, The Centennial of African Methodism*. New York: African Methodist Episcopal Zion Book Concern, 1895.

Johnson, R. J. *History of the Walker Baptist Association of Georgia*. Augusta: Chronicle Job Printers, 1909.

Jones, Charles Colcock, Jr. *Georgians during the War between the States: An Address Delivered Before the Confederate Survivors Association in Augusta, Georgia*. Augusta: Chronicle, 1889.

Jones, Charles Colcock, Jr., and Salem Dutcher. *Memorial History of Augusta, Georgia, from Its Settlement in 1735 to the Close of the Nineteenth Century*. 1890. Reprint, Spartanburg, S.C.: Reprint Company, 1980.

Jordan, Isabella. *"A Century of Service": First Baptist Church, Augusta, Georgia.* Augusta: n.p., 1921.

Kilpatrick, W. L. *The Hephzibah Baptist Association Centennial, 1794–1894.* Augusta: Richards and Shaver, 1894.

Laney, Lucy. "Address Before the Women's Meeting." *Proceedings of the Second Conference for the Study of Problems Concerning Negro City Life.* Atlanta University Publications, no. 2, May 25–26, 1897.

———. "The Burden of the Educated Colored Woman." *Southern Workman* 28 (September 1899): 341–44.

Longstreet, Augustus Baldwin. *Georgia Scenes, Character, Incidents, etc., in the First Half Century of the Republic.* 1835. Reprint, Savannah: Beehive Press, 1973.

Lynch, James. *The Mission of the U.S. Republic: An Oration Delivered by Rev. James Lynch, at the Parade Ground, Augusta, Ga., July 4, 1865.* Augusta: n.p., 1865.

Mays, Benjamin E. *Born to Rebel: An Autobiography.* New York: Charles Scribner's Sons, 1971.

McCrorey, Mary Jackson. "Lucy Laney." *The Crisis* 41 (June 1934): 161.

McTyeire, Holland N. *A History of Methodism.* Nashville, Tenn.: Publishing House of the Methodist Episcopal Church, South, 1904.

Milfort, Louis Leclerc. *Memoirs; or, A Quick Glance at My Various Travels and My Sojourn in the Creek Nation.* Savannah: Beehive Press, 1959.

Oglesby, Thadeus K. *A Vindication of the South against the "Encyclopedia Britannica" and Other Maligners.* Atlanta: Byrd, 1903.

Ovington, Mary White. *Portraits in Color.* New York: Viking Press, 1927.

Patrick Walsh: The Citizen, the Statesman, the Man. Augusta: Augusta Publishing Co., 1899.

Pegues, A. W. *Our Baptist Ministers and Schools.* Springfield, Mass.: Willey, 1892.

"The Petition of the Inhabitants of the Parish of St. George and St. Paul, including the ceded lands in the Province of Georgia," July 31, 1776. In *Collections of the New-York Historical Society for the Year 1872.* New York: privately printed, 1873.

Phillips, Charles Henry. *The History of the Colored Methodist Episcopal Church in America.* 1898. Reprint, New York: n.p., 1972.

The Possibilities of the Negro in Symposium: A Solution to the Negro Problem Psychologically Considered: The Negro Is Not a Beast. Atlanta: Franklin, 1904.

"Preston Papers." *Virginia Magazine of History and Biography,* 27 (1919): 309–25.

Pringle, Alex. *Prayer for the Revival of Religion in All the Protestant Churches.* Edinburgh: Schaw and Pillans, 1776.

Rawick, George P. *The American Slave: A Composite Autobiography.* New York: Greenwood Press, 1977.

———, ed. *The American Slave: A Composite Autobiography.* Vol. 13, *Georgia Narratives.* Westport, Conn.: Greenwood Press, 1974.

Rutherford, Mildred Lewis. *Historical Sins of Omission and Commission.* San Francisco: United Daughters of the Confederacy, 1915.

Sibley, Robert Pendleton. *Ancestry and Life of Josiah Sibley of Augusta, Georgia.* Augusta: Williams Press, 1908.

Simmons, William J. *Men of Mark: Eminent, Progressive, and Rising.* New York: Arno Press, 1968.

Smith, Charles Spencer. *A History of the African Methodist Episcopal Church.* Philadelphia: African Methodist Episcopal Church Book Concern, 1922.

Smith, George G., Jr. *The History of Methodism in Georgia and Florida: From 1785 to 1865.* Macon, Ga.: Jno. W. Burke, 1877.

———. *The Life and Letters of James Osgood Andrew.* Nashville, Tenn.: Southern Methodist Publishing House, 1883.

———. *The Life and Times of George Foster Pierce.* Sparta, Ga.: Hancock, 1888.

———. *A Hundred Years of Methodism in Augusta.* Augusta: Richards and Shaver, 1898.

Summers, T. O., ed. *Journal of the General Conference of the Methodist Episcopal Church, South,* 1866, 1879, 1874. Nashville, Tenn.: Publishing House of the M.E. Church, South, 1866–74.

"Through the Years at Asbury United Methodist Church." Pamphlet, Augusta Genealogical Society Library, Augusta.

U.S. Senate. Committee on Education and Labor. *Capital and Labor.* Washington, D.C.: U.S. Government Printing Office, 1885.

Wadley, Mary C. *One Hundred Years of the First Presbyterian Church of Augusta, Georgia, 1804–1904.* Philadelphia: Allen, Lane and Scott, 1904.

Watson, Thomas E. *Life and Speeches of Thomas E. Watson.* 2d ed. Thomson, Ga.: Jefferson, 1911.

White, W. J. *The Negro Problem, As Agitated in This Country: A Paper Read before the Sumner Literary and Historical Society of Augusta, Ga., Friday Evening, April 3, 1885.* Augusta: Georgia Baptist Print, 1885.

Whitson, L. D. *Sketches of Augusta, Sandersville, Sparta, Madison, Waynesboro, Georgia, and Aiken, South Carolina.* Atlanta: n.p., 1885.

Wood, Virginia Steele, and Ralph Van Wood, eds. *The Reuben King Journal, 1800–1806.* Vol. 15 of the *Collections of the Georgia Historical Society.* Savannah: Georgia Historical Society, 1971.

Works Progress Administration, Georgia. *Population Mobility: A Study of Family Movements Affecting Augusta, Georgia, 1899–1939.* Works Progress Administration of Georgia, Study no. 165-1-34-53, 1942.

Wright, Richard R., Jr. *Eighty Seven Years behind the Black Curtain.* Nashville, Tenn.: AME Sunday School Union, 1965.

SECONDARY SOURCES

Abbott, Shirley. *Womenfolks: Growing Up Down South.* New York: Ticknor and Fields, 1983.

Alexander, Gross. *A History of the Methodist Church, South, in the United States.* New York: Christian Literature, 1894.

The American Slave: A Composite Autobiography, Supplement. Ser. 1, vol. 4, *Georgia Narratives, Part Two.* Westport, Conn.: Greenwood Press, 1977.

Anderson, James D. *The Education of Blacks in the South, 1860–1935.* Chapel Hill: University of North Carolina Press, 1988.

Angell, Stephen Ward. *Bishop Henry McNeal Turner and African-American Religion in the South.* Knoxville: University of Tennessee Press, 1992.

Asher, Robert, Paul A. Gilje, and Howard Rock, eds. *American Artisans: Crafting Social Identity, 1750–1850.* Baltimore: Johns Hopkins University Press, 1995.

Ayers, Edward L. *The Promise of the New South: Life after Reconstruction.* New York: Oxford University Press, 1992.

Bacote, Clarence. "The Negro in Georgia Politics, 1880–1908." Ph.D. diss., University of Chicago, 1955.

———. "Some Aspects of Negro Life in Georgia, 1880–1908." *Journal of Negro History* 43 (1958): 186–213.

———. "Negro Proscriptions, Protests, and Proposed Solutions in Georgia, 1880–1908." *Journal of Southern History* 25 (1959): 471–99.

———. *The Story of Atlanta University.* Atlanta: Atlanta University, 1969.

Bailey, Fred Arthur. "The Textbooks of the 'Lost Cause': Censorship and the Creation of Southern State Histories." *Georgia Historical Quarterly* 75 (fall 1991): 507–33.

Bailey, Thomas A. *The American Spirit: United States History as Seen by Contemporaries.* 2 vols. Lexington, Mass.: D. C. Heath, 1978.

Baron, Ava, ed. *Work Engendered: Toward a New History of American Labor.* Ithaca, N.Y.: Cornell University Press, 1991.

Bartley, Numan V. *The Creation of Modern Georgia.* Athens: University of Georgia Press, 1983.

Beatty, Bess. "Textile Labor in the North Carolina Piedmont: Mill Owner Images and Mill Worker Response, 1830–1900." *Labor History* 25 (fall 1984).

Bederman, Gail. *Manliness and Civilization: A Multicultural History of Gender and Race in the United States, 1880–1917.*

Blassingame, John W. *The Slave Community; Plantation Life in the Antebellum South.* New York: Oxford University Press, 1972.

Bleser, Carol, ed. *The Hammonds of Redcliffe.* New York: Oxford University Press, 1981.

———. *In Joy and Sorrow: Women, Family, and Marriage in the Victorian South, 1830–1900.* New York: Oxford University Press, 1991.

Blewett, Mary. *Men, Women, and Work: Class, Gender, and Protest in the New England Shoe Industry, 1780–1910.* Urbana: University of Illinois Press, 1990.

Boatwright, Eleanor Miot. *Status of Women in Georgia, 1783–1860.* Brooklyn, N.Y.: Carlson, 1994.

Bonner, James C. *A History of Georgia Agriculture.* Athens: University of Georgia Press, 1964.

Boorstin, Daniel. *The Americans: The Colonial Experience.* New York: Vintage, 1964.

Bowden, Haygood S. *History of Savannah Methodism from John Wesley to Silas Johnson.* Macon, Ga.: n.p., 1929.

Brawley, Benjamin. *History of Morehouse College.* Atlanta: Morehouse College, 1917.

——. *Social History of the American Negro.* New York: Macmillan, 1921.

——. *Negro Builders and Heroes.* Chapel Hill: University of North Carolina Press, 1937.

Brawley, James P. *Two Centuries of Methodist Concern: Bondage, Freedom, and Education of Black People.* New York: Vantage Press, 1974.

Brooks, Walter H. "The Priority of the Silver Bluff Church and Its Promoters." *Journal of Negro History* 7 (April 1922):172–96.

Brundage, W. Fitzhugh. *Lynching in the New South: Georgia and Virginia.* Urbana: University of Illinois Press, 1993.

——, ed. *Under the Sentence of Death: Lynching in the South.* Chapel Hill: University of North Carolina Press, 1997.

Burr, Virginia Ingraham. *The Secret Eye: The Journal of Ella Gertrude Clanton Thomas, 1848–1889.* Chapel Hill: University of North Carolina Press, 1990.

Burton, Orville Vernon. *In My Father's House Are Many Mansions: Family and Community in Edgefield, South Carolina.* Chapel Hill: University of North Carolina Press, 1985.

Butterfield, Fox. *All God's Children: The Bosket Family and the American Tradition of Violence.* New York: Knopf, 1995.

Cade, John Brother. *Holsey—The Incomparable.* New York: n.p., 1964.

Caldwell, A. B. *History of the American Negro.* Atlanta: Caldwell, 1920.

Callahan, Helen. *Augusta: A Pictorial History.* Virginia Beach, Va.: Donning, 1980.

——. "The Irish in Augusta." *Richmond County History* 19–20 (1987–89).

Campbell, James T. *Songs of Zion: The African Methodist Episcopal Church in the United States and South Africa.* New York: Oxford University Press, 1995.

Candler, Allen D., ed. *The Colonial Records of the State of Georgia.* 30 vols. Atlanta: various printers, 1904–16.

Capeci, Dominic J., Jr., and Jack C. Knight. "Reckoning with Violence: W. E. B. Du Bois and the 1906 Atlanta Riot." *Journal of Southern History* 62, no. 4 (November 1996): 731–34.

Carlton, David. *Mill and Town in South Carolina, 1880–1920.* Baton Rouge: Louisiana State University Press, 1982.

Cash, Wilbur J. *The Mind of the South.* New York: Vintage, 1941.

Cashin, Edward J. "Thomas E. Watson and the Catholic Laymen's Association of Georgia." Ph.D. diss., Fordham University, 1962.

——. "Summerville, Retreat of the Old South." *Richmond County History* 5, no. 2 (summer 1973): 59.

———. "History as Mores: Walker Percy's *Lancelot*." *Georgia Review* 31 (winter 1977): 875–80.

———. *The Quest: A History of Public Education in Richmond County*. Augusta: Richmond County Board of Education, 1985.

———. *Colonial Augusta: Key to the Indian Country*. Macon, Ga.: Mercer University Press, 1986.

———. "Georgia: Searching for Security." In *Ratifying the Constitution*, edited by Michael Allen Gillespie and Michael Lienesch. Lawrence: University Press of Kansas, 1989.

———. *The Story of Augusta*. Augusta: Richmond County Historical Society, 1990.

———. *General Sherman's Girl Friend and Other Stories about Augusta*. Spartanburg, S.C.: Reprint Company, 1994.

———. *Old Springfield: Race and Religion in Augusta, Georgia*. Augusta: Springfield Village Park Foundation, 1995.

Cashin, Joan. *Our Common Affairs: Texts from Women in the Old South*. Baltimore: Johns Hopkins University Press, 1996.

Clark, Elmer T., ed. *The Journal and Letters of Francis Asbury*. London: Epworth Press, 1958.

Clary, George Esmond, Jr. "The Founding of Paine College: A Unique Venture in Inter-Racial Cooperation in the New South (1882–1903)." Ed.D. diss., University of Georgia, 1965.

———. "On the Origins of Methodism in Georgia and Richmond County." *Richmond County History* 1, no. 1 (winter 1969): 15–18.

Clinton, Catherine. *The Plantation Mistress: Women's World in the Old South*. New York: Pantheon, 1982.

Clinton, Catherine, and Michele Gillespie. *The Devil's Lane: Sex and Race in the Early South*. New York: Oxford University Press, 1997.

Cobb, James C. "Politics in a New South City: Augusta, Georgia, 1946–1971." Ph.D. diss., University of Georgia, 1975.

Cockburn, Cynthia. *Brothers: Male Domination and Technological Change*. London: Pluto Press, 1983.

Coleman, Kenneth. *Colonial Georgia: A History*. New York: Charles Scribner's Sons, 1976.

Coleman, Kenneth, and Charles Stephen Gurr. *The Dictionary of Georgia Biography*. 2 vols. Athens: University of Georgia Press, 1983.

Cook, Raymond A. *Thomas Dixon*. New York: Twayne, 1974.

Cooper, Walter G. *The Story of Georgia*. New York: American Historical Society, 1938.

Corley, Florence Fleming. *Confederate City: Augusta, Georgia, 1860–1865*. 1960. Reprint, Spartanburg, S.C.: Reprint Company, 1995.

Cornelius, Janet Duitsman. *"When I Can Read My Title Clear": Literacy, Slavery, and Religion in the Antebellum South*. Columbia: University of South Carolina Press, 1991.

Cott, Nancy F. *The Bonds of Womanhood: "Woman's Sphere" in New England, 1780–1835*. New Haven: Yale University Press, 1977.

Cottingham, Britt Edward. "'The Burden of the Educated Colored Woman': Lucy Laney and Haines Institute, 1886–1933." M.A. thesis, Georgia State University, 1995.

Coulter, E. Merton. *Georgia: A Short History*. Chapel Hill: University of North Carolina Press, 1960.

Craven, Martha Jacquelyn. "A Portrait of Octavia." *Richmond County History* 4 (summer 1972): 5–10.

———. "A Portrait of Emily Tubman." *Richmond County History* 6 (winter 1974): 5–10.

Crowe, Charles. "Racial Violence and Social Reform: Origins of the Atlanta Race Riot of 1906." *Journal of Negro History* 53, no. 3 (July 1968): 234–57.

———. "Racial Massacre in Atlanta, September 22, 1906." *Journal of Negro History* 54, no. 2 (April 1969): 150–73.

Currie-McDaniel, Ruth. *Carpetbagger of Conscience: A Biography of John Emory Bryant*. Athens: University of Georgia Press, 1987.

Davis, Harold E. *Henry Grady's New South: Atlanta, a Brave and Beautiful City*. Tuscaloosa: University of Alabama Press, 1990.

Davis, Leroy. *A Clashing of the Soul: John Hope and the Dilemma of African American Leadership and Black Higher Education in the Early Twentieth Century*. Athens: University of Georgia Press, 1998.

Derry, Joseph. *The Story of the Confederate States; or, History of the War for Southern Independence*. Richmond, Va.: B. F. Johnson, 1898.

Detreville, John R. "The Little New South: Origins of Industry in Georgia's Fall Line Cities, 1840–1865." Ph.D. diss., University of North Carolina, 1986.

Dillman, Catherine Matheny. *Southern Women*. New York: Hemisphere, 1988.

Dittmer, John. *Black Georgia in the Progressive Era, 1900–1920*. Urbana: University of Illinois Press, 1977.

Dodd, Donald B., and Wynelle S. Dodd. *Historical Statistics of the United States, 1790–1970*. Tuscaloosa: University of Alabama Press, 1973.

Drago, Edmund L. *Black Politicians and Reconstruction in Georgia: A Splendid Failure*. Baton Rouge: Louisiana State University Press, 1982.

Dublin, Thomas. *Women at Work: The Transformation of Work and Community in Lowell, Massachusetts, 1826–1860*. New York: Columbia University Press, 1979.

Duncan, Russell. *Freedom's Shore: Tunis Campbell and the Georgia Freedmen*. Athens: University of Georgia Press, 1986.

———. *Entrepreneur for Equality: Governor Rufus Bullock, Commerce, and Race in Post–Civil War Georgia*. Athens: University of Georgia Press, 1994.

Dvorak, Katharine L. *An African-American Exodus: The Segregation of the Southern Churches*. Brooklyn, N.Y.: Carlson, 1991.

Eskew, Glenn T. "Black Elitism and the Failure of Paternalism in Postbellum Georgia: The Case of Bishop Lucius Henry Holsey." *Journal of Southern History* 58, no. 4 (November 1992): 637–66.

Evans, Lawton B. *The Essential Facts of American History.* New York: Benjamin H. Sanborn, 1917.

Farnham, Christie Anne. *Women of the American South: A Multicultural Reader.* New York: New York University Press, 1997.

Fields, Barbara J. "Ideology and Race in American History. In *Religion, Race, and Reconstruction: Essays in Honor of C. Vann Woodward,* edited by J. Morgan Kousser and James M. McPherson. New York: Oxford University Press, 1982.

Fink, Leon. *Workingmen's Democracy: The Knight of Labor and American Politics.* Illinois, 1983.

Flamming, Douglas. *Creating the Modern South: Millhands and Managers in Dalton, Georgia, 1884–1984.* Chapel Hill: University of North Carolina Press, 1992.

Flynt, J. Wayne. "Southern Protestantism and Reform, 1980–1920." In *Varieties of Southern Religious Experiences,* edited by Samuel Hill. Baton Rouge: Louisiana State University Press, 1988.

Ford, Lacy K. *Origins of Southern Radicalism: The South Carolina Upcountry, 1800–1860.* New York: Oxford University Press, 1988.

Forgacs, David, ed. *An Antonio Gramsci Reader.* New York: Schocken, 1988.

Fox-Genovese, Elizabeth. *Within the Plantation Household: Black and White Women of the Old South.* Chapel Hill: University of North Carolina Press, 1988.

Franklin, V. P. *Black Self Determination: A Cultural History of African-American Resistance.* Brooklyn: Lawrence Hill, 1984.

Franklin, Vincent P., and James D. Anderson, eds. *New Perspectives on Black Educational History.* Boston: G. K. Hall, 1978.

Frazier, E. Franklin. *The Black Bourgeoisie.* New York: Collier McMillan, 1957.

Fredrickson, George N. *The Black Image in the White Mind.* New York: Torch, 1972.

Freeman, Douglas Southall. *George Washington: A Biography.* 7 vols. New York: Charles Scribner's Sons, 1949–57.

Friedman, Jean F. *The Enclosed Garden: Women and Community in the Evangelical South, 1830–1900.* Chapel Hill: University of North Carolina Press, 1995.

Gaines, Kevin K. *Uplifting the Race: Black Leadership, Politics and Culture in the Twentieth Century.* Chapel Hill: University of North Carolina Press, 1996.

Gallay, Alan. *The Formation of a Planter Elite: Jonathan Bryan and the Southern Colonial Frontier.* Athens: University of Georgia Press, 1989.

Gaspar, David Barry, and Darlene Clark Hine. *More than Chattel: Black Women and Slavery in the Americas.* Bloomington: Indiana University Press, 1996.

Gatewood, Willard. *Black Americans and the White Man's Burden, 1898–1903.* Urbana: University of Illinois Press, 1975.

———. "Aristocrats of Color, North and South: The Black Elite, 1890–1920." *Journal of Southern History* 54, no. 1 (February 1988): 3–20.

———. *Aristocrats of Color: The Black Elite, 1880–1920.* Bloomington: Indiana University Press, 1990.

Genovese, Eugene D. *Roll, Jordan, Roll: The World the Slaves Made.* New York: Vintage, 1976.

———. *From Rebellion to Revolution: Afro-American Slave Revolts in the Making of the New World.* New York: Vintage, 1979.

German, Richard Henry Lee. "The Queen City of the Savannah: Augusta, Georgia, during the Urban Progressive Era, 1890–1917." Ph.D. diss., University of Florida, 1971.

———. "The Augusta Strike of 1898–1899." *Richmond County History* 4 (winter 1972): 35–48.

Gillespie, Michael Allen, and Lienesch, Michael. *Ratifying the Constitution.* Lawrence: University Press of Kansas, 1989.

Gillespie, Michele. "Fruits of Their Labor: White Artisans in Slaveholding Georgia, 1790–1860." Unpublished manuscript, in possession of author.

———. "Planters in the Making: Georgia Artisans in the Early Republic." In *American Artisans: Crafting Social Identity, 1750–1850*, edited by Howard B. Rock, Paul A. Gilje, and Robert Asher. Baltimore: Johns Hopkins University Press, 1995.

———. *Free Labor in an Unfree World: White Artisans in Slaveholding Georgia, 1789–1860.* Athens: University of Georgia Press, 1999.

Gilmore, Glenda Elizabeth. *Gender and Jim Crow: Women and the Politics of White Supremacy in North Carolina, 1896–1920.* Chapel Hill: University of North Carolina Press, 1996.

Ginzberg, Lori D. *Women and the Work of Benevolence: Morality, Politics, and Class in the Nineteenth Century United States.* New Haven: Yale University Press, 1990.

Grant, Donald S. *The Way It Was in the South: The Black Experience in Georgia.* Secaucus, N.J.: Carol Publishing Group, Birch Lane Press, 1993.

Gravely, William B. "The Social, Political, and Religious Significance of the Formation of the Colored Methodist Episcopal Church (1870)." *Methodist History* 18 (October 1979): 3–25.

Greene, Jack P. *Landon Carter: An Inquiry into the Personal Values and Social Imperatives of the Eighteenth Century Virginia Gentry.* Charlottesville: University Press of Virginia, 1965.

Griffen, Richard W. "The Augusta (Georgia) Manufacturing Company in Peace, War, and Reconstruction." *Business History Review* 1, no. 32 (1958): 60–73.

———. "The Origins of the Industrial Revolution in Georgia: Cotton Textiles, 1810–1865." *Georgia Historical Quarterly* 42, no. 4 (December 1958).

Griggs, A. C. "Lucy Craft Laney." *Journal of Negro History* 19 (1934): 97–102.

Grob, Gerald. *Workers and Utopia: A Study of Ideological Conflict in the American Labor Movement, 1865–1900.* Evanston, Ill.: Northwestern University Press, 1961.

Gunderson, Joan R. "Kith and Kin: Women's Networks in Colonial Georgia." In *The Devil's Lane: Sex and Race in the Early South*, edited by Catherine Clinton and Michele Gillespie. New York: Oxford University Press, 1997.

Gutman, Herbert. *The Black Family in Slavery and Freedom, 1750–1925*. New York: Pantheon, 1976.

Guy-Sheftall, Beverly. "'Daughters of Sorrow': Attitudes toward Black Women, 1880–1920." Ph.D. diss., Emory University, 1984.

Hale, Grace. *Making Whiteness: The Culture of Segregation in the South, 1890–1940*. New York: Pantheon, 1998.

Hall, Jacquelyn Dowd. *Revolt against Chivalry*. New York: Columbia University Press, 1979.

Hall, Jacquelyn Dowd, Robert Korstad, and James Leloudis. "Cotton Mill People: Work, Community, and Protest in the Textile South, 1880–1940." *American Historical Review* 91 (April 1986): 245–86.

Hall, Jacquelyn Dowd, James Leloudis, Robert Korstad, Mary Murphy, LuAnn Jones, and Christopher B. Daly. *Like a Family: The Making of a Southern Cotton Mill World*. Chapel Hill: University of North Carolina Press, 1987.

Hamilton, William. "Political Control in a Southern City: Augusta, Georgia, in the 1890s." Honors paper, Harvard University, 1972.

Hammond, Edmund Jordan. *The Methodist Episcopal Church in Georgia*. N.p., 1935.

Harper, Keith. *The Quality of Mercy: Southern Baptists and Social Christianity, 1890–1920*. Tuscaloosa: University of Alabama Press, 1996.

Harris, Eula Wallace, and Maxie Harris Craig. *Christian Methodist Episcopal Church through the Years*. Rev. ed. Jackson, Tenn.: n.p., 1965.

Harris, J. William. *Plain Folk and Gentry in a Slave Society: White Liberty and Black Slavery in Augusta's Hinterland*. Middletown, Conn.: Wesleyan University Press, 1985.

Harris, Waldo P., III. "Daniel Marshall: Lone Georgia Revolutionary Pastor." *Viewpoints Georgia Baptist History* 5 (1976): 51–65.

Harris, Waldo P., III, and James D. Mosteller. *Georgia's First Continuing Baptist Church: A History of the Kiokee Baptist Church in Georgia*. Appling, Ga.: Kiokee Baptist Church, 1997.

Harvey, Diane. "The Terri, Augusta's Black Enclave." *Richmond County History* 5, no. 2 (summer 1973): 60–75.

Herring, Harriet. *Welfare Work in Mill Villages: The Story of Extra-Mill Activities in North Carolina*. Chapel Hill: University of North Carolina Press, 1929.

Hewitt, Nancy. *Women's Activism and Social Change: Rochester, New York, 1822–1872*. Ithaca, N.Y.: Cornell University Press, 1988.

Hild, Matthew J. "The Knights of Labor in Georgia." M.A. thesis, University of Georgia, 1996.

Hildebrand, Reginald F. *The Times Were Strange and Stirring: Methodist Preachers and the Crisis of Emancipation*. Durham, N.C.: Duke University Press, 1995.

Holt, Thomas. *Black over White: Negro Political Leadership in South Carolina during Reconstruction.* Urbana: University of Illinois Press, 1977.

Hornsby, Anne R. Lockhart. "Shifts in the Distribution of Wealth Among Blacks in Georgia, 1980–1915." Ph.D. diss., Georgia State University, 1980.

Hunter, Tom. "The Harrisburg Story." *Augusta Magazine* 2, no. 3 (1984).

Inscoe, John C., ed. *Georgia in Black and White: Explorations in the Race Relations of a Southern State, 1865–1950.* Athens: University of Georgia Press, 1994.

Jenkins, William Sumner. *Proslavery Thought in the Old South.* Gloucester, Mass.: Peter Smith, 1960.

Jensen, Joan, and Sue Davidson, eds. *A Needle, a Bobbin, a Strike: Women Needleworkers in America.* Philadelphia: Temple University Press, 1984.

Johnson, Michael P., and James L. Roark. "Strategies of Survival: Free Negro Families and the Problem of Slavery." In *In Joy and Sorrow: Women, Family, and Marriage in the Victorian South, 1830–1900,* edited by Carol Bleser. New York: Oxford University Press, 1991.

Johnson, Paul E. *African-American Christianity.* Berkeley and Los Angeles: University of California Press, 1994.

Johnson, Whittington B. "Free Blacks in Antebellum Augusta, Georgia: A Demographic and Economic Profile." *Richmond County History* 14 (1982): 12.

Jones, Anna Olive. *A History of First Baptist Church, Augusta, Georgia, 1817–1967.* Columbia, S.C.: R. L. Bryan, 1967.

Jones, Edward A. *A Candle in the Dark: A History of Morehouse College.* Valley Forge, Pa.: Judson Press, 1967.

Jones, Jacqueline. *Labor of Love, Labor of Sorrow: Black Women, Work, and the Family from Slavery to the Present.* New York: Random House, 1986.

———. *Soldiers of Light and Love: Northern Teachers and Georgia Blacks, 1865–1873.* Athens: University of Georgia Press, 1992.

Jordan, Ervin L., Jr. *Black Confederates and Afro-Yankees in Civil War Virginia.* Charlottesville: University Press of Virginia, 1995.

Kahn, Kenneth. "The Knights of Labor and the Southern Black Worker." *Labor History* 18 (winter 1977): 47–70.

Ken, Sally, and Eileen Law. "A Study of the Chinese Community." *Richmond County History* 5, no. 2 (summer 1973): 23–43.

Kendall, Anne W. "Lucy Craft Laney: The Mother of the Children of the People." Unpublished paper, May 1972. Special Collections, Atlanta University, Atlanta.

Kerber, Linda K. *Women of the Republic: Intellect and Ideology in Revolutionary America.* Chapel Hill: University of North Carolina Press, 1980.

Kessler-Harris, Alice. *Out to Work: A History of Wage Earning Women.* New York: Oxford University Press, 1982.

Kierner, Cynthia A. "Hospitality, Sociability, and Gender in the Southern Colonies." *Journal of Southern History* 62, no. 3 (August 1996): 449–80.

Kousser, J. Morgan. *The Shaping of Southern Politics: Suffrage Restriction and the Establishment of the One-Party South, 1880–1910.* New Haven: Yale University Press, 1974.

———. "Separate but *Not* Equal: The Supreme Court's First Decision on Discrimination in Schools." Social Science Working Paper no. 204, California Institute of Technology, March 1978.

Kousser, J. Morgan. "Separate but Not Equal: The Supreme Court's First Decision on Racial Discrimination in Schools." *Journal of Southern History* 46, no. 1 (February 1980): 17–44.

Kousser, J. Morgan, and James M. McPherson. *Religion, Race, and Reconstruction: Essays in Honor of C. Vann Woodward.* New York: Oxford University Press, 1982.

Knight, Jack C. "Reckoning with Violence: W. E. B. Du Bois and the 1906 Atlanta Riot." *Journal of Southern History* 62, no. 4 (November 1996): 731–34.

Lakey, Othal Hawthorne. *The Rise of "Colored Methodism": A Study of the Background and the Beginnings of the Christian Methodist Episcopal Church.* Dallas: n.p., 1972.

———. *The History of the CME Church.* Memphis, Tenn.: CME Publishing House, 1985.

Lamon, Lester C. *Black Tennesseans, 1900–1930.* Knoxville: University of Tennessee Press, 1977.

Lamplugh, George R. "The Importance of Being Truculent: James Gunn, the Chatham Militia, and Georgia Politics, 1782–1789." *Georgia Historical Quarterly* 80, no. 2 (summer 1996): 227–45.

Lane, Mills. *The Rambler in Georgia.* Savannah: Beehive Press, 1973.

Langley, A. M., Jr., and Mary L. Langley. *Trolleys in the Valley: A History of the Street and Interurban Railways of Augusta, Georgia.* N.p., 1972. Special Collections Room, Reese Library, Augusta State University, Augusta.

Laurie, Bruce. *Artisans into Workers: Labor in Nineteenth-Century America.* New York: Hill and Wang, 1989.

Lebsock, Suzanne. *The Free Women of Petersburg: Status and Culture in a Southern Town, 1784–1860.* New York: W. W. Norton, 1984.

Leslie, Kent Anderson. "A Myth of the Southern Lady: Pro-Slavery Rhetoric and the Proper Place of Women." *Sociological Spectrums* 6 (1986): 31–49.

———. *Woman of Color, Daughter of Privilege: Amanda America Dickson, 1849–1893.* Athens: University of Georgia Press, 1995.

Leslie, Kent Anderson, and Willard B. Gatewood Jr. "'This Father of Mine . . . a Sort of a Mystery': Jean Toomer's Georgia Heritage." *Georgia Historical Quarterly* 77, no. 4 (winter 1993): 789–809.

Lewis, David Levering. *W. E. B. Du Bois: Biography of a Race.* New York: Henry Holt, 1993.

Litwack, Leon. *Trouble in Mind: Black Southerners in the Age of Jim Crow.* New York: Alfred A. Knopf, 1998.

Lockley, Timothy J. "A Struggle for Survival: Non-elite White Women in Low-Country Georgia, 1790–1830." In *Women of the American South*, edited by Christie Ann Farnham. New York: New York University Press, 1997.

Logan, Rayford. *The Betrayal of the Negro: From Rutherford B. Hayes to Woodrow Wilson*. London: Collier, 1965.

MacLean, Nancy. *Behind the Mask of Chivalry: The Making of the Second Ku Klux Klan*. Oxford, 1984.

Magrath, Peter. *Yazoo: Law and Politics in the New Republic; the Case of Fletcher v. Peck*. Providence, R.I.: Brown University Press, 1966.

Malone, Henry Thompson. *The Episcopal Church in Georgia, 1733–1957*. Atlanta: Protestant Episcopal Church in the Diocese of Atlanta, 1960.

Mathews, Donald G. *Slavery and Methodism: A Chapter in American Morality, 1780–1845*. Princeton, N.J.: Princeton University Press, 1965.

Matthews, John Michael. "Studies in Race Relations in Georgia, 1880–1930." Ph.D. diss., Duke University, 1970.

McCommons, Mrs. W. C., and Miss Clara Stovall. *History of McDuffie County*. Tignall, Ga.: Boyd, 1988.

McCoy, Carl Lavert. "A Historical Sketch of Black Augusta, Georgia, from Emancipation to the Brown Decision, 1865–1954." M.A. thesis, University of Georgia, 1984.

McCrorey, Mary Jackson. "Lucy Laney." *Crisis* 25 (June 1934): 471.

McCurry, Stephanie. "The Two Faces of Republicanism: Gender and Proslavery Politics in Antebellum South Carolina." *Journal of American History* 78 (March 1992): 1245–64.

McFeely, William S. *Frederick Douglass*. New York: W. W. Norton, 1991.

McLaurin, Melton. *Paternalism and Protest: Southern Cotton Mill Workers and Organized Labor, 1875–1905*. Westport, Conn.: Greenwood Press, 1971.

———. *The Knights of Labor in the South*. Westport, Conn.: Greenwood Press, 1978.

McMillen, Neil R. *Dark Journey: Black Mississippians in the Age of Jim Crow*. Urbana: University of Illinois Press, 1990.

McMillen, Sally G. *Motherhood in the Old South: Pregnancy, Childbirth, and Infant Rearing*. Baton Rouge: Louisiana State University Press, 1990.

Meier, August. *Negro Thought in America, 1880–1915: Racial Ideologies in the Age of Booker T. Washington*. Ann Arbor: University of Michigan Press, 1963.

Milkman, Ruth, ed. *Women, Work, and Protest: A Century of U.S. Labor History*. Boston: Routledge and Kegan Paul, 1985.

Miller, Perry. *The New England Mind: The Seventeenth Century*. Boston: Beacon Press, 1961.

Miller, Vincent M. D. "United Methodism in Black Augusta: A Historical Study." M.A. thesis, Emory University, 1982.

Mitchell, Broadus. *Rise of the Cotton Mills*. Baltimore: Johns Hopkins University Press, 1921.

———. *William Gregg: Factory Master of the Old South.* Chapel Hill: University of North Carolina Press, 1928.

Mohr, Clarence L. *On the Threshold of Freedom: Masters and Slaves in Civil War Georgia.* Athens: University of Georgia Press, 1986.

Montgomery, William E. *Under Their Own Vine and Fig Tree: The African-American Church in the South, 1865–1900.* Baton Rouge: Louisiana State University Press, 1993.

Morgan, Edmund S. *Virginians at Home: Family Life in the Eighteenth Century.* Williamsburg, Va.: Colonial Williamsburg Foundation, 1952.

Moses, William Jeremiah. *Wings of Ethiopia: Studies in African-American Life and Letters.* Ames: Iowa State University Press, 1990.

Moses, Wilson. *The Golden Age of Black Nationalism, 1850–1925.* New York: Oxford University Press, 1989.

Murray, Dorothy Hayne. "William John Henning: The Man, the Publisher." *Richmond County History* 2, no. 1 (winter 1970): 7–12.

Murray, Pauli. *Proud Shoes: The History of an American Family.* New York: Harper and Row, 1956.

Newby, I. A. *Plain Folk in the New South: Social Change and Cultural Persistence, 1880–1915.* Baton Rouge: Louisiana State University Press, 1989.

———. *Black Carolinians: A History of Blacks in South Carolina from 1895–1968.* Columbia: University of South Carolina Press, 1973.

Norwood, John Nelson. *The Schism in the Methodist Episcopal Church 1844: A Study of Slavery and Ecclesiastical Politics.* Philadelphia: Porcupine Press, 1976.

O'Donnell, James H., III. *Southern Indians in the American Revolution.* Knoxville: University of Tennessee Press, 1973.

Olwell, Robert. "'Loose, Idle, and Disorderly': Slave Women in the Eighteenth-Century Charleston Marketplace." In *More than Chattel: Black Women and Slavery in the Americas,* edited by David Barry Gaspar and Darlene Clark Hine. Bloomington: Indiana University Press, 1996.

Orr, Dorothy. *A History of Education in Georgia.* Chapel Hill: University of North Carolina Press, 1950.

Owen, Christopher H. *The Sacred Flame of Love: Methodism and Society in Nineteenth-Century Georgia.* Athens: University of Georgia Press, 1998.

Ownby, Ted. *Subduing Satan: Religion, Recreation, and Manhood in the Rural South, 1865–1920.* Chapel Hill: University of North Carolina Press, 1990.

Patton, June O. "The Black Community of Augusta and the Struggle for Ware High School, 1880–1899." In *New Perspectives on Black Educational History,* edited by Vincent P. Franklin and James D. Anderson. Boston: G. K. Hall, 1978.

Percy, Walker. *Lancelot.* New York: Farrar, Straus and Giroux, 1977.

Pope, Liston. *Millhands and Preachers: A Study of Gastonia.* New Haven: Yale University Press, 1942.

Ramage, Thomas. "The Bloody Tenth Congressional District Election of 1892." *Richmond County History* 7, no. 2 (summer 1975): 65–76.

Range, Willard. *The Rise and Progress of Negro Colleges in Georgia, 1865–1949.* Athens: University of Georgia Press, 1951.

Reed, Florence. *The Story of Spelman.* Atlanta: Spelman College, 1961.

Reed, Merl E. "The Augusta Textile Mills and the Strike of 1886." *Labor History* 14, no. 2 (spring 1973): 228–246.

Richardson, Harry V. *Dark Salvation: The Story of Methodism as It Developed among Blacks in America.* New York: Doubleday, Anchor Books, 1976.

Robertson, Heard. *Notes upon the History of St. Pauls: James Seymour.* Augusta: n.p., 1974.

Rodgers, Daniel T. "In Search of Progressivism." *Reviews in American History* 10 (December 1982): 113–32.

Roediger, David R. *The Wages of Whiteness: Race and the Making of the American Working Class.* New York: Verso, 1991.

Rotundo, Anthony. *American Manhood: Transformations in Masculinity from the Revolution to the Modern Era.* New York: Basic Books, 1993.

Schweninger, Loren. "Property-Owning Free African-American Women in the South, 1800–1870." *Journal of American History* 1 (winter 1990): 13–44.

Scott, Ann Firor. *The Southern Lady from Pedestal to Politics, 1830–1930.* Chicago: University of Chicago Press, 1970.

Shaw, Barton C. *The Wool Hat Boys: Georgia's Populist Party.* Baton Rouge: Louisiana State University Press, 1984.

Soltow, Lee, and Aubrey C. Land. "Housing and Social Standing in Georgia, 1798." *Georgia Historical Quarterly* 64 (1980): 448–58.

Spalding, Phinizy. *Oglethorpe in America.* Chicago: University of Chicago Press, 1977.

Spruill, Julia Cherry, *Women's Life and Work in the Southern Colonies.* New York: W. W. Norton, 1972.

Stansell, Christine. *City of Women: Sex and Class in New York, 1789–1860.* Urbana: University of Illinois Press, 1986.

Stevenson, Brenda E. *Life in Black and White: Family and Community in the Slave South.* New York: Oxford University Press, 1996.

Stowell, Daniel Wesley. "'The Negroes Cannot Navigate Alone': Religious Scalawags and the Biracial Methodist Episcopal Church in Georgia." In *Georgia in Black and White: Explorations in the Race Relations of a Southern State, 1865–1950*, edited by John C. Inscoe. Athens: University of Georgia Press, 1994.

———. "Rebuilding Zion: The Religious Reconstruction of the South, 1863–1877." Ph.D. diss., University of Florida, 1994.

———. *Rebuilding Zion: The Religious Reconstruction of the South, 1863–1877.* New York: Oxford University Press, 1998.

Strickland, Reba Carolyn. *Religion and the State in Georgia in the Eighteenth Century.* New York: Columbia University Press, 1939.

Sweat, Edward Forrest. "The Free Negro in Antebellum Georgia." Ph.D. dissertation, University of Michigan, 1957.

Swint, Henry Lee. *The Northern Teacher in the South, 1862–1879.* Nashville, Tenn.: Vanderbilt University Press, 1941.

Terrell, Lloyd P., and Marguerite S. Terrell. *Blacks in Augusta: A Chronology, 1741–1977.* Augusta: Preston, 1977.

Thompson, Holland. *From the Cotton Field to the Cotton Mill: A Study of the Industrial Transition in North Carolina.* New York: MacMillan, 1906.

Thorton, J. Mills, III. *Politics and Power in a Slave Society: Alabama, 1800–1860.* Baton Rouge: Louisiana State University Press, 1978.

Tillman, Manie Norris, and Hortense Woodson. *The Hammond Family of Edgefield District.* Edgefield, S.C.: Advertiser Press, 1954.

Tilly, Louisa A., and Joan W. Scott. *Women, Work, and Family.* London: Methuen, 1978.

Torrence, Ridgely. *The Story of John Hope.* New York: Macmillan, 1948.

Tullos, Allen. *Habits of Industry: White Culture and the Transformation of the Carolina Piedmont.* Chapel Hill: University of North Carolina Press, 1989.

Turner, Darwin T. Introduction to *Cane,* by Jean Toomer. New York: Liveright, 1975.

Van Doren, Mark, ed. *Travels of William Bartram.* New York: Dover, 1955.

Voss, Kim. *The Making of American Exceptionalism: The Knights of Labor and Class Formation in the Nineteenth Century.* Ithaca: Cornell University Press, 1993.

Wade, John Donald. *Augustus Baldwin Longstreet: A Study of the Development of Culture in the South.* Athens: University of Georgia Press, 1969.

Wade, Richard C. *Slavery in the Cities: The South, 1820–1860.* New York: Oxford University Press, 1964.

Wagner, Clarence M. *Profile of Black Georgia Baptists.* Gainesville, Ga.: n.p., 1980.

Walker, Clarence E. *A Rock in a Weary Land: The African Methodist Episcopal Church during the Civil War and Reconstruction.* Baton Rouge: Louisiana State University Press, 1982.

Walsh, Julia. " 'Horny-Handed Sons of Toil': Mill Workers, Populists, and the Press in Augusta, 1886–1893. *Georgia Historical Quarterly* 81, no. 2 (summer 1997): 311–44.

———. " 'Horny-Handed Sons of Toil': Workers, Politics, and Religion in Augusta, Georgia, 1880–1910." Ph.D. diss., University of Illinois at Urbana-Champaign, 1999.

Washington, George R. "A Study of Eight Nineteenth Century Documents Found in the Richmond County Courthouse Bearing on the History of Mount Zion African Methodist Episcopal Zion Church." Undergraduate thesis, Paine College, 1978.

Watson, E. O. *Builders: Sketches of Methodist Ministers in South Carolina.* Columbia, S.C.: Southern Christian Advocate Press, 1932.

Wax, Darold D. "'New Negroes Are Always in Demand': The Slave Trade in Eighteenth-Century Georgia." *Georgia Historical Quarterly* 63, no. 2 (summer 1984): 216–18.

Weaver, Gordon. *Selected Poems of Father Ryan.* Jackson: University and College Press of Mississippi, 1973.

Welter, Barbara. "The Cult of True Womanhood: 1820–1860." *American Quarterly* 18 (summer 1966): 151–74.

———. *Dimity Convictions: The American Woman in the Nineteenth Century.* Athens: Ohio State University Press, 1976.

Werner, Randolph. "Hegemony and Conflict: The Political Economy of a Southern Region, Augusta, Georgia, 1865–1895." Ph.D. diss., University of Virginia, 1977.

Whitaker, John. "Central Christian Church, 1882–1982: A Brief History." Augusta: n.p., 1982. Reese Library, Augusta State University, Augusta.

White, Deborah Gray. *Ar'n't I a Woman? Female Slaves in the Plantation South.* New York: W. W. Norton, 1985.

Whites, LeeAnn. "Southern Ladies and Millhands: The Domestic Economy and Class Politics, Augusta, Georgia, 1870–1890." Ph.D. diss., University of California at Irvine, 1982.

———. *The Civil War as a Crisis in Gender: Augusta, Georgia, 1860–1890.* Athens: University of Georgia Press, 1995.

Williams, Darlene. "An Inquiry into the Early History of the Colored Methodist Episcopal Church, with Special Attention to the Development in Augusta, Georgia, Up to 1875." Undergraduate thesis, Paine College, 1976.

Williamson, Joel. *New People: Miscegenation and Mulattoes in the United States.* New York: New York University Press, 1980.

Wills, Gregory. *Democratic Religion: Freedom, Authority, and Church Discipline in the Baptist South, 1785–1900.* New York: Oxford University Press, 1997.

Wingo, Horace Calvin. "Race Relations in Georgia, 1872–1908." Ph.D. diss., University of Georgia, 1969.

Wood, Betty. *Women's Work, Men's Work: The Informal Slave Economies of Lowcountry Georgia.* Athens: University of Georgia Press, 1995.

Woodson, Carter G. *The Education of the Negro Prior to 1861.* 1915. Reprint, New York: Arno Press, 1968.

———. "Free Negro Owners of Slaves in the United States in 1830." *Journal of Negro History* 9 (January 1924): 41–85.

Woodward, C. Vann. *Origins of The New South, 1877–1913.* 1951. Reprint, Baton Rouge: Louisiana State University Press, 1993.

———. *Tom Watson: Agrarian Rebel.* New York: Oxford University Press, 1963.

———. *The Strange Career of Jim Crow.* 3d ed. New York: Oxford University Press, 1974.

Wright, Gavin. *The Political Economy of the Cotton South: Households, Markets, and Wealth in the Nineteenth Century.* New York: W. W. Norton, 1978.

———. *Old South, New South: Revolutions in the Southern Economy since the Civil War.* New York: Basic Books, 1986.

Wright, George C. *Racial Violence in Kentucky, 1865–1940: Lynchings, Mob Rule, and "Legal Lynchings."* Baton Rouge: Louisiana State University Press, 1990.

The Contributors

EDWARD J. CASHIN graduated from Marist College in Poughkeepsie, New York, and obtained his Ph.D. from Fordham University. He taught in high schools in the Bronx and in Miami, Florida, before returning to Marist College, where he served as academic vice president. He returned to his native Augusta in 1969 and held the position of department chair at Augusta State University from 1975 to 1996. He has received the E. Merton Coulter Award and the Malcolm and Muriel Bell Award, both from the Georgia Historical Society; the Fraunces Tavern Award from the New York Revolution Round Table; the Hugh McCall Award from the Georgia Association of Historians; and the Governor's Award in the Humanities. Upon retirement in 1996, he inaugurated the Center for the Study of Georgia History and is currently its director.

BOBBY J. DONALDSON is a member of the church founded by the subject of his essay, William Jefferson White. He attended Davidson Fine Arts School in Augusta and did his undergraduate work at Wesleyan University in Middletown, Connecticut. He obtained his M.A. at Emory University in 1996 and completed his Ph.D. there in 2000. He is now an assistant professor of history at the University of South Carolina in Columbia. In his short academic career he has received seven awards and grants, among them the Huggins-Quarles Award from the Organization of American Historians in 1998. Dartmouth College awarded him its Thurgood Marshall Dissertation Fellowship for the year 1998–99. His doctoral dissertation is a study of black intellectuals in Georgia at the turn of the century.

GLENN T. ESKEW earned his bachelor's degree from Auburn University in 1984 and his master's and doctorate from the University of Georgia in 1993. Since then he has taught at Georgia State University in Atlanta. He published *But for Birmingham: The Local and National Movements in the Civil Rights Struggle* (Chapel Hill: University of North Carolina Press, 1997), which received the 1997–98 Francis Butler Simpkins Award, given jointly by the Southern Historical Association and Longwood College in recognition of the best first book by an author in the field of southern history over a two-year period. An earlier study tangential to his contribution in this volume, "Black Elitism and the Failure of Paternalism in Postbellum Georgia: The Case of Bishop Lucius Henry Holsey," was published in the *Journal of Southern History* (November 1992).

MICHELE GILLESPIE received her undergraduate degree in history from Rice University and her doctorate from Princeton. She has taught at Agnes Scott College in Atlanta and currently holds the rank of associate professor of history at Wake Forest University. She has edited two books with Catherine Clinton, *The Devil's Lane: Sex and Race in the Early South* (New York: Oxford University Press, 1997) and *Taking Off the White Gloves: Southern Women and Women's History* (Columbia: University of Missouri Press, 1998). Her *Free Labor in an Unfree World: White Artisans in Slaveholding Georgia, 1789–1860* (Athens: University of Georgia Press, 2000) is a broader study of her pioneer work in this volume. She is currently editing *Neither Lady nor Slave: Working Women of the Old South* with Susanna Delfino.

KENT ANDERSON LESLIE obtained her degrees at Queens College and Emory University, with additional study at the Penland School of Crafts. She has taught at Agnes Scott College, Georgia State University, and Emory University. From 1994 through 1998 she directed the Women's Studies Program at Oglethorpe University. Her biography of Amanda America Dickson, *Woman of Color, Daughter of Privilege* (Athens: University of Georgia Press, 1995), evaluates the aristocracy of color. An article " 'This Father of Mine . . . a Sort of Mystery': Jean Toomer's Georgia Heritage," coauthored with Willard Gatewood, appeared in the *Georgia Historical Quarterly* (winter 1993).

JULIA WALSH, a native of England, graduated from Cambridge University in 1991 and obtained her master's and doctoral degrees from the University of Illinois at Urbana-Champaign. She is currently assistant professor of history at Webster University in Saint Louis. She has received support from a number of sources, including a Pew Program in Religion and American History Fellowship from Yale University and a fellowship in the Center for the Study of Georgia History awarded by the Richmond County Historical Society. Her research explores the ways in which religious identity shaped and interacted with other forms of identity, particularly in the political arena.

LEEANN WHITES has chosen Augusta as the focus of much of her study. Her doctoral dissertation at the University of California, Irvine was entitled "Southern Ladies and Millhands: Class Politics and the Domestic Economy, Augusta, Georgia, 1870–1890," and she has published the book *The Civil War as a Crisis in Gender: Augusta, Georgia, 1860–1890* (Athens: University of Georgia Press, 1995). She has contributed to four anthologies other than this volume and has presented numerous papers at professional conferences. From 1982 to 1989 she held the rank of assistant professor at Virginia Polytechnic Institute and State University, and since 1989 she has taught at the University of Missouri–Columbia, where she is an associate professor of history.

Index